CARLOS TEVEZ

WELCOME TO MANCHESTER

CARLOS TEVEZ

WELCOME TO MANCHESTER

THE BIOGRAPHY OF MANCHESTER CITY'S SUPER STRIKER

IAN MACLEAY

JOHN BLAKE

Published by John Blake Publishing Ltd,
3 Bramber Court, 2 Bramber Road,
London W14 9PB, England

www.johnblakepublishing.co.uk

First published in hardback in 2010

ISBN: 978-1-84454-828-6

British Library Cataloguing-in-Publication Data:
A catalogue record for this book is available from the British Library.

Design by www.envydesign.co.uk

Printed in Great Britain by CPI William Clowes, Beccles, NR34 7TL

1 3 5 7 9 10 8 6 4 2

Papers used by John Blake Publishing are natural, recyclable products
made from wood grown in sustainable forests. The manufacturing processes conform
to the environmental regulations of the country of origin.

Every attempt has been made to contact the relevant copyright-holders, but some were
unobtainable. We would be grateful if the appropriate people could contact us.

For Marie

CONTENTS

The world is divided into two classes. Those who believe the incredible and those who do the improbable
OSCAR WILDE

CHAPTER ONE
SLUMDOG MILLIONAIRE

Carlos Tevez is the Argentine prophet for the 21st century.
MARADONA

I just think that human life is considered so insignificant now that the only thing one can do in order to do anything at all is to become famous.
MORRISSEY

C arlos Tevez is the original slum boy millionaire. He's the stuff that Hollywood movies are made of – a boy who rose from a difficult start in life to become a superstar footballer playing for the world's richest club.

Tevez was a product of his time. Only two options were open to him when he was young: crime or football. There was very little else on offer for a boy from a poor Argentine family. But Tevez became a heroic figure, a fellow with integrity who climbed very rapidly to the top of his profession thanks to his skill, intelligence and toughness. This is the story of the archetypal penniless kid who used his towering ambition to become one of the most famous players in the world. It is also the story of 21st-century football, at a time when dubious deals and mystifying transfers went hand in hand with greed, avarice and egoism.

Carlos Alberto Martinez was born on Sunday, 5 February 1984 in Ciudadela, Buenos Aires. 1984 is one of those years that stand out. It is the title of the dystopian novel by George Orwell, predicting the rise of a sinister organisation called Big Brother. On a Sunday a quarter of a century later, when this book was being written, the biggest star of a TV show called *Big Brother* was getting married in a star-studded media event. The bride, Jade Goody, was dying of cancer and the corporate media's agenda was to exploit it to the max. Orwell had been correct all along.

In 1984 some of the big biggest singles in the charts were 'Pride' by U2, 'Robert De Niro's Waiting' by Bananarama and 'White Lines' by Grandmaster Flash. *Miami Vice* first appeared on TV.

Two days after Carlos was born, his future employers Manchester United drew 2-2 with Birmingham City at St Andrews. The Reds' goalscorers in that first division game were Hogg and Norman Whiteside. A few weeks later United beat Barcelona 3-0 at Old Trafford in a European Cup-Winners' Cup match. Bryan Robson scored twice in one of the most magnificent games staged there. Trailing 2-0 after the first leg, United overwhelmed the Catalan side, which included Argentine legend Maradona. United finished fourth that season, 16 points behind champions Liverpool. It is interesting to note that the two teams occupying second and third place were Southampton and Nottingham Forest, both now exiled from the big time.

United's run in the Cup-Winners' Cup ended in the semi-finals, against Juventus. In the FA Cup a Bournemouth side managed by a young Harry Redknapp knocked them out in a 2-0 victory – the last time United were beaten in the third round of the competition for 26 years. West Ham United finished in ninth place in the League that season.

Argentina is the second largest country in South America and the eighth largest in the whole world. In 1982 the country's loss to the British in the Falklands war discredited the Argentine dictator Leopoldo Galtieri and led to free elections in the year before Carlos Martinez was born. His birthplace, Buenos Aires, is the capital of Argentina and its largest city. Football ran deeply throughout the young Carlos's life, and even his birthplace had a football connection. In 1978, the World Cup was held in Argentina and the home side won. The ruling military regime at the time were determined to hide the poorer elements of the city from the tourists and visiting dignitaries. They were particularly concerned about the acres of slum dwellings that stretched from the international airport to the city centre. The dwellings were a vast shantytown known as Villa Miseria. 'Villa' means 'village' or 'small town' while 'Miseria' means 'abject poverty'.

Those shantytowns consisted of tiny houses or, more often, shacks made of wood, tin or whatever could be salvaged. The streets were unpaved and there was no sanitation system. The inhabitants came from many backgrounds and the majority of them were migrants from poorer provinces. Others came from nearby countries such as Paraguay (birthplace of Manchester City striker Roque Santa Cruz) and Bolivia. There were always a great number of children in these squalid areas; some of them were the grandchildren of the original settlers who had been unable to improve on their desperate lot in life. The famous Argentine painter Antoni Berni produced a series of heart-rending portraits entitled *Juanito Laguna* – 'Slum Children'.

The dilapidated shantytowns were also havens for criminals, ranging from petty thieves and pickpockets to serial armed robbers, kidnappers, gunmen and drug dealers.

Eventually, the downtrodden were moved from the Villa Miseria to a series of high-rise developments. The whole project was overseen by the then mayor of Buenos Aires, Osvaldo Cacciatore. A series of 13 areas, known as nodes, was constructed, each consisting of three tower blocks and a water tower. The new area was called Ejercito de los Andes (Army of the Andes). It was originally designed to house around 25,000 people, but current estimates of the population put it at around three times that number. Some estimates place it at over 100,000. This was a sink-or-swim kind of environment.

It was a tough area; it made the estate in Peckham where the Ferdinand brothers were raised look like the Jumeirah Palm hotel complex in Dubai. In fact, it was probably one of the most dangerous places to live in the world. There was a community of drug dealers living there, who were caught up in a vicious gang war. A local crime reporter dubbed the area Fuerte Apache (Fort Apache) after a brutal turf war ended up in a bloody shoot-out that looked like the finale of the seminal Samuel Peckinpah movie *The Wild Bunch*.

The leader of the gangs for a while was a colourful character called El Loco Jerry, who ordered that no crime was to go on within the area. 'El Loco' was killed by a rival gang leader in another deadly battle. Legend had it the killer literally danced on his grave. The violence that beset so many of the inhabitants of Fuerte Apache grew so bad it was said that the police would not venture into the area.

When Carlos was young, the buildings were new but today some have been deemed unsuitable for human habitation. In 2000, the tower blocks in 'nodes' eight and nine were demolished for health and safety reasons.

Carlos was born and bred there, and he was lucky to be

part of a close-knit family. His parents, Raimundo and Adriana, had a daily struggle to feed him and his four younger siblings, Diego, Miguel, Ricardo and Debora. Carlos has spoken to the *Man Utd 24* website of his impoverished childhood there. 'There were tough times, growing up in Fuerte Apache. When it was dark and you looked out of the window, what you saw would scare anyone. After a certain hour you could not go into the street. It was incredible.'

When he was just 10 months old, Carlos was scalded by boiling water. He was in intensive care for nearly two months with third-degree burns to his face, neck and chest. The accident occurred when his mother was making tea. Little Carlos was crawling about in the kitchen and, as lively as ever, he waved his arms around and hit the handle of the kettle. Its boiling contents spilled all over him. Carlos was scarred for life, but he has always rejected any chance of cosmetic surgery to improve the disfigurement.

When he was asked about the scar Carlos told the *Man Utd 24* website: 'It was a defining experience – it marked me for life. I won't have plastic surgery. You either take me as I am or you don't. The same goes for the teeth. I don't change the way I am.'

Tevez's teeth are broken and crooked as a result of two incidents. The first was when a girl accidentally head-butted him in school, breaking a front tooth. The second was when he took a whack during a street fight over money. Even this stemmed from a game of street football. Carlos was trying to hustle coins from people betting on the outcome of the games. He loved those games as much as the Champions League battles he was to play in later life. He told *soccerphile.com*: 'Street soccer is the greatest thing in the world. There is just you and your friends against the rest. If someone feels he has to stick a foot in your throat, he will.'

Football was Carlos's life literally from the moment he could walk. He threw himself into the game and took solace from it. It was his ticket out of Fort Apache and his tremendous focus on the sport helped him steer clear of drifting into crime. As he told the *Man Utd 24* website: 'I could have started doing drugs and ended at the bottom, but instead I made it to the place where I am now. In fact, my childhood was nice. I learned then all the values that grace me now: respect, humility, sacrifice.' Those three values were to be watchwords throughout his career. Carlos had a very close friend who unfortunately took the wrong path and ended up being part of the local gang. This friend was later killed in a shoot-out – an interesting statistic about Fort Apache was that 7 out of every 10 arrests in the area were for minors carrying guns. Tevez was devastated at the loss of his friend. His career was just taking off at the time and he was participating in the Under-17 World Cup, which was being staged in Trinidad & Tobago. He told the *Guardian*: 'The news came just after we were defeated by France, and it finished me off.'

Carlos had a happy childhood and was brought up eating the traditional *morcillas* (blood sausages) and *empanadas* (stuffed pasties). He developed a liking for music from an early age, and his favourite type of music was *Cumbia Villera*, best defined as the Argentinean equivalent of gangsta rap. Even at an early age he was acquiring nicknames; one was 'Apache', derived from his birthplace. Another nickname he acquired in Fuerte Apache was 'Manchado' ('Spotty'), a rather cruel reference to the red marks he inherited from the scalding. When he joined Manchester United the fans dubbed him 'Sir Charles'.

Football was always Carlos's driving passion. He started off by playing football on the *potrero* (playground) near the tower blocks. From there, his mother could keep an eye on him and he would spend most of the day just kicking a ball around. All the kids had to play with was a cheap plastic ball from the bargain shop. Sometimes, when their ball was punctured or literally kicked to pieces, they would have to make do with a smaller tennis ball. This helped Carlos improve his ball skills as the smaller ball was harder to control and would bounce off at strange angles. The ground was littered with broken glass and jagged cans, so any slip on the treacherous surface would result in painful cuts. Most of the skill that the great Argentinean players have had was developed by playing on bad pitches with ill-fitting boots, or sometimes with no boots at all. In recent years greater numbers of playing areas have disappeared, with the relentless building of more and more tower blocks. Football is such a part of the social fabric that coaches are becoming concerned that the skill factor may start to decline.

Carlos certainly learnt from the football 'school of hard knocks'. Years later, when questioned about the punishing tackles dished out in the Premier League, he thought of his early days in Fort Apache, smiled and slowly shook his head. When he was younger, Carlos played against much older boys who would try to intimidate the little kid with kicks and punches. If he could not bet money on the games, he would play for the street teams in exchange for food or drink. Whatever he obtained, he would take home to share with his family. A downturn had hit the economy and his father was finding it increasingly hard to get work. Had he not been blessed with his God-given football skills, Carlos would have tried to find work with his father in the construction business.

7

Grinding poverty was everywhere and this drove him on. Carlos told the *soccerphile.com* website: 'Sometimes we had little to eat because my old man could not find a job as a bricklayer, but to hear "I love you" from my parents was enough to help the hunger pass. Seeing them struggle gave me inner strength and made me what I am today.'

Soon he was banging in goal after goal for his local junior sides, Estrellas del Uno, Santa Clara and Villa Real. Doctors offered to improve his scars with surgery, but he turned this down because it would have meant missing four months' football. Carlos joined the youth system of Second Division team All Boys in 1992, at the age of 8, and stayed with them until he was 13. Young Tevez was lucky that his skill at football had lifted him out of the slums, but for every Carlos there were thousands of boys who missed that opportunity to be spotted and signed up by a big club.

Carlos was discovered by the talent scout Ramon Maddoni, the man who had discovered some of Argentina's biggest names, including Juan Roman Riquelme and Pablo Aimar. In an interview with *Absolutely United* he explained: 'I have worked with many talented young players and one of Carlos's great virtues is his desire to be as good as he can be and never accept defeat. Tevez has the ability to go as far as he wants.

'I remember when I first saw him. He was fearless in the way he played against older and bigger boys, and was not bothered if they tried to kick him. I helped him develop, but when a player has natural talent you only have to guide him for the talent to shine through.'

Carlos had fond memories of Ramon and used the same article to express them. 'I remember when Ramon Maddoni, who was like a father to me, discovered me. I was just a kid, eight. The game had finished and I was still kicking around and two men came up to me and said, "We have been looking for you everywhere." I had no idea what they wanted. I joined a team called Club Parue but did not like it because they made me dribble around cones. Practising for hours. I went home saying I would not be back. But they came to collect me again and I am very grateful.'

The word quickly spread around Fort Apache that the young man was a red-hot prospect and he soon became a local celebrity. Boca Juniors were the biggest name in Argentinean football and had a huge network of scouts constantly looking for talent; they had already started to monitor his progress. It was estimated that over one and a half million boys like Tevez had trials for football clubs annually. Most of the kids spent hour after hour practising; a fair amount dropped out of education completely. If they did not make it by the time they reached the age of 18 or 19, they had nothing.

In 1997 Carlos, now aged 13, changed his name to Tevez – his mother's maiden name. This was common in Argentinean football and was a ploy used to switch young prospects around different clubs and to obtain passports. Boca Juniors snapped Carlos up and put him in their youth team. In four years he scored over 70 goals at youth level as he continued to make a name for himself. At the age of 17 he was promoted to the senior side and made his debut for the Boca Juniors first team in a friendly in August 2001 against a team called Union, scoring a fine goal. His first game in the Argentinean First Division came in October against Tellers de Cordoba, but he was on the losing side as they went down 1-0. In all, he made 11 appearances that season, scoring once.

In August 2002 Boca played at Old Trafford in a friendly for the charity Unicef. The game was anything but friendly, and Tevez was sent off for elbowing United legend Paul Scholes. Before his departure, though, Tevez had been the game's outstanding player; putting in a tremendous amount of work and displaying great composure. Sir Alex Ferguson was watching the match with great interest, always one the lookout for players who could combine a huge appetite for work with silky skills. Carlos Tevez was certainly a player to watch in the future. After the match the United boss gave instructions that the young Boca starlet's progress should be monitored. Liverpool manager Rafael Benitez was a fan of players with Tevez's background and told the *Sunday Times*: 'It is clear that when you have a good Argentinean player, it's really good. They are very good and they have South American technique.'

Carlos had to wait until 2003 to win his first trophy when, under the shrewd coach Carlos Bianchi, Boca Juniors won the Copa Libertadores, the South American equivalent of the Champions League. Having taken part in the South American Under 20s competition, he missed the opening phase of the Copa Libertadores. Bianchi had previously dropped Carlos as he was concerned about his fitness, but in the end, the trophy was won, thanks to a series of great performances by Tevez. A particularly strong individual display came against a side from Chile, Cobreloa, in the away leg. Feuntes put the home side ahead after 10 minutes, but tremendous play by Tevez set up the equaliser for Guillermo. In the second half, the same player shot the winner after a powerful shot by Tevez bounced back off the crossbar. The Argentinean sports paper *Ole* gave him a rating of 10/10 for his audacious exhibition of skill.

In the entire competition he played in seven matches and scored a total of five goals. Three came in the two legs against America de Cali and he also scored in the return leg of the Cobreloa tie. His crowning moment, though, came in the final against Santos of Brazil. The match was billed as a duel between the two rising stars of South American football: Tevez of Boca and Argentina, and Robinho of Santos and Brazil. Like Carlos, Robinho (who later played for Manchester City) had been brought up in a very poor neighbourhood. Robinho has admitted that in his younger days he often could not afford to eat three meals a day. For both men, football was their way out of the impoverished underclass. Making it in football was not just doing something they loved, but also getting a better way of life.

Like Tevez, Robinho was to make it all the way, with a transfer to Real Madrid followed by a lucrative move to the Premier League. Now he is on around £160,000 a week. On that day back in 2003, though, he was completely outshone by Carlos Tevez. The Boca battler even managed to score a goal and celebrated it by flapping his arms up and down. Boca's greatest, most bitter rivals were River Plate. Think Rangers/Celtic, Arsenal/Spurs or United/Liverpool. River's nickname was the *gallinas* (hens), or in the eyes of the Boca fans, 'chickens'. Carlos's flapping gesture was deliberately aimed at offending their supporters – and it did.

That victory was the defining moment in his career and things were never quite the same again for him. The goal celebration and his unconfined joy at winning his first major honour for his beloved team were more than he could bear. Carlos wept uncontrollably when he was presented with his first medal and then managed to get his hands on the clunky trophy known as the Copa Libertadores. They could not wrest the cup from his grip; it was his, it was his people's. He had won it for them wearing the blue and yellow Boca shirt.

2003 was some year for Boca and their 19-year-old hotshot, as it was also their treble-winning season. The team added the Argentinean League (Apertura) and the Intercontinental Cup to the booty already won. Carlos described the moment to the *Ole* newspaper: 'This is so thrilling, so emotional words cannot describe it. I dedicate it to all the Boca fans.'

His brilliant play continued in the Argentine league. The problem was that he was in such irresistible form the only way his opponents could stop Carlos was by resorting to fouling him. A fellow Boca Junior, Roberto Trotta, told the press: 'Nothing short of a shot in the back of the neck will stop him.' Actually, a hard tackle by Felix Benito of Independiente stopped him in November 2003 – and as a result he sustained a pulled side ligament in his left knee which put him out of the rest of the competition. Carlos spoke to *Ole* again about the treatment he received in some matches. 'They want to get me off the pitch and they did it. The refs do not look out for me. I am scared to go on playing and not being able to walk; they come out and hit me at full strength, but I have to take it as all part of football. Otherwise I should not play any more.'

Already the durability and hard edge to his play was starting to show. Boca still had enough momentum to win the title despite the loss of their star player in the closing stages. Carlos scored eight goals in the 11 matches he played. The third leg of that treble-winning year was the Intercontinental Cup final against AC Milan, the winners of the European Champions League. Carlos came off the bench to replace

Guillermo in the game, despite still not being fully fit following his injury. He did enough in that period to have the Italian scouts reaching for their phones. Boca won the match on penalties. Tevez was fifth on Boca's hit list of penalty takers but his talents were not required as the Italians had already missed out with their allocation. The tears came again and Carlos told *Ole*: 'I wept like a madman, much more than at the Morumbi, I am telling you the truth, I could not even speak.' Those were genuine tears of joy. Tevez was, as Sir Matt Busby once described Duncan Edwards, 'utterly indefatigable'.

The honours were coming thick and fast for him now. In 2003 he won the Copa Libertadores' Most Valuable Player award, the Silver Olimpia (Argentine Footballer of the Year) and the South American Footballer of the Year award. Earlier in the year he had won a medal for helping his country clinch the South American U20 Championship.

Boca moved Carlos and his family out of Fort Apache to a residential area of the capital. Life improved for them all. The Boca directors insisted the move should take place because they were worried about the safety of their star man. Their concerns were unfounded – Tevez, like Maradona, was assuming a cult status amongst the Argentine public. The only problem was that with the fame came the attention of the press. The following season was marred by the constant intrusion of the press into his personal life. Carlos made the front page for the wrong reasons when they broke the news that he was dating the beautiful model Natalia Fassi. At the same time, though, Carlos himself announced that his girlfriend Vanessa Mansillo was pregnant with his child. The backlash began there and soon Carlos was fighting the photographers in the street and requesting the public give him some space. His form dipped and his fitness suffered. The 2004–5 season was his last for Boca; he played only nine games and scored twice.

His final game for Boca was highly emotional, because they won the Copa Sudamericana against Bolivar of La Paz. The Cup was played over two legs and Boca lost the first leg in Bolivia by a solitary goal. Martin Palermo grabbed an equaliser for Boca early in the return leg at the Bombonera and then Tevez shot the winner to spark a near-riot. It was his last goal for Boca, though he has always said he will return there one day. From the first minute of his Boca career to the last, Tevez's fighting spirit was undiminished. Despite his problems earlier in the year and the controversy following his departure, he was given a great send-off. At one stage during the celebrations he draped himself in a Boca flag.

For the second year running he won the Argentine Player of the Year award and also the South American Footballer of the Year award. It was interesting to note that his fellow countryman Javier Mascherano was second, with Robinho third. While his domestic form had suffered as a result of the problems he'd had with press intrusion, Carlos's form for his country was outstanding. He had made his debut for Argentina that spring and in the summer he was a member of the Argentina team that took part in the Olympics in Athens. They won gold by winning all six matches and the hard-shooting Tevez netted eight of their 17 goals. It was an outstanding performance and earned him the Olympic Golden Boot. Tevez was also awarded the Argentine Sportsperson of the Year award.

Carlos had signed for the Brazilian side Corinthians in an

$18m deal that rocked the world of South American football. The deal was financed by Media Sports Investment (MSI), a highly mysterious organisation with 33-year-old Kia Joorabchian as its president. Kia's identity was shrouded in mystery. Details of company records he controls or used to control tell of a Kia Joorabchian, who was born on 14 July 1971 and who holds a British passport.

Kia was born in Iran and after the 1979 Islamic revolution moved to Britain, where his family started a Mercedes-Benz dealership in Kent. Educated at the University of London, he then joined the family business. Kia became friendly with a businessman called Roy Azim, who introduced him to the Russian oligarch Boris Berezovsky. One of Boris's partners was Roman Abramovich, the owner of Chelsea. In November 2004 Arsenal fan Joorabchian and MSI leased the Brazilian team Corinthians for 10 years in exchange for wiping out the club's toxic debts of £11.5m and providing money for investment in new players. Corinthians went on an Abramovich-style spending spree and snapped up Carlos Tevez, Javier Mascherano, Carlos Alberto and Jo.

The Corinthians fans had mixed feelings about the purchase of Tevez, the player many believed to be the natural successor to Maradona. His ability was unquestioned but it was said that Brazilians were only interested in Brazilians. People were puzzled at the purchase of arguably the best player in the world, outside of Europe. Tevez was the kind of player that the European superclubs snapped up. The fee for him was four times the previous record fee for a Brazilian club. Fernando Hidalgo was the agent who had brokered the deal between Boca and Corinthians. The super-agent had close links with Pini

Zahavi, the intermediary who had helped Abramovich purchase Chelsea from Ken Bates.

The purchase of Carlos Tevez blew the wage structure of Corinthians away in a tsunami of dollars. The president of the club was critical of the signing, as were the older, hardcore fans who were worried about the identity of their club being lost. In the dressing room, the imbalance in players' wages caused immediate disharmony. Soon Tevez was in the media spotlight; again for the wrong reasons. A stand-up fight on the training ground with Brazilian team-mate Marquinhos was caught – on camera and quickly splashed all over the news. More trouble followed when he picked up a ban for swearing at a referee. He was also fined for making sexist comments about female match officials.

Despite these problems, Tevez cut through it all with the greatest gift he had at his disposal – his talent. The truly great can always produce when the odds seem stacked highest against them. There is footage somewhere on the internet of Marvin Gaye, perhaps the greatest soul singer of all time, being interviewed on a beach in Belgium. Gaye was exiled there after leaving Motown and being hounded for huge tax debts. He said: 'They can take away my money, they can take away my car, they can take away my home, but they can never take away my talent.' Within a year he was back on top of the USA charts with his song 'Sexual Healing'. Tevez was the same – nothing could diminish his will to succeed and his extraordinary talent. Appointed captain of Corinthians, he soon won the hearts of the fans with his honesty and hard work. He smashed in 25 goals in just 38 games as Corinthians won their first title in six years.

Once again, honours followed. The most prestigious was the CBF Campeonato Brasilero; the 'Best Player of the Year' award. This was the first time in 29 years that a non-Brazilian player had won the award – an amazing achievement considering the chaos that had ensued following his arrival and the initial antipathy that he had experienced. For the third year running he was voted the South American player of the year. The problem was that nothing good lasts for long.

Tevez was keen to meet Ronaldo – not the one at Old Trafford; their paths were to cross a bit later. This was the Brazilian version and Carlos revealed that he had a big poster of him in his home in Buenos Aires. It was a dream of his that they would meet in a World Cup clash so that they could exchange shirts. Carlos had a good World Cup in the summer of 2006. In Gelsenkirchen he scored the fifth goal for Argentina as they thrashed Serbia and Montenegro 6-0. Many people thought of Argentina as favourites to win the competition. In *Shoot* magazine Tevez was asked what he thought was his best performance in a match. This was his reply: 'Probably the 2006 World Cup quarter-final against Germany. I played really well but we still lost on penalties after leading 1-0. It was a very hard defeat for us all because we should have won that one. It's the game I would go back in time to change the result of.'

Tevez's stock rose even higher after his showing in the World Cup. He was now constantly linked with a move to Europe, and things quickly soured for him in Brazil after he expressed his desire to leave Corinthians. It did not help matters when he turned up for a press conference wearing a Manchester United shirt. The club were in turmoil as internal problems tore them apart; there was constant conflict between Corinthians and the MSI men. In 18 months they had been through seven different managers. All but five of the players in the squad were owned by MSI.

Things quickly deteriorated on the pitch too, and after losing seven games in a row Corinthians were at rock bottom. The fans turned on Carlos, and in a nasty incident they surrounded his car, with his wife and daughter inside. Shaken by the incident, Tevez missed training and flew back to Buenos Aires, telling the Brazilian media that he had played his last game in Brazil. His future seemed uncertain.

CHAPTER TWO

EAST ENDER

I came to West Ham intending to become an idol. I was prepared mentally and physically, ready to give maximum effort. But what happened to me is incredible. Never have I experienced anything like it.
CARLOS TEVEZ

The speculation about Carlos's future was centred on rumours of him going to either Italy or Spain. The hot money was on a move to Spain, where he could speak the language. England did not seem a realistic option; he had no foot in the door with any of the big clubs. Manchester United had him on their radar but were unsure about his ownership. Chelsea were still flush but Jose Mourinho, then in charge, was not keen on star names and Didier Drogba was already in fine form. When Tevez and Mascherano ended up at West Ham after an 11th-hour transfer deadline deal it was the biggest shock to hit the East End since Dirty Den came back from the dead. West Ham's official statement was:

'West Ham United are delighted to announce the double signing of Argentinean World Cup stars Tevez and Mascherano from Brazilian club Corinthians. The pair have been signed for an undisclosed fee and put pen to paper on permanent contracts with the club this afternoon. All other aspects of the transfers will remain confidential and undisclosed. The transfers represent a massive coup for the Hammers, who have beaten off some of Europe's biggest clubs to secure the services of the duo.'

The deal was done on 31 August 2006, the last day of the transfer window. Kia Joorabchian agreed the deal with the then chairman Teddy Brown and chief executive Paul Aldridge. The key words in the statement were 'permanent contracts' and 'undisclosed'. After the signing Tevez and Mascherano rejoined the Argentina squad, preparing for the friendly against Brazil which was to be played at Arsenal's Emirates Stadium.

Did West Ham need the hassle of acquiring Argentina's equivalent of the Chuckle Brothers? That is what the Hammers fans were asking themselves, but they should have been wary of drawing assumptions based on geography. In their first season back in the top flight, 2005–6, West Ham finished a very respectable ninth. They had also come within a whisker of winning the FA Cup, eventually losing on penalties to Liverpool in the final after leading 2-0 at one stage. Only a brilliant equaliser by Stevie Gerrard had hauled the Scousers back into the match. The game eventually ended in a 3-3 draw after extra time.

West Ham were at that time managed by ex-Crystal Palace defender Alan Pardew, who had joined them in 2003. The season had started badly when top striker Dean Ashton was ruled out for the duration before a ball had been kicked in anger. Ashton had broken a bone in his foot while training with the England squad, an injury that was to eventually end his career. West Ham fans were delighted at the new international signings and thought that the club could now really build on their encouraging start. Some were even talking in terms of European football being in the offing.

This was before the credit crunch and stars from all over the world were flocking to what was known as the 'Golden Age' of the Premier League. The stampede was on for the huge salaries being paid by the fat cats of the upper echelons. Tevez knew he was arriving in a major football city as soon as his plane touched down at Heathrow. It was the Promised Land, where the streets were paved with football gold.

London was a bit of a culture shock. Carlos admitted that the only thing he knew about West Ham was that the club's insignia was two little hammers (this hammer image would be a recurring motif in his game in the coming months). The shopping was fantastic, though, and he was interested in checking out the world-famous music scene. But he soon started to feel homesick and told *Shoot* magazine: 'I miss my friends and family. Living in England is great and people treat me very well, but the hardest thing for me has to be the language followed by the weather. The weather is very different from what we have in Buenos Aires where it does not rain that much. I cannot believe how, during the English winter, it gets dark at 3pm.'

At that stage no West Ham fan understood how the club had managed to end up with South America's most promising youngsters. The deal looked to be the smartest since hard-headed svengali Sir Alex Ferguson had acquired Eric Cantona from Leeds. It transpired, though, that West Ham were only borrowing the players for an unspecified period. Moreover, West Ham had broken the rules set out by the Premier League by obscuring the third-party ownership of Tevez and his pal.

Speaking on the West Ham website, Carlos explained why he had gone to West Ham: 'One of my ambitions was to play in the Premiership, which is one of the biggest leagues in the world and this is why I am at West Ham. There were reports that other clubs were interested in signing me but that is all it was.' The list of those clubs ranged from Chelsea to Inter Milan, from Arsenal to Lyon. 'West Ham showed a lot of interest in us and that is why we are here. I first heard about the possibility of joining West Ham 48 hours before the transfer deadline and from the moment we met the manager, Alan Pardew, we were impressed with what he had to say and are very proud to have signed for such a big club.'

Carlos drew comfort from a parallel with his idol and mentor, Maradona, and his glory days with Napoli. West Ham, like Napoli, were a small club living in the shadows of their wealthy rivals. Both clubs had fanatical hardcore supporters, brought up on a culture of good football, who stuck with them no matter what. They were also chronic underachievers with delusions of grandeur. For a short while Napoli's dreams came true as, singlehandedly, Maradona led them to two Serie A titles and the UEFA Cup. Surely Maradona was living proof that the 'one man does not make a team' argument was not always true.

At first Alan Pardew could not believe his luck, landing players of that quality, and did not question their arrival or the motives behind it. The fact was, though, that West Ham was being used as a vehicle to showcase the unique talents of the pair. The Hammers had to issue a statement denying that they were contractually obligated to play Tevez and Mascherano in every game. In hindsight, had the pair been integrated into the side from the start of the season it might have made things a lot easier for all concerned.

The acquisition by West Ham of Tevez and Mascherano not only flabbergasted their fans but also their Argentina team-mates. 'Really?' said an astonished Javier Saviola when he learnt of the amazing transfer. Alan Pardew was delighted with the first training session to include the two new boys from Argentina. Carlos had only had two light training sessions in the preceding three weeks and looked short of full fitness. Javier was ahead of him in terms of fitness and looked ready to take on the world. Such was Carlos's eagerness to play and his desire to succeed, though, Pardew was impressed and decided to blood them both as quickly as possible.

Tevez made his tentative debut in England on 10th September 2006 in a home match against Aston Villa. Before the game he gave an interview to the *People*: 'I am ready to play but the decision depends on the manager. I have talked with him and made it clear that I am not at my top level but I cannot wait to start helping West Ham and repaying the confidence in me. I am just a young player with a lot of desire to be a big success in England. I will score many goals this season and I already know my first one will be dedicated to the fans. I am conscious of the fact that I am going to be kicked in the Premiership but I am a professional and it is part of my salary. But I am here to play at West Ham for many years. I am not here for convenience or professional interests.'

The game ended 1-1. Liam Ridgewell gave Villa an early lead, but Bobby Zamora equalised for West Ham after 52 minutes. Pardew was satisfied with the performance but admitted to the press that the little striker was still some way off attaining full fitness. Tevez had come on after 61 minutes to replace Marlon Harewood, and Alan Pardew knew that Carlos would have to put in a lot of work over the coming weeks to reach the required level. The game was shown live in Argentina because of the interest that had been generated over there by the club's acquisition of two of their biggest stars.

Tevez claimed that he had followed West Ham because he had a friend called Lionel Scaloni in Argentina, who had 13 games for them on loan from Deportivo La Coruna. Lionel replaced the departed Tomas Repka and played in the FA Cup Final. They watched Hammers games together and Scaloni advised him of the background and gossip on the players. The ex-Estudiantes defender was always sorry that West Ham could not agree a deal for a permanent move for him.

The seating at Upton Park is very close to the pitch, and over the years there have been numerous incidences of players running at high speed and colliding with the advertising hoardings. For a player like Tevez, whose style was to play with his head down, there was the omnipresent threat of dribbling the ball off the field and into the hoardings, out of the ground and down Green Street. The fact that the crowd could reach out and touch the players amazed Tevez; the absence of fences, barriers and wire had been a great surprise to him. In Argentina it would have been impossible to deal with the crowds without those things. Mind you, there was a time when similar methods were employed in Britain. Around the time Carlos was born, the then Chairman of Chelsea FC, Ken Bates, had introduced an electric fence at Stamford Bridge following crowd disturbances reportedly involving the West Ham ICF hooligan group. The famous 'Chicken Run' section of the ground received its name because of the wire that surrounded it.

Carlos was already striking up a special relationship with the Hammers fans, and he quickly found that he could relax more in England. In South America, superstar football players were treated like the huge pop stars of the sixties, who were mobbed wherever they went. A relatively simple task like taking his daughter to the local park was an impossibility for Tevez once he had attained a certain level of success and fame in Brazil. The West Ham fans had more respect for his privacy. Some would come up to him and shake his hand. They were proud that a player of his stature had come to play for their club. Some wanted autographs but it was always done very quietly and efficiently.

West Ham had a great history of wonderful players of all races, colours and backgrounds. The only requirement of the fans was that they could play the beautiful game. Their three most famous players were of course Bobby Moore, Geoff Hurst and Martin Peters – the most quintessentially English players of all time and arguably the most famous; certainly the most successful. Bobby Moore was the coolest footballer ever, on and off the field. Just imagine if Moore circa 1966 was marking Tevez. What a duel that would have been! Geoff Hurst was still the only player to score a hat-trick in a World Cup Final. As former Chelsea chairman Brian Mears so memorably put it, 'Dinosaurs will walk the earth before that happens again.'

Last of the trio was Martin Peters, a player England manager Sir Alf Ramsey said was '10 years ahead of his time'. People scoffed at the time, but his words have a chilling accuracy now. Martin Peters was the first postmodern player. Looking at some of the current England squad, Peters still looks a decade ahead. On their way to 1966 glory, a solitary goal by Geoff Hurst knocked out a ferocious Argentina side in the quarter-finals. Carlos heard the coaches at Boca talking about those battles; it was part of Argentina's modern history. Football gives such a perception of a nation. Tevez was respected almost immediately by the fans in England because he was seen as a tough, street kid with great skill and a huge appetite for work. This was a player of the same lineage as Maradona, Kempes and Villa, as characteristic of his culture as the image of Bobby Moore was to the English fans.

Another two West Ham legends were Billy Bonds and Julian Dicks, both incredibly hard players who would sweat blood for the cause of West Ham United. Tevez was cut from the same block of granite as those players. The fans sensed this early on in their relationship; they could spot a phoney a bus ride away. Despite their fearsome reputation at the height of the hooligan wars, the West Ham crowd were highly supportive of one of the first black players to break through in the 1970s. The player's name was Clyde Best (ask your grandparents). The big Bermudian made his debut against Arsenal in August 1969 and went on to score 58 goals over the next seven seasons. His legacy still hovers over the modern West Ham team. There were also some notable coloured members in the notorious IFC hooligan gang. Cass Pennant, whose blistering life story was told in the successful eponymous film, was of mixed parentage.

At West Ham there was always this great contradiction of image. There was the sort of xenophobia typified by Alf Garnett in *'Til Death Us Do Part* – the archetypical bigoted West Ham fan – and yet juxtaposed with this was the West Ham supporters' reputation as the most knowledgeable, appreciative fans in London, if not the whole country. An incident that typified the spirit of the fans occurred back in the seventies, when West Bromwich Albion were the visitors. The Midlands side that day included three black players: Laurie Cunningham, Brendan Baston and Cyrille Regis. Cunningham was the first black player to win England honours and was signed by Real Madrid for the then astonishing fee of £995,000 in 1979. A dazzling, ball-playing winger with a louche swagger, Cunningham was the first black player to be signed by the Spanish giants and won La Liga with them in 1980. He was tragically killed in a car smash in Spain in 1989, at the age of 33.

Cunningham led the West Ham defence a merry dance all night but it was Regis who stood out even more, with his speed and strength, which terrorised the Hammers' defence. If a player like Clyde Best punched a large hole in the wall of race hate, then Regis helped kick it down. A custom in those days, if that was the word for it, was the habit of fans throwing bananas at the black players. This vile practice didn't just happen at West Ham; there is the famous picture of John Barnes at Liverpool kicking a banana out of his path, shortly before a Merseyside derby. Today a storm would rightly rage for weeks if something like that happened, but in less enlightened times it was an all too common sight.

A small bunch of bananas was launched out of the crowd and landed at the feet of Cyrille Regis. With the ball cleared upfield, Regis proceeded to sit down on the pitch. He made a pantomime out of choosing one of the bananas and then ate it. Not satisfied at that, he chucked the skin back into the crowd. As he ran back up the field, a spontaneous round of applause broke out from the Hammers fans. The next time he played at Upton Park, the big centre-forward was presented with a bunch of bananas before the game by a group of fans, in tribute to his humour and tolerance. Cyrille continued the joke by saying that the ones chucked at him were tastier. A wonderful little anecdote showing how a despicable action was turned into something far more pleasant. It could only have happened at West Ham.

Carlos spoke of how happy he felt when he first heard the chants of 'Argentina, Argentina' being recited by the Hammers fans after he had scored a vital goal. This chant was later picked up by the Manchester United fans and included in their loop of chants and songs. Quite amazing when you think that England was at war with Argentina less than a generation before. Carlos told *World* Soccer: 'For someone like me who had a relative who fought in the Malvinas [Falklands] and who knows the feeling that existed after the war, it was incredible to hear that chant. I was amazed that I could be an idol for English fans, it made a huge impression on me.'

It was soon apparent that Carlos was a very big fish in the relatively small pond of Upton Park. He was surrounded largely by home-grown players who had come through the youth system. A few years earlier the West Ham youth academy had given the world a brilliant crop of youngsters who went on to become stars at the biggest Premier League clubs. Rio Ferdinand and Michael Carrick were at Manchester United, Frank Lampard and Joe Cole at Chelsea, Jermaine Defoe at Tottenham, and Glen Johnson at Portsmouth. In February 2009 England manager Fabio Capello called Carlton Cole, Matthew Upson and Robert Green into the international squad for a friendly match against Spain.

Lifelong West Ham fan Greg Kimberley was interviewed about the impact the Argentinean pair made on Hammers' season: 'Newspaper reports that West Ham had signed these two Argentine internationals was the first I had heard of Tevez. I have to admit I had not heard of either player, but was excited at the prospect of them joining us.'

The success of reaching the FA Cup final the previous season had already raised expectation levels and now with two world-class players joining the squad, anticipation was at a dangerous level. The first home game against Villa began with Alan Pardew addressing an eager crowd with a speech underlining the need to be patient. This was going to be hard as everyone, as is so often the case in football today, expected immediate results. From the start it was thought that Tevez and Mascherano were players on a different level; for Mascherano this proved to be a problem. Evidently he needed more time to settle into a struggling side.

Tevez, on the other hand, had the luxury of being a hardworking, highly competitive forward who obviously frightened defences. His early mistakes did not matter so much in his 'holding role' in midfield. Alan Curbishley said later, when Tevez was scoring goals for fun, that the reason he did not start Carlos in more games was because he was still working out his best position. The fact that he played as the main striker for Argentina might have given him a clue!

Soon it became clear to Carlos and Javier that Alan Pardew had no place for them in his team. Carlos admitted that to all intents and purposes he was starting his career over again. The fact that he had a huge reputation in South America counted for nothing in England. To the average English fan, Argentinean football began and ended with Diego Maradona. For a young man like Carlos to have achieved what he did in such a short space of time was a remarkable achievement, but the punters had no reference point. The relevance of being the Argentinean Player of the Year was lost on them. If you were up early on a Saturday morning before the latest racing news on Channel 4, there was a little programme about football from around the world, with clips of the action, but that was about it.

Carlos was still struggling for match fitness; it took him months to be anywhere near fit enough for the punishing Premier League. When he arrived in England he had never seen a Premier League game live. West Ham were performing badly and people were saying that the bad run of form was caused by the disruption of having to accommodate Mascherano and Tevez. Looking back this was nonsensical, because the talent that was being added to the team was of the highest quality. Any squad in the Premier League would have been enhanced by their presence. The proof of this particular pudding was that both players would go on to make a huge impression on their next employers.

But West Ham went nine games without a win, seven of them without even scoring a goal. The strike force of Sheringham, Zamora and Harewood was looking increasingly impotent. The West Ham fans thought that Carlos was being underused by Pardew; they knew their football and all of them believed that Tevez and Mascherano should be in the team. Carlos Bianchi had been one of Carlos's coaches at Boca Juniors and was confident that Tevez could transfer his particular brand of brilliance to the English game. Alan Pardew had to reconfigure the West Ham attack, though, and he explained to the *People*: 'Tevez is a star but he needs a coach with a very attacking mind who is prepared to pick the team to suit his needs. The

West Ham team needs a player who will do the work so Tevez can feed on that.' A highly perceptive view there, from his former coach. The player that could perhaps have helped Carlos most was Dean Ashton, who sadly thanks to injuries never had the chance to line up alongside him in the claret and blue.

The Hammers' next home fixture in the Premier League, on 17 September, was against Newcastle; then coached by Glenn Roeder, another ex-Hammers boss. Our Argentinean hero was hoping to get off the mark for his new club and early on in the first half he rattled the crossbar with one of his special free kicks. That was the high spot of the game for Carlos, because at half-time he was substituted and replaced by Marlon Harewood. Second-half goals by ex-Chelsea winger Damien Duff and Obafemi Martins gave the Geordies victory and raised doubts about Tevez's future in the big time. Mascherano did not play the full 90 minutes either and the game ended with both of the new boys on the bench. Alan Pardew spoke about his decision on the West Ham website: 'Tevez was not injured. I felt he showed "moments" for us but in the end, we ran out of options with him and I tried to change it.

'Tevez took it well, but I have not had too many chances to work with him and he has not played a lot of football, either. Alongside Javier Mascherano, I thought they both looked a little bit tired today but those two were not the only players who looked tired out there.

'I don't want to focus on the arrival of the Argentinean guys too much. Yes, there have obviously been changes to the spirit and the squad, and whenever that happens to our group, we always need to re-focus to make sure that it does not affect us.

'Overall, I think that we have handled the situation well but we cannot get away from the fact that we are going through a transitional period following the arrival of the new boys and if you were to put me under a lie-detector test, I probably would have a problem giving you my best team, right now.

'After all, no manager can name his best eleven when new players first arrive, and at the moment, I cannot guarantee anyone a first-team place, especially after that performance.'

Hindsight is a wonderful thing but reading that quote now, it is possible to sense how Pardew was distancing himself from the Argentinean pair, implying their arrival had unsettled the club. The West Ham bubble was about to burst. Soon, reports started appearing in the tabloids that Tevez was set to leave again. This time, Spanish aces Atletico Madrid were believed to be weighing up a bid for the diminutive striker. PSV Eindhoven had bid for him at Boca and there were persistent rumours that they were again interested in him.

Meanwhile, Palermo outplayed the Hammers in their UEFA Cup ties and beat them 4-0 on aggregate over the two legs. West Ham had managed to qualify by virtue of their appearance in the FA Cup the previous season, but their European sojourn was a short one. Carlos played in both of the matches, being subbed in the Hammers' home fixture as the Italians won by a solitary goal.

The new boys hardly played that autumn, but they both appeared at White Hart Lane in October, where Hammers went down by a solitary goal. That reversal left West Ham in nineteenth position in the Premier League. In a match with about as much action as a Harold Pinter play, the only incident of note occurred when former Hammer Jermain Defoe was accused of biting Javier Mascherano on the arm after the two men clashed in a midfield skirmish. The hot-blooded Mascherano was annoyed at the coverage this particular episode received in the media – despite being used to the madhouse of South American football, both Argentinean players were stunned at the tactics used by the press to highlight confrontations.

Alan Pardew spoke to the *Sun* about Mascherano: 'I feel sorry for Javier because his training and his work for us have been of the highest order – but he just can't seem to get an opening. The problem is that he is blocked by Hayden Mullins and I cannot play them both in the same team.' Hayden Mullins was always a solid, tidy player in the mould of Scott Parker. In the January 2009 window Mullins joined Portsmouth. Whether he was indeed more worthy of a place in the West Ham starting eleven than Mascherano, who finished the 2006–7 season by playing in a Champions League final having made the move to Liverpool, is questionable.

Making his first appearance for seven weeks, Carlos started on the right wing on 18 November in a tough away game against Chelsea. It was his first appearance at Stamford Bridge, against a club that made no secret of their admiration for him. In a typical functional performance Chelsea, with a visit to Manchester United in the offing, won 1-0. Geremi scored the solitary goal with a thunderous free kick which left West Ham goalkeeper Robert Green helpless. One of the few high spots in the match was Carlos's duel with Chelsea full-back Ashley Cole. Carlos seemed to be in the mood for taking out his frustrations on Chelsea, but found Cole a formidable opponent.

Nevertheless, Carlos had produced his best game in the claret-and-blue shirt to date, putting in a strong performance as he ran around like a man possessed. The stats indicated that he made 35 passes, 27 of which were accurate. The *Sun* gave him 7/10 for his showing against Chelsea; no West Ham player had a higher rating. Importantly he had played for the full 90 minutes. He was unable to create any goal chances though, as Mourinho's men did what they did best under his command: ground out a result. Alan Pardew was gushing in his praise of Carlos as he told the *Sun*: 'Tevez is 22 and bursting on to a league that's completely different to anything he's played in. We have to give him time and our patience has been rewarded. Now it's down to Tevez to show the same diligence and work rate. If he does that with the undoubted ability he has, then he is going to be a handful.

'He has had problems with injury since he came here and the past couple of weeks have been his first real run on the training ground. He has got a burly chest like Wayne Rooney and people mistake that for excess weight, but he's actually in good condition. In fact, he's lighter now than he has ever been in Argentina or Brazil.'

The fortunes of West Ham changed at the end of November 2006, when the club was taken over by Eggert Magnusson and his Icelandic backers. At the time of the takeover, Magnusson spoke of the EastEnders' huge potential and proud traditions. But the acceptance of the £85m bid by Magnusson left some question marks over the future of the two Argentinean players. Carlos had yet to score for the Hammers; the press were already prepared to write him off, but the fans believed in him and, more importantly, he believed in himself. Tevez told *Sky Sports*

News: 'If the new owner wanted me to leave, that is what I would have to do. I would respect what he wanted as if it is his club. But I would prefer that and manager Alan Pardew wanted to keep me.'

Tevez's rebellious side surfaced in the next game, a home match against Sheffield United. In the 67th minute of the game, Alan Pardew substituted Tevez for Teddy Sheringham. This incensed Carlos, who stormed out of the ground. Pardew, who spent most of the second half prowling around the touchline like a footballing Uriah Heep, was furious and demanded an apology from the player. To give him his due, Carlos turned up at training on the Monday morning and offered his apologies to his manager and team-mates. He was particularly anxious to convey to them that he meant no disrespect to the manager, his colleagues and especially to the loyal fans. This was duly accepted, but the players were allowed to determine the amount he should be fined, which was to be donated to Great Ormond Street Hospital. They also decided to come up with a forfeit for Carlos as further punishment. It must have been an amusing scene at the training ground when this matter was discussed! Finally, it was decided – Carlos would be made to wear a Brazil shirt in training. Tevez was horrified and told Argentinean radio station *Mitre*: 'I think that my team-mates have gone crazy. I will never use Brazil's national team shirt. My team-mates have a great sense of humour and they have asked me to do that, but they know that it will be impossible. I have respect for Brazil because I have played there, but I would never use that shirt because I am Argentinean.' Javier Mascherano joined in the joke, suggesting that nobody outside of the training ground would know about it – but in the end the

Brazil shirt never saw the light of day at the Chadwell Heath training ground.

So, it would seem that team spirit was still fairly buoyant. Carlos was also starting to understand the quirky, almost indecipherable humour of his new countrymen. But there were still questions. Teddy Sheringham was finding it hard to make regular starts because of the competition for places, mainly from Carlos. Speaking to the *Daily Mirror*, he denied that the West Ham camp had been divided by the arrivals of the Argentineans: 'There is no turmoil. The South American lads are learning English even if, like typical foreigners, they probably know more than they make out at the moment,' he said. 'They are not stupid, they understand the situation and know we have a good team and spirit here before they arrive. It's only a matter of time before they make their presence felt.'

It was a rather strange quote from Teddy; the phrase 'like typical foreigners' jarred a bit, but Carlos was putting his head down and trying to make a go of it. Alan Pardew had employed the services of a full-time interpreter to improve the communication problems, but the latest rumour from the mill was that he was heading back to Boca Juniors in time for next year's Copa Libertadores.

Everton away on a blustery early December afternoon was his next outing and again he put in a highly impressive individual performance, which should have earned his side at least a draw. The West Ham team controlled the first half and forced 12 corners without being able to score. Second-half goals from Everton duo Leon Osman and James Vaughan sunk them, though, as they plunged down to 17th spot. West Ham had gone over 10 hours without scoring a goal away from home in a dreadful spell. Speaking about the match on the West Ham website, Carlos stated: 'I do not think the result fairly reflected the way we played and we definitely deserved something from the game. We worked really hard, especially in the first half, and it was very frustrating not to score a goal.

'Yes, the conditions were hard, but it was the same for both teams. We should have used the wind to our advantage in the first half because they certainly did in the second half. At the end of the day they were just more clinical in their finishing.'

Carlos's lack of clinical finishing was a constant problem. Slowly, though, he was getting used to the Premier League. The increase in speed and the stamina required were the hardest aspects of the English game for him, but he talked about his improvement in the same interview: 'I definitely feel that little by little, I am getting to where I want to be in terms of the level of my performances. I feel good in myself, I have had a few kicks and knocks, but I understand that is part and parcel of the Premiership so it is not a problem. It makes me stronger as a player.'

Flashes of the kid from Fort Apache were starting to emerge, as Carlos refused to be physically intimidated by bully-boy defenders. All his life he had been riding tackles and avoiding flailing boots, fists and elbows. There was nothing new to face here; it held no fear for him. Like all great players Tevez had that toughness. If you were to make a list of the greatest players – Pelé, Maradona, Cruyff and Best – the characteristic common to them all would be their bravery and ability to stand up to the most ferocious tackling. If you were born in a tower block in Buenos Aires and had played street football since you were a toddler, what was the problem?

Alan Pardew was sacked in mid-December as Eggert Magnusson cleared the decks for a fresh start at his new club. West Ham had taken two bad beatings in the last two matches: 0-2 at Wigan and 0-4 away to a revved-up Bolton. Carlos had played in both of them. The board moved quickly to appoint former Charlton boss Alan Curbishley in Alan Pardew's place. Curbishley had the right credentials on his CV in that he too was a product of the Hammers youth academy and had played for them for four years. Born in Forest Gate, he still has the record of being the youngest-ever Hammer to appear on a team sheet, even though he did not play in that particular match. He was no Joe Cole, though; more an Alan Dickens. Another steady, effective player, who became a steady, effective manager. He had built a reputation as one of the very few English managers to cut it at the highest level. Strangely enough, Pardew was to swap places with Curbishley as he took over at the Valley.

The fans' reaction to Alan Curbishley's appointment was mixed – some doubted he had the flair to produce the style of football that West Ham demanded. Nevertheless he got off to a good start, beating Manchester United in his first home game. Carlos took no part and could only watch as the team whose shirt he once wore at a Corinthians press conference went down to a late goal from the marauding Nigel Reo-Coker, after a mistake by Rio Ferdinand.

Carlos was of the opinion that Alan Pardew had failed to utilise his talents to their fullest extent and he told the *News of the World*: 'I was surprised to see how long Pardew held on to the job in the end. In Argentina or Brazil he would have been out long ago. It was clear the team did not react as he wanted – it wasn't going right. I was never given the chances I thought I would be given and I was told to play out of position against my will. I had to sacrifice myself for the team, which I don't think helped. I was playing in ways I did not understand well and I lost a lot from my own game. It did not fit where he put me, but I wanted to help.'

There was no doubt that the arrival of Tevez and Mascherano did not help prolong Pardew's career. He was too good a manager not to be aware of their unquestioned talent, but how much he knew of the overall picture is unclear. If he was aware, as it has been claimed, that Tevez and Mascherano were just passing through then he could hardly be blamed for not wanting to build a team around them.

Carlos pledged his support to the cause of keeping the Hammers from relegation and vowed to support Curbishley. It was his ambition to start scoring goals and to help West Ham win matches. Things were going to get worse before they got better, though, as the Hammers went on a 10-game winless Premier League run from late December to March. 2007 started in the best possible way for Carlos, though, as he played a starring role in the 3-0 thrashing of Brighton and Hove Albion in an FA cup third-round tie. He still failed to get on the scoresheet, but he had a brilliant game and had a hand in all three of the second-half goals scored by Mark Noble, Carlton Cole and Haydn Mullins. West Ham were receiving a lot of bad press, but after the game Alan Curbishley defended the summer signings.

Tevez started the next match, the home game against Fulham, which ended in an error-riddled 3-3 draw. He lasted only 15 minutes, though, before limping off with a calf strain, but he was back for the home match against Watford on 2 February, coming on as a second-half sub for

Bobby Zamora. On two occasions he was unlucky to score, first firing a free kick just wide and then having a shot kicked off the line. The Hammers went down to a penalty kick, and things now looked dire.

Javier Mascherano left to join Liverpool in the January transfer window. This gave the first indication that all might not be as it seemed with regard to Tevez and Mascherano – when the Merseyside club completed the transfer and the paperwork was checked, questions began to be asked about the Argentinean duo's transfer history. Javier started only three games for West Ham, with two further appearances as a substitute. Many would say this was a criminal waste of his talents, and after he left, he established himself as possibly the best holding midfield player in Europe and a cornerstone of the Liverpool team. On a personal level, Carlos was sorry to see Javier go – they had been friends since both of them had played together for Argentina's Under-20 squad and later in Brazil with Corinthians. Speaking to *World Soccer,* Carlos added: 'Going to Liverpool was the best thing that could have happened for him. He was not happy at West Ham; he was really depressed because there was no place in the team for him. I was thrilled he got to the Champions League final.'

Mascherano did appear in the Champions League final that year, when Liverpool played Italian giants AC Milan. Fresh from the Kaka-inspired victory over Manchester United in the semi-finals, Milan won 2-1. Both goals came from the frisky Filippo Inzaghi.

Back at West Ham, Alan Curbishley purchased Luis Boa Morte from Fulham for £5m, but he failed to make any impact. Ex-Arsenal defender Matthew Upson joined for £6m, but injury hindered his first season as he tried to resurrect his career. As the winter wore on, the Hammers' chances of staying in the top flight seemed even more remote. The relationship between Carlos and Curbishley seemed as uncomfortable as the one he had enjoyed with Alan Pardew. Lack of communication was at the heart of it. In an interview with Charlie Wyett of the *People*, he revealed that he barely spoke to the ex-Charlton boss: 'The manager speaks to you very little. They put the set pieces on a blackboard and you have to go up to read it? It's a much colder way of doing things. I am not thinking about leaving; I do not want a situation to happen here like the ones that happened at Boca Juniors and Corinthians where, for reasons beyond football, I had to leave, and I left in a bad way.'

At the end of February, West Ham were demolished 4-0 by Charlton as they put up an appalling display. The West Ham fans, in utter despair, chanted, 'You're not fit to wear the shirt,' at their broken, dejected team as they were ripped apart by their London neighbours. Carlos was probably the only West Ham player who had looked fit to wear the famous claret-and-blue shirt. As West Ham folded under the Charlton onslaught, Tevez never gave up running and striving, displaying great ball control throughout. But the season looked a hopeless cause now, as the trapdoor to the Championship beckoned. The game was described as the £50million relegation shoot-out; that was the estimate figure that a relegated club would ultimately lose out on. It was reported that some bookmakers were giving 66-1 on for West Ham to be relegated.

Spurs at home on the first weekend of March was the game where it all changed for Carlos. He finally scored a goal, and after that all the old confidence and swagger came flooding back. Coupled with that was the important fact that after more than six months in England, he had finally attained a good level of fitness. His first goal for West Ham came from a curling free kick, which saw him rip off his shirt and exuberantly jump into the crowd in celebration. When he finally re-emerged he was, of course, booked. It ended his 20-game goal drought and sparked a huge outburst of affection from the home fans. They wanted him to know how highly they rated him and how pleased they were that all the faith they had placed in him had been repaid by his superb goal. Tevez's painstaking pursuit of excellence was gathering momentum. In a thrilling game, West Ham led 3-2 with less than 90 seconds to go, but ended up losing 3-4. The winning goal was scored by Tottenham substitute Paul Stalteri in stoppage time. Prior to that, Dimitar Berbatov equalised for Spurs, also from a free kick. It was the first time their paths had crossed.

After the game Curbishley described the last-minute defeat as 'naïve', but he was encouraged by the work rate and effort of the players. The lack of confidence worried him, as did the players' inability to close a game out. Tevez's goals that season would prove more controversial than anyone could have imagined, but overlooked in all the hubbub was his part in the win at Blackburn on 17 March. With 70 minutes gone at a rainy Ewood Park, the Hammers were trailing to a 50th-minute Christopher Samba goal, and apparently spinning out of the Premier League. Then Carlos scored from the spot, after he had been brought down by Brett Emerton. The penalty decision sparked an angry exchange between the two sides. Emerton and Zamora were cautioned as things boiled over.

The pressure was on Tevez as he stepped up to take his

first penalty kick in England. He simply had to score to keep his team in the big time – no pressure, then. In goal for Blackburn was top-class keeper Brad Friedel, but Carlos beat him with a perfectly-placed shot – low and to the left. Among the 18,591-strong crowd that night was a large following of Hammers fans. They gave their team tremendous support throughout the game but when their hero scored, they increased the decibel level even higher in demented euphoria.

The Hammers went looking for the winner – and they got it, with the most bizarre goal that Tevez had ever been involved in. West Ham's Lee Bowyer appeared to handle the ball, and then substitute Bobby Zamora fired a shot goalwards. Carlos was standing on the goal line, in an offside position. The ball hit his boot and was deflected out. It did not appear to have crossed the line at any point. Amazingly, though, the referee gave a goal and West Ham left the ground with three priceless points. The goal should have been disallowed on three counts: firstly, Carlos was standing in an offside position, clearly interfering with play. Secondly, Lee Bowyer had clearly handled the ball before it had been struck by Bobby Zamora. And in any event, the ball had not crossed the line.

Truly bewildered, Rovers' left-back Stephen Warnock confirmed this: 'It was never over the line; there was a handball by Lee Bowyer and Tevez was in an offside position. If the officials cannot pick up one of those things between them, you wonder what game they are watching.'

The quick-thinking Carlos had started wildly celebrating for a goal even though the ball had not crossed the line, which further confused the issue. Carlos figured that in that split second, the assistant referee would be far more likely to signal for a goal if a West Ham player was already celebrating, as opposed to standing around looking guilty. It is entirely possible the linesman was affected by this, and also by the fact that behind him 4,000 West Ham fans were screaming at the top of their voices for a call.

The win was to spark the most amazing 'great escape' in the modern history of the game.

CHAPTER THREE
(SHEF)FIELD
OF DREAMS

I don't think there is another town in the world that can beat Sheffield for sport. There is such a hearty love for outdoor recreation amongst the "grinders" that on the occasion of a good match at cricket or football, Bramall Lane is bound to see thousands of spectators assembled within its anything but classic precincts.
THE ATHLETIC NEWS (1877)

The crowd kept singing for him. It put pressure on me.
ALAN CURBISHLEY

I am a person that likes to fight for everything until the end.
CARLOS TEVEZ

Carlos Tevez had gone 1,146 minutes without scoring a goal before he scored against Spurs. Now he was on a roll, and scored again in the 2-0 victory over Middlesbrough at the end of March. It was a vital win because it closed the gap on Sheffield United, then lying in 17th spot on the table, to 5 points.

Carlos set up the first goal for Bobby Zamora in the opening moments to set the game alight from the start. He won the ball out on the right and crossed hard, his run of good fortune continuing as it deflected off a Boro defender and fell to Zamora, who fired home. Just on half-time, Carlos netted his third goal of the campaign with a quick turn and low drive into the corner. Full-back George

McCartney had provided the cross and Tevez pounced when Andrew Taylor failed to close him down.

Middlesbrough played badly that afternoon and the Hammers ran out easy winners. Alan Curbishley was admitting now that his early assessment of Tevez was based on the fact that he had not scored a goal and the fact that his standard of finishing had failed to impress. Curbishley told *The Times*: 'Alan Pardew and myself struggled a little bit how to use Tevez best. He was doing a lot of his work outside the box and not really being in the danger area. We have asked him to concentrate on being in the danger area. Every time he gets the ball now he is further up the field and he has caused problems. It has dawned on him that in our position you have got to put that effort in to give yourself a chance. Now the others are starting to follow. He and Mark Noble have sparked us off today.'

Curblishley's statement about things 'dawning on Carlos Tevez' did not quite ring true; he had been putting in the effort since he had first kicked a ball in anger. That was the only way he knew to play the game. He was correct, though, about the improvement in Mark Noble's game since Tevez's influence had grown in the team.

Curbishley had also made the point that the crowd had always put him under pressure to play their new idol. The love affair between the West Ham fans and Tevez continued to grow. The fans had warmed to him in a manner not seen at the Boleyn ground since Paolo Di Canio had strutted his stuff there. Curbishley drew a comparison between the Italian winger and his striker: 'Tevez and Di Canio do share that indulgent touch. We will have to see how long Tevez is here before we can tell whether he will be remembered like Di Canio.'

In the next few weeks Carlos was going to show exactly

why he will be remembered like Paolo. The stats were already pointing to an upturn in Carlos's fortunes. He had so far recorded two goal assists, 20 shots on target, 20 off, 18 tackles won, 178 completed passes, 25 dribbles, 21 crosses, one clearance and three interceptions during his time at Upton Park.

The next week, the Hammers had a great win at the Emirates Stadium to increase their chances of staying up. They were the first team to beat Arsenal at home in their new stadium. It gave them a unique double over Arsène Wenger's stylish team, as the previous November (without Tevez) West Ham had pulled off a shock win over them.

Bobby Zamora scored one of his best-ever goals for West Ham late in the first half to clinch the points, but it was Robert Green who had the game of his life to deny Arsenal a goal. Stats indicated the Gunners had 25 attempts at goal. The West Ham programme for the next home match, against Chelsea, featured Green as the cover star, thanks to his superb display against Arsenal.

It was another steep learning curve for Tevez, playing against an outstanding team in their magnificent new ground. With his team under the cosh for nearly all of the game, he had few chances to shine and was well policed by the classy Gael Clichy. The closest he came to scoring was when Zamora almost played him in for a one-on-one with Jens Lehmann. Near the end of an exhausting battle, Kepa Blanca came on to replace a shattered Carlos. There was a real feeling that West Ham could escape relegation after that result. In his weekly column in the *Guardian*, Russell Brand asked how a team could beat the likes of Arsenal and Manchester United, yet still be in relegation trouble.

The next week, though, all the old weaknesses and nerves

returned as West Ham were crushed 3-0 by Sheffield United at Bramall Lane. They were outclassed and once again looked destined for relegation. Tevez had a poor game and missed a good chance to equalise when the score was 0-1. The incident happened after 62 minutes when the Hammers' saviour-elect brilliantly cut inside two Sheffield defenders and found himself clear and about 8 yards out. He should have buried the chance instantly, but snatched at it and skied it way over the bar.

On such moments teams are saved or relegated, and within minutes former United winger Keith Gillespie sent over a perfect corner and Phil Jagielka leapt above Zamora to rocket home a header. Jagielka was seen as a growing force in the game and the undoubted jewel in the Sheffield crown. Tevez's day of misery was complete when he was booked in the closing minutes.

West Ham were a shambles that day and the Sheffield boys must have felt ultra-confident of retaining their status in the top flight. That evening, Sheffield United boss Neil Warnock appeared on *Match of the Day* and his interview gave the impression that his team had already done enough to stay up in the Premier League. Mathematically, the Hammers could survive if they won all their remaining games and other results went their way, but the message from Bramall Lane was that they had already done enough to stay up. They were almost home and very nearly dry. Substituted near the end, Carlos's mediocre showing gave no indication that he would be able, by some superhuman effort, to save them from impending disaster. But he had not given up hope and told *Sky Sports*: 'Just because I have won everything in South America does not mean I could automatically come to Europe and sign for the biggest club.

You have to grow and learn how European football is and prove yourself; you have to have patience. I did not arrive thinking I would play in the team all the time.

'It is good for me to be in a team like this. I am getting experience in European football and it's a club with a lot of ambition. Every day I need to improve myself a little bit more. I am starting to understand English football and how to play the game. It is fast and physical, but I am not afraid of that.'

Abramovich's all-stars (AKA Chelsea) drove across town the following Wednesday on a mild, bright April evening for a match at Upton Park. They were greeted by a brick through the window of the team coach, aimed at the West Ham fans' hate figure, Frank Lampard. Mark Bosnich, who played for both Manchester United and Chelsea, once told the author that Abramovich had a personal army of 80 bodyguards. How many of them were in the cavalcade is not known, but soon Green Street looked like a scene from *24*. The whole evening had an air of the surreal about it after that. In a strange gesture, the Icelandic owner Eggert Magnusson hired his country's top opera singer to deliver a pre-match rendition of 'I'm Forever Blowing Bubbles'. The West Ham crowd were slightly stunned, while the Chelsea fans tried to drown it out.

Champions Chelsea were still in hot pursuit of Manchester United at the top of the Premier League and were in no mood to show any charity to their neighbours, but Tevez scored another fine goal for the Hammers in the first half. The problem was, it was sandwiched between two goals from Shaun Wright-Phillips, who was making a rare start for Chelsea. Wright-Phillips scored the opening goal, his first in the Premiership for Chelsea, on the half-hour when he rode a feeble challenge from Yossi Benayoun and then cut inside ex-United defender Jonathan Spector to fire home.

It was a great goal, but Carlos scored an even better one to equalise 4 minutes later. This was a fabulous angled drive that whistled past Petr Cech, the Chelsea keeper. Some critics blamed the huge custodian but he was so rarely beaten from long range that it was more a testimony to the accuracy and power of the shot. The cameras panned round to Jose Mourinho for his reaction to Tevez's goal. His handsome features were scowling; he was not used to his star keeper being beaten from that range. The Hammers fans were desperate to beat Chelsea and they saw Carlos as their best hope of springing a surprise. Curbishley had been disappointed with Tevez's performance at Bramall Lane and was looking to him to produce something against Chelsea.

Mourinho was, at that stage, making an extraordinary bid to capture the quadruple of Premier League, Champions League, Carling Cup and FA Cup trophies. In the end, Chelsea had to settle for the last two, but that night they kept their title hopes alive by instantly roaring back to make it 2-1. The Portuguese manager preferred more physical players than Wright-Phillips (hence his rumoured interest in Carlos Tevez) but the 25-year-old scored the best goal of his Chelsea career with a tremendous volley from Wayne Bridge's overlap. Wright-Phillips was something of a bête noire to the Hammers that season. The West Ham fans knew that Dean Ashton's injury had been caused by a collision with a Chelsea player in the England training camp, and the hot money was on the despised figure of John Terry, but in fact Ashton had clashed with Wright-Phillips.

Carlos was the lone hero who battled against the most

organised back four in the Premier League, and West Ham had a great chance to pull the game back to 2-2 early in the second half. Bobby Zamora fluffed it, though, after Tevez found him unattended at the far post with a perfect pass. That was it; the chance was gone and the Kalashnikovs were now pointed at the Hammers' defence. Shortly afterwards, Salomon Kalou forced the ball over the line following a huge scrimmage. After 62 minutes Didier Drogba smashed in number four, his 31st goal of the campaign, after a slip-up by Lucas Neill.

Didier decided to celebrate by the corner flag with one of his famous dance routines. This incensed the West Ham fans, who surged forward. Carlos strolled over to try and calm things down. Some fans chucked tea at 'the Drog'; the referee booked him. Just for a while Carlos thought he was back home at Boca. Thousands of West Ham fans decided to head for home, though nearly 30 minutes of the game were left. The Chelsea fans taunted the EastEnders with chants of 'We'll never play you again!'. Relegation had never looked so near, as the game ended 1-4. For Tevez's team, things were desperate. Drogba's goal had been the 58th they had conceded; they had scored just 27, of which Carlos notched 4. They had 29 points, 5 behind Sheffield United. Both sides had played 34 games. Alan Curbishley told the *Evening Standard*: 'We have to win three of our last four games now. That would give us 38 points, which would at least give ourselves some sort of chance. We are in the position now that whatever the team is, whoever the substitutes are, whoever is not happy, we just have to get on with it. What is important is what happens on the pitch.'

The tabloids were convinced West Ham were down, eager to claim the sacking of Alan Pardew had been a mistake.

Tevez's burst of form and goals were seen as coming too late to save them. But the first part of West Ham's Mission Impossible was successfully carried out, when they beat Everton 1-0 at home in front of an excited crowd of 34,945 – just 21 fewer fans than had witnessed their trouncing by Chelsea. Bobby Zamora scored the only goal, his fierce curling shot flying into the net after just 13 minutes. All afternoon, Tevez had a running battle with the Everton defence.

Meanwhile, the storm regarding the legality of the signings of Tevez and Mascherano was gathering. On 2 March, West Ham were charged by the Premier League for breaching their rules with regard to the signing of the duo. In early April, a three-man panel was appointed by the League to investigate the transfer. Then on 26 April, five days after the Everton game, the hearing began. The next day it was announced that West Ham were to be fined £5.5m after being found guilty of fielding the two ineligible Argentinean players. The amount was a world record sum for 'acting improperly and withholding vital documentation'. The salient point, though, was whether Tevez would still be allowed to play. West Ham were given three choices:

1. They could stop playing Tevez in the team
2. They could bring the third party agreement with Kia Joorabchian into line with FA Premier League's Rule 18, effectively meaning Joorabchian could not materially influence the club's policy
3. They could terminate the agreement with Joorabchian, on the basis that they would then assert their rights over Tevez.

West Ham went for the third option as they were desperate

to have Tevez available for the last three matches of the season. If they had announced that Tevez was not playing due to some clerical mix-up, the fans would have dismantled the Bobby Moore stand, piece by piece. Instead they decided to terminate their agreement with MIS and assert their rights over the player. They were ripping up their contract with Joorabchian, which would then leave them open to be sued by him for breach of contract.

As one Sheffield United fan wrote on the club's message board, it was tantamount to him ripping up his mortgage contract and informing his bank that they would not be receiving any more payments. In other words, it appeared that West Ham had ripped up a third party agreement without informing the third party. Tevez was only allowed to play in those final three games after West Ham assured the Premier League that the ownership agreements had been terminated. Did the Premier League seriously think that a businessman like Kia Joorabchian would walk away from an asset that had cost him £14m in 2003? There would be more to come in this particular saga.

The pressure had been building on Carlos over the weeks, and he had responded in the only way he knew – by working even harder and scoring even more important goals. Once the hearing had begun, though, the knives came out again and the snipers started firing in his direction. Carlos Tevez was blamed for West Ham's fall from FA Cup finalists to relegation certainties. Once again, the allegations that he had caused dressing-room disharmony and cost Alan Pardew his job were hauled out. The tabloids were saying that West Ham's season was the most chaotic in the history of the Premier League. Angered by the situation, Carlos spoke to the *Daily Mirror*: 'The people who have blamed me and

Mascherano for everything do not understand football. These problems have never been caused by us, either because of the transfer or the problems on the pitch. Javier is a big player, and I cannot say about myself, but we are not to blame. Anyone who says that is wrong. I care for this club and have only ever done everything I can as a player and as a person to help West Ham this season.'

Carlos finished off his statement with a promise that he would keep Hammers up: 'The miracle is still possible. We have three matches to play and 9 points to win. I have faced more difficult situations in Argentina and Brazil than this, even though this one is very complicated.' This was fighting talk from Carlos, the street kid showing through. The goal he had blasted past Petr Cech was the best he had scored so far in the Premier League, but he had more tricks up his sleeve. Alan Curbishley had made the point that when he took over the squad he thought that there were a lot of young players in it who had great potential, but in his own words, 'had not been dragged through the mill too much'. Tevez was the exception, battle hardened in the combat zones of South America.

Cleared to play by the FA, Tevez was raring to go at Wigan on 28 April. A statement on the West Ham website said that his actual registration had not been called into question and that he remained a West Ham player approved by the Premier League. The Hammers had an easy 3-0 victory over Wigan to keep their dream alive with two matches left. It was a sweet victory, not least because Wigan chairman Dave Whelan had been vociferous in his outcry over West Ham not incurring a points deduction for their breach of the rules.

Tevez did not score, but he had a tremendous game. In the

first 25 minutes, he created two chances that went narrowly wide. The much criticised Luis Boa Morte put Hammers ahead with a neat chip. That was how it stayed until with 30 minutes left, Carlos figured in a high-speed passing move that ended with Benayoun slotting in the second. Shortly afterwards, Tevez should have been rewarded for all his efforts with a goal for himself and Zamora sent him through on goal with a gem of a pass. Once again, though, his shooting let him down and he crashed a shot against the post when really he should have scored. Reo-Coker pounced on the rebound, but defender Leighton Baines cleared off the line.

It was a fantastic match, with the Hammers repeatedly hitting Wigan on the break and numerous chances being created and squandered by both sides. Eventually West Ham got their third goal of the afternoon when Tevez contributed to another high-tempo move which ended with sub Marlon Harewood rolling the ball home.

On TalkSport Alan Curbishley spoke in awed tones about the 6,000 Hammers fans who had made the trip to Wigan. They had out-sung and out-chanted the home fans. Carlos emphasised their importance to the cause when he spoke again to the *Daily Mirror*: 'We have needed the help of the fans in these key moments. After we won at Wigan, I enjoyed the best moments of this campaign because I saw our fans and people so happy.'

There were two matches left, and the first was a home game against Bolton on the first weekend in May. Before the game, Tevez was presented with the award for being voted Hammer of the Year for the 2006–7 campaign. It was a landslide victory – Tevez polled a staggering 84.5% of the ballot. What more evidence could there be of Carlos's impact on the team? And this came before arguably his greatest performances in West Ham colours. Pictures of Carlos collecting the trophy from Eggert Magnusson were splashed all over the tabloids. With the chairman's bald head and Tevez's Dracula hairline it was an extraordinary image.

In the film *Jerry Maguire*, sports agent Tom Cruise accused his client, played by Cuba Gooding Jr., of being a 'pay-cheque' player – playing with his head instead of his heart, and being more concerned with the value and the duration of his contract than with his actual game. Tevez was the complete opposite of the 'pay-cheque' player. Although he was at the centre of one of the most high profile incidents in the modern game, a controversy that was all about money, ownership and the machinations of the transfer system, Tevez always played with his heart.

In a way, winning the West Ham Player of the Year award was one of his greatest achievements. At Manchester United he was surrounded by world-class players. The player voted the best in the world, Cristiano Ronaldo, was his wing-mate. He was guided by the greatest manager in the world; the most experienced, the shrewdest judge of a player and the best motivator. At West Ham he had nothing remotely like that. Raw, promising youngsters or players past their best were his team-mates and both of his managers ended up being sacked. Tevez had come to a foreign country where he could not speak a word of the language, and in just a few months he had overcome massive problems, prejudices and setbacks. He had won over one of the toughest crowds in the world and had them eating out of the palm of his hand. Even more impressive than the vast amount of skill he displayed was his sheer strength of character. Tevez was truly a magnificent character, and he was also a confident player. At that moment in time, his confidence was sky-high. The whole of the East End adored him and he was the King of Upton Park. How could he fail?

Carlos spent a great deal of the build-up to the Bolton game in an oxygen tent following a bad knock he received on his ankle in training. Nothing could spoil his big moment, though. He had been inducted into the Hammers' Hall of Fame alongside the likes of Bobby Moore, Geoff Hurst, Martin Peters, Billy Bonds, Johnny 'Budgie' Byrne and Tony Cottee.

You could have bet your mortgage on Carlos scoring for West Ham that day, and in fact he scored twice and claimed an assist for another goal as they overwhelmed Bolton 3-1 to keep their Premier League dreams alive. The first came after 10 minutes when Carlos smashed home a free kick to send the crowd wild. A recently promoted former Liverpool midfielder Sammy Lee became the new boss at Bolton, following the departure of Sam Allardyce to Newcastle. Both men had short tenures, but Lee (sacked after one win in 11 games) had a real baptism of fire as the Hammers, inspired by you know who, simply engulfed them with wave after wave of attacks.

Tevez neatly slotted home the second goal to record his first double in the English game. His marker that day was veteran ex-Real Madrid star Ivan Campo, who was operating as a makeshift right-back. In the first half he was simply obliterated by Tevez's surging runs. Spanish-born Campo had a hairstyle almost as interesting as Carlos's. The third goal was set up by Tevez with a perfect cross, which the exciting prospect Mark Noble volleyed home. Canning Town-born Noble would be celebrating his 20th birthday a few days later, and Tevez's inch-perfect delivery was better than any birthday present he could have imagined. Fittingly enough, that goal won the award for the best Hammers goal of the season, and it is still burned into the memories of all West Ham fans. In an interview with John Cross of the *Daily Mirror*, Mark Noble rhapsodised about his team-mate: 'Carlos has set up every goal I have scored. He headed it down for me against Brighton, chested it down against Tottenham and he has played a wonderful ball for me again today. He's a fantastic player. Even if you play just little passes into him, he makes angles for you. He's such a great player he makes you lift your game and it's fantastic to have him in our side. 'When he first came here, he was not really putting in the performances but now we are seeing what the South Americans have been watching for the last two or three years.'

However that performance brought down the curtain on Carlos's career at Upton Park. There was one final act of the drama to be played out, though, at the most famous venue of them all. West Ham's fiercest warrior had a date with destiny in the Theatre of Dreams – Old Trafford. Before the game Carlos spoke to the *Daily Mirror* about the ongoing transfer saga: 'This controversy, the fine and everything, will not affect me. I am only a player and I only think about my game. I leave everything else to the lawyers. I am not worried about anything else but football and I will not let it damage my performance as a player. I am just looking forward to a game and playing in a stadium I have always dreamed about. We go to Old Trafford to play the Champions. To play in this stadium is something emotive because it is one of the greatest in history and I have always wanted to be part of that. I have spoken to Juan Sebastian Veron about the atmosphere and he told me it is sensational. I have so much desire to play there.' Carlos was obviously anxious to make a big impression at Old Trafford. Speaking before the game, he said: 'The match at Bolton was the key. For me it was like a Cup Final, nearly the Copa Libertadores because the victory meant we left the relegation zone. The team has changed totally in the last weeks. With our hard work and results, West Ham is no longer in the relegation zone.'

Manchester United were already Champions, although at one stage it had looked as though Jose Mourinho's Chelsea machine might wear them down. A remarkable 4-2 win at Everton, where United came back from a 2-0 deficit, was the pivotal moment of the run-in. The same afternoon Chelsea dropped two vital points in a 2-2 home draw with Bolton. On the evening of 9 May 2007, Chelsea entertained Manchester United. The TV companies had guessed this would be the fixture that decided the destination of the title, but in fact that had already been determined after United's victory over City in the Manchester derby. The game at Stamford Bridge was an anti-climax and ended goalless. Shortly afterwards the two great houses of English football had another date at Wembley in the FA Cup final and their 0-0 draw was only the dress rehearsal, with the understudies, juvenile leads and bit-part players taking centre stage in place of the big guns.

Despite reclaiming the Premier League title, the one aspect of United's play that concerned Sir Alex Ferguson was a lack of firepower. Ruud Van Nistelrooy had been sold to Real Madrid, Ole Gunnar Solskjaer was losing his lengthy battle against a knee injury and a great deal depended on the injury-prone Wayne Rooney and new sensation Ronaldo, whose star status was rapidly increasing. It was an open secret in football that Sir Alex was looking south for a new striker. Dimitar Berbatov was a favourite but the recent emergence of Tevez at West Ham had him drooling.

After their anaemic 0-0 draw with Chelsea, the United squad adjourned to a plush watering hole in Mayfair to celebrate depriving Jose Mourinho and Roman Abramovich of the title. One of the guests of honour was Carlos Tevez, bizarrely dressed in some clubby gear that may have suited the Ministry of Sound but not the private members' club United had hired for the occasion.

Three days later, in first-half injury time, Tevez scored the only goal of the game at Old Trafford. It kept West Ham in the Premier League, relegated Sheffield United to the Championship and caused a controversy that raged for two years afterwards. The value of that goal to West Ham was incalculable, though the result made little difference to Manchester United, who collected their ninth Premier League trophy after the game. Tevez's goal denied them a record-breaking 29 wins, but it simply meant they won the League by 6 points instead of 9. Of the five games United had lost, two of them had been to West Ham, the only team besides Arsenal to do the double over them that season. United failed to score against West Ham in either game. Tevez had stated before the match that he thought the fact that United would be celebrating their title win was a positive thing for West Ham. Ever since he had joined the club, he had made a point of expressing how much he cared for it.

Carlos's goal, however, ended up being possibly the most contentious goal ever scored in the Premier League. One of the most infamous, certainly, ranking alongside his friend Maradona's 'Hand of God' against England in the 1986 World Cup. The move that started it was a long, powerful clearance from Robert Green that was headed on by Bobby Zamora to Tevez. The striker held off a challenge by Michael Carrick and played the ball back to Zamora. Carlos's fellow striker gave him a poor ball back but Tevez managed to win it from Wes Brown to go into the box and beat Van der Sar.

At half-time, Premier League chief executive Richard Scudamore switched his seat, as he had been sitting directly in front of Kia Joorabchian. The unease he felt was nothing compared to the storm that was about to break over the matter. Neil Warnock, subsequently sacked as manager of Sheffield United, was soon to call for Scudamore to resign over his handling of the Tevez transfer.

In the second half United, without ever really raising the tempo, laid siege to the West Ham goal. Robert Green, playing as well as he had done at the Emirates, kept them at bay. Green was voted Man of the Match in front of the match winner Tevez. Ole Gunnar Solskjaer, playing what was to be his last Premier League game for the Reds, had a chance saved but the East End side hung on to take all 3 points and ensure they avoided relegation.

On the same day, Sheffield United lost 2-1 at home to Wigan. All they had to do to stay up was to stop Wigan from scoring, but they failed to do so and the result relegated Sheffield but kept Wigan in the top flight on goal difference. The Wigan owner, Dave Whelan, vowed to keep up the legal battle to relegate West Ham. At one point Sheffield United had been 10 points ahead of West Ham. It would get messy now, very messy. Whelan was unhappy with the team that Sir Alex had fielded against West Ham, which did not include Nemanja Vidic. Cristiano Ronaldo, Ryan Giggs and Paul Scholes came on for the last 30 minutes, but theirs were low-key performances.

Greg Kimberley, a staunch West Ham fan, discussed that last game:

'Did Tevez keep West Ham up? You would have to say yes, or at the very least he was solely instrumental in reviving our fortunes. The team and crowd grew in confidence and collectively drew from his unique talisman-like presence; you felt everything was going to be okay because we had Tevez. I knew he had the same impact in South America. He is definitely regarded as one of the greats at West Ham even after just one season.

'The Old Trafford game had everything at stake and just sometimes the underdog wins. West Ham had just finished many places behind a magnificent Premiership winning Manchester United wide, yet ironically it meant more to West Ham's travelling fans that were going potty in celebration beside the rather muted home fans celebrations. My son Luke watched the game in the Boleyn club and he said the place erupted at the end, with beer flying everywhere and fans singing and dancing on pool tables. The atmosphere was brilliant, with total strangers hugging each other. The Old Trafford game is the reason why any of us watch football. It's not the result that kills you, it's the hope.'

The statistics relating to Carlos's performances in the last five games made impressive reading. Those five games started with the home defeat by Chelsea. Tevez scored 44% of the Hammers' goals and was directly involved in 55% of them. In that same period he had 30.4% of their shots and created 16.3% of their goalscoring chances.

Tevez played the whole 90 minutes in all of those matches. The accuracy of his completed passing was an astonishing 81% compared to the overall team's performance of 72%. Let us not forget that West Ham, despite their appalling performances in patches that season, finished incredibly strongly. Apart from the glitch against Chelsea they had beaten all of the top six teams in the final two months of the season. The *Sun* went back further, to 4 March, when Tottenham had beaten West Ham 4-3, but when Tevez converted his free kick everything changed for him. Tevez had scored seven goals. (Top scorer was Benny McCarthy of Blackburn with eight, but Carlos was second in the table. Bobby Zamora had chipped in with a handy five, including the beauty at Arsenal). In that five-game period, Tevez had 25 attempts at goal but was way down the overall list, trailing behind Cristiano Ronaldo with 39. Also above him was Wayne Rooney with 27 shots at goal, and someone called Berbatov who had peppered the goal with 26 attempts. Carlos also increased his goal assists to 3. Aside from setting up the famous Noble goal, he had added 2 more assists. Bobby Zamora was the recipient of both; the 'assistance' rendered at Blackburn in that bizarre incident and also the goal he conjured up against Middlesbrough.

The *Sun* went on to say Tevez had earned West Ham 6 points with his efforts and re-jigged the league table to show the difference in the positions had those points been deducted. This re-imagined league table showed that, without the perceived influence from Tevez, West Ham would have gone down and Sheffield United would have stayed up in the Premier League. Against Middlesbrough at home, had Carlos not scored one goal and set up another, the score would have been 0-0 and West Ham would have received 2 points fewer than they earned for their actual 2-0 victory. In the game away to Blackburn, which West Ham won 2-1, had Tevez not scored from a penalty kick, the result would have been 1-1 and West Ham would have picked up just 1 point instead of 3. Tevez scored twice in the home game against Bolton and made the third, so a case could be made for all 3 points being gleaned by him.

Finally, only Carlos could have scored a goal like the one that gave West Ham a 1-0 win over Manchester United – had he not scored, the result would have been 0-0 and West Ham would have again ended up with 1 point instead of the 3 points they actually picked up from that match.

That makes 9 points in all. Football is, of course, a finite business, based on argument and speculation. The argument might be made that other players in the West Ham squad could have turned in those match-winning, season-saving performances. Bobby Zamora scored five goals in the last five games of the season, but once Tevez left the East End and Bobby moved onto Fulham, his performances and goalscoring dipped. Teddy Sheringham had been a fantastic player, but he was past his best and his next destination was Colchester United. Could Alan Curbishley have purchased another star striker had Tevez departed in the January transfer window, along with Javier Mascherano? Curbishley was strongly linked with Ashley Young, then at Watford, who subsequently blossomed into an England winger when he joined Aston Villa. Marcus Bent, who later joined Spurs, was another player that Curbishley tried to bring to West Ham. The fact remains, though, that for West Ham to have a player like Tevez available made a tremendous difference, because he really was that good.

CHAPTER FOUR
THE DEBATE

I wanted this book to be as fair as possible. The story of Carlos Tevez is as fascinating as any ever written, and one that showcases both the good and the bad sides of the world's greatest game. I used to follow Chelsea when I was young. I was brought up on the great players like Greaves, Osgood, Hudson, Charlie Cooke and later Pat Nevin, Gianfranco Zola and Ruud Gullit. When Abramovich took over, something died for me. When people like Peter Kenyon started running the club, and a player as mundane (to my mind) as John Terry became captain of England, I stopped going. Manchester United re-kindled my love for football; I always admired players like George Best, Bobby Charlton and Denis Law, and now that admiration has carried on with Ronaldo, Rooney, Berbatov and, of course, Tevez.

This book could easily have become a legal textbook, with all the complexities and nuances of the case. I have no axe to grind with either West Ham or Sheffield United. I used to visit both grounds and found the fans as knowledgeable and freethinking as anywhere else. I am simply trying to show both sides of the story and be fair to both clubs, and that is why I have tried to explain the good and bad points of both sides. The crux of the matter is: can one man make a team?

Gianfranco Zola, probably the best and easily the nicest player of his generation, makes the point that one player does not make a team. In an interview with the *Guardian,* the now West Ham manager stated: 'During my time at Napoli, I do not remember one occasion when Maradona won the game on his own and was the best player in the world. Obviously a great player can make a hell of a difference, but you still need all the other players to support you.'

Who am I to dispute the views of a player who was truly a legend? After all, he was the apprentice to the greatest one-man band of all time – Diego Maradona.

If you stuck a gun to my head and asked me, though, I would say that in my opinion Carlos Tevez did keep West Ham up. He galvanised the team and the crowd, and created a life force so strong it was, for a few weeks, unbeatable. At Old Trafford and Wigan the home sides faced not just 11 men, but 6,011; Tevez's greatest gift was that he gave the players and the fans hope.

THE WEST HAM CASE

West Ham would argue that Sheffield United blew it all by themselves and were simply not good enough to survive in the Premier League. Neil Warnock was lulled into a false sense of security. When the crunch came, his only hope was that West Ham would be deducted points. It has been pointed out that Sheffield United beat the Hammers 3-0 in April 2007. Why didn't they instigate proceedings at the time if they were unhappy with Tevez's registration? At that time, though, they looked safe from relegation.

Despite Tevez's brilliant form in the closing matches, West Ham were destabilised at the start of the season by the introduction of both the Argentinean players. If Tevez had scored his goals at the start of the season instead of the end, no one would have argued that he single-handedly saved the Hammers from relegation. West Ham's statement at the time of the FA arbitration ruling was: 'We do not accept that one player's contribution can be placed over that of the team as a whole, nor used as the basis for judging the results of a 38-game season.'

Freelance sports writer Frank Joseph has been a West Ham fan since the days of Clyde Best. His take on the situation was as follows: 'In reference to West Ham's unenviable and unwanted attachment to the Tevez affair, this can be included on the list of what is wrong with the English game. As far as I am concerned, the board at West Ham should have ensured that the documents were in order before allowing Tevez to put on a West Ham shirt. However, the club were duly fined £5.5m for "non-disclosure of documentation" regarding ownership of Tevez. Therefore, that should be the end of the matter. But the board of Sheffield United wanted to pursue this issue because they had lost out on future television revenues due to being relegated. However, if the situation were reversed with West Ham losing to Manchester United and Sheffield gaining a point against Wigan, then there would not be a case to answer. When you look at the facts, Sheffield United did not accumulate sufficient points or recruit enough players of Premiership quality. On the other hand, Tevez did not single-handedly win the last game of the 2006–7 season away to Manchester United. He was a major influence in the latter stages of the season, though.'

THE SHEFFIELD UNITED CASE

West Ham admitted the crime. Consequently, they were fined the unprecedented amount of £5.5m. Sheffield United would argue that a fine so large surely shows that West Ham's actions were beyond the pale, and in situations like this a normal punishment would be a deduction of points. Most Sheffield fans did not want automatic relegation for West Ham; just a points deduction, which they believed would be fair, given the FA's ruling.

Actor Sean Bean is best known for his role as a soldier in the Napoleonic Wars drama series *Sharpe*, but he is also a die-hard Sheffield United fan. In June 2007 he led a delegation of Blades fans to the House of Commons to lobby MPs over the Tevez affair. He told the *Daily Mirror*: 'We played by the rules – we have done everything right. West Ham, by their own admission, have broken the rules and we have been punished for that.'

The crux of the problem was the grey area around the Premier League's ruling in April 2007 that allowed Tevez to continue playing. The terms of this mandated that West Ham had to clarify Carlos's situation, ensuring that he was 100% owned by the club. Did the East End club comply with the judgement? If they did, why did Kia Joorabchian appear to continue trying to peddle Tevez around the top clubs in Europe? We have seen the effect Tevez had on West Ham's fortunes when he was allowed to play on in the final three matches of the season.

According to the laws that surround the game of football there is no such thing as 'third party ownership'. A player can only be owned by the club holding his registration. No individual or consortium can hold a player's registration, and no private deals amounting to even some cursory form of third party ownership are allowable.

Sheffield United felt they were hard done by, that things had not been done legally. They believed that the Premier League failed to impose a tougher penalty on West Ham when the club was asked to explain its dealings with those who owned the little Argentinean's playing rights. Tevez netted five times in the relegation run-in; exactly what impact this had on Sheffield United's fortunes can never truly be gauged.

My personal take on it is that Sheffield United went down by 3 points. In the next two seasons Tevez went on to play for the World and European Champions and harvest a fistful of honours. Sheffield failed to return to the big time. There is a huge gulf in class now between the worlds that Carlos Tevez and Sheffield United inhabit. A world-class player like Tevez can make a huge difference to a club.

As a direct result of their relegation, Sheffield United lost out on nearly £22m in television and merchandising rights, in addition to bonus payments. They also factored into their inventory of losses ticket sales, sponsorship deals and the capital loss incurred on the sale of Phil Jagielka. The overall calculation was based on the difference in income and expenditure of being in the Championship as opposed to the Premier League.

THE FALL-OUT

On 15 May 2007, FIFA said they would investigate the Premier League's ruling over the transfer affair. The next day, Sheffield United filed arbitration proceedings against the Premier League, in an attempt to overturn the decision not to deduct any points from Tevez's team. The chairman of the Premier League, Sir Dave Richards, and his chief executive, Richard Scudamore, had written a six-page letter to the chairmen of all the other clubs in the Premier League defending their decision in the case.

On 22 May, the Premier League agreed to set up an arbitration tribunal over Sheffield United's grievances. Shortly after this, Brighton had written to the FA, seeking clarification on Tevez's eligibility to play in their 2007 FA Cup third round clash. Brighton had been on the receiving end of his escalating form and fitness, and he had hit them like a hurricane in a 3-0 rout. Good try, but no cigar for Brighton.

The storm caused by 'Tevezgate' was having widespread implications. In June 2007, the Premier League agreed a new rule forcing clubs to disclose every shred of documentation connected to player transfers. The reasoning behind this was to improve clarity. Before the independent arbitration panel started, the Sheffield United PLC chairman Kevin McCabe threatened to turn to the European Commission to seek compensation if the panel rejected their pleas.

On the first day of the hearing, Sheffield United called on the Liverpool chief executive Rick Parry, as senior executive of the Premier League, to answer questions about when the rules governing third-party ownership were instituted. The hearing was concluded on 19 June, but the panel's deliberations were not announced until early July. The ruling was that Sheffield United's claim should be dismissed.

Angered by this, the Blades investigated the possibility of an appeal in the High Court. The basis of such an appeal was that the arbitration panel made an 'error in law' by not referring the Tevez case back to the original independent panel which had slapped the £5.5m fine on West Ham back in May.

Meanwhile, Tevez's dream move to Manchester United was nearing completion. It was ironic that once again the deal was held up by problems over his ownership. The League were insisting the transfer fee should be paid to West Ham rather than to MSI and Kia Joorabchian. Carlos Tevez put in an official request to West Ham for them to cancel his contract.

Sheffield United had a private hearing at the High Court, in an attempt to gain leave to appeal the arbitration panel's decision, but this was refused. Around that time, a fake Sheffield United 'banknote' was in circulation around Bramall Lane. The fake note was for £30m and had a likeness of Carlos Tevez on the front, with Trevor Brooking pictured on the reverse side. The Sheffield fans suspected ex-West Ham legend Brooking had used his influence on the Premier League and had persuaded them not to deduct any points from West Ham.

On 17 July Tevez flew into Manchester airport for a medical, but the ongoing wrangling between United and West Ham cast huge doubts over the deal. The next day United chief executive David Gill made a statement that the club would ask FIFA to arbitrate on the transfer. FIFA, however, recommended the case be referred to Court of Arbitration for Sport. Kia Joorabchian then decided to issue High Court action against the Hammers and sued them for the release of Tevez. Shortly afterwards, it was announced that the parties had reached a £4m settlement and Tevez was now free to join United. A statement was issued by Manchester United confirming that he had joined the club. A two-year loan agreement was agreed, with the option to sign the player permanently at the end of that period. Meanwhile, Tevez had been playing in the Copa America in Venezuela; Argentina won through to the final, but they were beaten 3-0 by Brazil. His personal terms were believed to be in the region of £90,000 a week, and the fee for the two-year deal was thought to be £6m.

On the eve of the 2007–8 season, Sheffield United publicised their intention to sue West Ham for the cost of their relegation from the Premier League. West Ham replied that it was a 'desperate' action. The following month, a Football Association arbitration hearing ruled in favour of Sheffield United in their claim for compensation from West Ham. The claim was not agreed until the spring of 2009.

CHAPTER FIVE

A NEW CAREER IN A NEW TOWN

The most important thing is he's already proved himself in the
English game. There's no doubt in my mind his performance
saved West Ham from relegation.
SIR ALEX FERGUSON

Carlos Tevez made his debut for Manchester United in a Premier League match against Portsmouth on 15 August 2007, down at Fratton Park. At last, the bureaucratic red tape that had encircled his move to Old Trafford had been sorted out and he was cleared to play for the new champions. It was a dream come true for Carlos, but he was nowhere near fit.

Sir Alex had received over £13m from the sale of two strikers, Giuseppe Rossi and Alan Smith, which had more than covered the cost of Carlos's fees for the two-year loan period. But Carlos had missed the pre-season endurance training, which to any footballer is absolutely vital. Even more so for a player who has just joined a new club. The complications had already seen him miss United's Charity Shield victory over Chelsea and a tepid 0-0 draw with Reading at Old Trafford in the season's opening Premier League fixture.

Wayne Rooney had sustained a hairline fracture of his left

foot in that match and with Ole Gunnar Solskjaer's glittering career about to end, United had little option but to give Tevez his first taste of Mancunian football. Sir Alex Ferguson told the *Daily Mirror*: 'He has come at the right time for us. Certainly with Wayne out in the forthcoming weeks. He will go straight in the team against Portsmouth. He trained very hard on Saturday and Sunday so today and tomorrow it will be lighter sessions to get him ready.'

Carlos was second-last out of the tunnel and the fans' first glimpse of him revealed that he had the number 32 on his back. He looked shorter in the flesh than in the TV clips and his crow-black hair was shorn. The first foreign player to break into the Manchester United first team was also called Carlos, but his surname was Sartori. The ginger-haired midfielder was born in Calderzone in Italy. His parents moved to Collyhurst and the youngster signed for United in 1963 when he was 15. He made his debut for United in October 1968 in a 2-2 draw at Tottenham Hotspur; Denis Law was among the scorers. In all, Sartori played 40 games, scoring six goals before leaving the club in 1972.

A generation later, our Carlos slotted into Wayne Rooney's traditional role and immediately won the approval of the travelling United fans as he neatly turned Pompey defender Paramot to send Nani sprinting away. For the first time, cries of 'Argentina' came from the Manchester contingent. Nani returned the favour a few minutes later when he slickly exchanged passes with the debutant on the edge of the Portsmouth box. Carlos held off Paramot and slipped the ball through to Scholes, who scored with a crisp right-footed shot.

So far, so good! Less than a quarter of an hour gone in the game and already an assist to chalk up. Tevez should have added a goal to that when Portsmouth keeper David James spilled a Ronaldo thunderbolt – he was just millimetres away from connecting with the rebound. He missed an even simpler chance just after half-time when Scholes put him in and he blazed wide. The *Sun's* chief sports writer, Steven Howard, was covering the match and dubbed him 'Careless Tevez' after that miss. It was to prove costly because the let-off encouraged Portsmouth and Benjani equalised soon afterwards.

All hell broke loose in the closing minutes as both the Portsmouth midfielder Sulley Muntari and Cristiano Ronaldo were sent off. Ronaldo walked for an apparent head-butt on Pompey sub Richard Hughes. Just before the incident Tevez should have won the match for United when Ronaldo's curling drive was somehow kept out by James and Carlos failed to convert it.

Sir Alex Ferguson had wanted to introduce Carlos to the United fans by giving him a baptism of fire in the Manchester derby, to be played the following Sunday at Eastlands. Circumstances dictated that Carlos's debut had come earlier, and a few extra days training may have made all the difference to his finishing. As it happened, United lost 0-1 to City, who at the time were coached by former England boss Sven-Goran Eriksson. The only goal was scored by Geovanni after 31 minutes, when his shot flew in off Vidic. The Serb made the fatal error of turning his back on the City winger and his shot flicked off his leg. Carlos was United's best player of the match, and proved to be a constant threat to the City defence.

In direct opposition to him was the teenage defender Micah Richards, who had already been capped by England. At that time, Richards was considered to be an outstanding prospect. The duel between the Argentinean and the rookie was the high spot of the afternoon. Only a string of brilliant tackles by Richards nullified the omnipresent Tevez. After 21 minutes Carlos surged ahead of Micah and was about to pull the trigger in front of goal when the youngster robbed him of the ball with a perfect challenge. Five minutes later he did the same thing after Carrick's surreptitious pass had put Carlos in again for a second chance.

Richards was built like a young George Foreman and his sheer physical prowess at times out-muscled the 5'5" Tevez. In injury time, Carlos headed wide from a yard out. Pictures of the incident showed Tevez virtually on the goal line, twisting in mid-air with the ball flying over the bar. Peter Schmeichel's son Kasper, City's custodian that afternoon, was on the ground and was just another helpless onlooker. Sir Alex thought the ball was in, so hard did it look to miss the chance. United's manager rose, arms aloft, to celebrate until he saw Carlos beat the ground with his fists.

The defeat rankled with Ferguson. United were 16th in the table, the poorest start to a season since 1992. It would have been easy for him to panic then and to lose confidence in his players and tactics, with the press writing it up as if it was the biggest disaster since the *Titanic*. United had torn City apart at times, yet came away with nothing.

Fortune smiled on United the following week, though, when they beat Tottenham 1-0. It was almost due to a Tevez goal. After 67 minutes, Owen Hargreaves, another new addition to the squad, turned in the semi-circle and fed Wes Brown, who passed to Chris Eagles. Spurs defender Anthony Gardener intercepted Eagles' forward pass to Tevez, but his clearance only went as far as Nani. The young forward was more than 30 yards out, but fired a shot in against the then Spurs keeper Paul Robinson. It dipped and brushed Carlos's head before swerving past the England stopper. You could not exactly call it a header; there were even some Spurs fans who swore that it had gone in the net via Tevez's shoulder.

In the press conference after the game, Sir Alex was keen to credit Carlos with the goal. Common sense prevailed, however, and the goal was credited to Nani. He only managed another three that season, so to deprive the poor chap seemed a bit harsh. Sir Alex was keen to bolster Tevez, though, as he knew that the longer a new forward went without scoring a goal, the more the pressure built. The Uruguayan Diego Forlan had joined United for £7.2m in 2002, but had taken eight months to find the net – and even that was a penalty.

A minute before Nani's match-winning shot, the same player had fired in another one, which Robinson weakly punched out to the feet of Tevez. Reacting fast, Carlos knocked it back past Robinson but Spurs midfielder Jermaine Jenas cleared off the line. Thus, Tevez was denied a goal against the team from White Hart Lane. Speaking of the legitimacy of goals, Dimitar Berbatov was playing up front for Spurs that afternoon and had two sound claims for penalties turned down.

Carlos's next game for United was against Sunderland, also at Old Trafford. It ended in a 1-0 victory to the home side, and once again Carlos was too eager to impress, snatching at an early chance. United had struggled in the opening weeks of the season with Rooney's injury and Ronaldo's suspension, but the energy and experience brought to the side by Carlos helped stabilise things.

It was a melancholic afternoon. The legendary Norwegian striker Ole Gunnar Solskjaer had announced his retirement from the game after succumbing to the injury to his left knee sustained nearly four years before. Solskjaer, who had scored the winning goal in the 1999 Champions League final against Bayern Munich, was one of the most deadly substitutes in the history of the game. Renowned for his accurate finishing, Ferguson had scoured the earth looking for an adequate replacement.

Tevez was the latest in a long line but their styles were as different as their appearance. Ole had the nick-name of the 'Baby-faced Assassin', while Carlos had the sort of face only a mother could love. Solskjaer had come from a Scandinavian country and was serene and calculating; Tevez was a product of South America, volatile and excitable. In front of goal Ole was coolness personified, the Chet Baker of strikers. Carlos's finishing was not in the same class; he still tended to snatch at chances in his eagerness to score.

It was an open secret in the game that Sir Alex was still casting longing glances at Dimitar Berbatov, whose brittle relationship with Tottenham was souring. Berbatov's performance in United's previous home game had intensified his suitor's interest but, like a couple involved in an extra-marital affair, the final outcome would be messy and expensive.

Berbatov reminded Sir Alex a great deal of Ole Gunnar Solskjaer, with his detachment and magnificent football brain. Now it was time to say goodbye to one of the club's finest servants as Ole came onto the pitch before the game. The ceremony was watched by a former team-mate of his, and a legend of the same lineage, Roy Keane, who was then managing Sunderland. The man always referred to as 'The Irishman' by the late Brian Clough embraced his old pal Solskjaer before returning to his players. His thoughts must have returned to his last day at Old Trafford as a player. He wistfully told Tom Humphries of the *Irish Times*: 'I lost the love of the game that Friday morning. I thought football was cruel, life is cruel. They had a statement prepared and they were thanking me for eleven and a half years of service. I had to remind the chief executive David Gill I had been there twelve and half years.'

You may detect early signs of Keane's growing disenchantment with the game, but for Tevez the whole business was totally new, adjusting to the culture and the hysteria that surrounded the biggest club in the world. He was also part of one of the strongest dressing rooms in the world. Each game brought a new set of characters from the United hall of fame. It was Tevez's time, then; the cruelties of life and football had not yet visited him.

The Sunderland game failed to live up to expectations. Another United striker whose career had been ravaged by injury came off the bench to grab the winner, with Louis Saha netting his first league goal in nine months. Carlos had a steady game, hustling and harrying. United moved further up the table. In his column in *The Times*, Oliver Kay warned the fans, 'not to expect too much too soon from Tevez.'

Carlos played at Goodison Park in another solitary goal victory by the Reds. This time, their victims were a stubborn Everton side. Seven minutes from time, Vidic headed the winner from Nani's left-wing cross. Carlos then flew to Lisbon with the team for his first taste of European action as they took on Sporting Lisbon. In the end he didn't play for long; just 3 minutes, in fact, as he replaced Ronaldo. The Portuguese wizard had already worked his magic, scoring the only goal of the game on his return to Lisbon. He was given a tremendous ovation by the fans when Carlos replaced him; all four sides of the ground rose as one to honour him. Carlos was impressed by the reception his colleague received; he noted that when Ronaldo scored against his old team, his celebrations had been muted to the point of non-existence.

Around that time there was a feeling in the club that it might just be a special season. Ronaldo started scoring goals for fun, the feisty Rooney was a real powerhouse, and they were galvanised by Tevez. He had fitted in easily, working incredibly hard and chipping in with some vital goals. It was as if he offered an express invitation to the other superstars to strut their stuff. This extended to the crowd, too, and soon it would become intoxicating.

The addition of Owen Hargreaves had strengthened United's midfield and gave added protection to an already solid defence. However, the problem was that the tendonitis which had punctuated Hargreaves' career was again starting to make him miss games. Outside of Old Trafford, events also started to go their way. A few days before his team was scheduled to play United, Jose Mourinho sensationally left Chelsea. Roman Abramovich's billionaire fortune had given the West London team the clout to become United's biggest domestic rivals.

The young oligarch had made his fortune quickly in a Russia where the ruthless and those with powerful friends were able to become fabulously wealthy. Under the shrewd tutelage and sabre-rattling of Jose Mourinho, Chelsea had won the two Premier League titles back to back before Sir Alex reorganised United and reclaimed the trophy as the balance of power swung back towards the North. This had a deeper effect on the Chelsea psyche, and the cracks between Mourinho and his demanding employer started to show. This culminated in the sudden departure of Jose for reasons which were never made public. Chelsea never really recovered from the loss of Mourinho, their most dominant figure in recent history, who for a short while had the rest of the Premier League in subjugation. We will probably never know the real story, but came as a tremendous blow to most of the players and nearly all of the supporters, who were fanatical in their admiration of the Portuguese coach.

United could not have played Chelsea at a better time. Morale was low and their future uncertain. Avram Grant, the director of football, was in charge of the team that sunny late autumn afternoon. He was to remain in charge for the rest of the season and, despite the size of the task in front of him, he was to perform beyond most people's expectations.

One player determined to do well that afternoon was Carlos Tevez, who had been a Chelsea transfer target in the past. He scored his first goal for United that day, and it could hardly have been more vital. Sensing the turmoil Chelsea were in, United tore into them from the start. Rooney glided past John Terry and hit in a curling drive that Cech tipped past the post. United were desperate to cut the points gap between themselves and Chelsea; also to gain revenge for their Cup Final defeat the previous May. Carlos had still been on West Ham's payroll then, but nobody played with more heart than him.

Goal number one of his Old Trafford career was a rarity for Carlos; a diving header. Ryan Giggs arrowed over a corner that was partially cleared, but Wes Brown latched onto the loose ball and passed back to the evergreen Giggs. His inch-perfect cross was met at the near post by Carlos, who had stolen ahead of Terry to thump the ball into the net. The goal was scored 3 minutes into stoppage time at the end of the first half. After Mikel Jon Obi had been sent off for a wonky two-footed tackle on Patrice Evra, the game had over-run. Louis Saha then wrapped the game up with a late penalty after Tal Ben Haim chopped him down. For Carlos it was a watershed moment on the emotional journey he had made from Fort Apache to the Theatre of Dreams.

Carlos spoke to *World Soccer* about his feelings on the goal: 'It was great. I always like to appear in the big games and for a player like me it is always important to score. Sometimes you do not get the chance to do that and you feel frustrated because you know that you have done everything that you can. That has already happened to me a few times at Manchester United, but I trust in myself and in my team-mates.

'The most important thing about me getting my first goal was it meant that those people who had placed a lot of faith in me by bringing me here in the first place were able to relax a bit.'

Tevez's next goal there was in the 4-0 demolition of Wigan on 6 October. It came in the 54th minute after stubborn resistance by Wigan. They had thrown up a screen of five players in midfield to try and halt the rampaging Red machine. The goal was a beauty; Anderson threaded the ball through to the irresistible Carlos, who powered through the defence leaving Titus Bramble and Kevin Kilbane trailing in his wake. An emphatic left-footed strike finished off the move. Rooney and Ronaldo shared the remaining three goals between them, the Portuguese winger notching two of them. Nani came on for Carlos with 9 minutes left, but he had already done enough to earn himself the highest rating of 8/10 in the *Guardian*.

After a string of 1-0 victories United had found their shooting boots, and in four out of their next five games, they notched up four goals. Aston Villa were next to be put to the sword as United ransacked Villa Park. Carlos was not among the scorers but had a simply marvellous game. Gabriel Agbonlahor headed Villa ahead early on from a cross provided by Ashley Young; the two youngsters were seen as key elements in the emerging team that Martin O'Neill was assembling. A ruthless three-goal burst just before the break crushed the Villa insurgents and Carlos, looking ominous in the all-black away strip, was at the heart of it all. His interchanges with Rooney were little short of brilliant. Wayne Rooney had levelled for United from Nani's low cross with his marker Zat Knight preoccupied with Tevez's run into the box.

The spotlight was on Rooney, following a bizarre performance for England a few days before in Moscow. England were beaten by Russia in a game that was ultimately to cost them a place in the 2008 European finals. Rooney scored a brilliant goal to put England ahead but then in a reckless moment had given away the penalty that put Russia back in the game. The jury was still out on his rambunctious international form, but his impact for Manchester United was unquestioned. Could it be that if he had a partner of the stature of Tevez alongside him in the England set-up, things might be different? Rooney's back-up players in Moscow, the Chelsea pair Joe Cole and Shaun Wright-Phillips, had been particularly ineffective.

Back in Birmingham, Rooney and United's second goal of the evening came courtesy of Carlos, as ex-Everton striker Rooney peeled off from his marker to collect Tevez's pass and fire home. Just on the break the game as a contest was over when Rio Ferdinand bundled in a third from close range. Villa's Nigel Reo-Coker was sent off for two yellow cards and keeper Scott Carson was then dismissed for bringing down Carlos. Rooney had put in Tevez with a wonderfully weighted pass. Carlos took the ball round Carson, but was brought down as he shaped to roll the ball home. It was an indisputable penalty but the interplay between Rooney and Tevez had been dazzling.

Carlos should have taken the penalty kick as Ronaldo was on the bench, but Rooney opted to take it. Stuart Taylor was brought on to go in goal and his first action was to save the penalty, hit rather weakly in the end by Rooney. A few minutes later, Rooney nearly brought the bar down on Taylor's head when he crashed a shot against it from another Tevez pass. The Argentinean and the Scouser were blood brothers – both products of hard-as-nails environments, both hailed prodigies, and both had fought their way to the very top of an utterly ruthless world. Darren Fletcher replaced Carlos with 17 minutes to go as Sir Alex looked to tighten up and conserve, and then Ryan Giggs scored the fourth goal with a deflected drive. Villa were beaten out of sight.

Rio Ferdinand was still marvelling at Tevez's set-up for Rooney's second goal as he talked to the *Guardian* about the dynamic duo: 'The myth about Tevez and Rooney not being able to play together was finally put to bed. We knew that as a team, but I think on Saturday they put it on show and their movement and awareness around each other was unbelievable.'

Rio was on the scoresheet again when he opened the scoring by nodding in a Giggs free kick in Kiev. The globetrotting Carlos made the trip to Eastern Europe for the fixture against Dynamo. It was his first visit to Russia, and as Arthur Daley once put it, the world was his lobster.

Rooney put the Reds 2-0 up from Ronaldo's cross before Dynamo pulled a goal back. Giggs, having a fine game, set up Ronaldo for the third before Carlos, who had been zipping all over the pitch, got into the act midway through the second half. A hard-hit cross from him was blocked by Goran Gavranic and the referee had no hesitation in awarding the penalty kick. Once again he was denied the opportunity to take it as Ronaldo sent Kiev keeper Shovkovskiy the wrong way from the spot. The final score was 4-2; Carlos was replaced by Nani after 72 minutes.

Sir Alex was excited by what he saw that night, and told the press how excellent United's forward play had been. On their first night in Kiev, the team had gone to the stadium for a training session. It was a freezing night at the start of the Russian winter, and when the session finished Ferguson noticed Rooney and Tevez still on the pitch practising their shooting. They were both keen to continue, smashing the ball from all angles. Two young men, rich beyond their wildest dreams, kicking a ball about in extreme temperatures and loving every moment of it. Feigning irritability, Ferguson gesticulated at the pair to finish, muttering about the cold and shaking his head. Secretly he was delighted; he knew that as long as his superstar players still had that love for the game that they had cultivated since boyhood then his team would be a match for anyone. It was such a perfect image; the two of them out there in the cold, a couple of scruffs from the backstreets. Always looking for that perfect moment; when they kicked leather and it just flew...

Carlos showed no after-effects from his trip to Ukraine when he plundered two goals against Middlesbrough the following Saturday. That day the Tevez–Rooney partnership was in full cry. It was the last Saturday in October but

Christmas came early that day and the party started when Nani scored after just 3 minutes with one of his long-range specials. Middlesbrough surprisingly equalised through ex-Arsenal striker Jeremie Aliadiere, and it was a landmark goal on two counts. Firstly, because Boro became the first Premier League opposition side to score at Old Trafford that season, and secondly, because the last player to score against United at home had been one Carlos Tevez back in May, in that last feverish game for West Ham.

United edged back in front through Wayne Rooney just before half-time. The second half belonged to Carlos, though, who scored his first brace for United. Rooney made the first for him with an audacious back-heel. The build-up started with Anderson finding Carlos, whose neat pass found Rooney. He ran into the box, but appeared to have gone into a cul-de-sac when he was cornered by a pack of tussling defenders. The move seemed to have broken down but Rooney suddenly unleashed the back heel for Carlos to crack into the net. The goal was constantly replayed on television as it combined so many of the ingredients of good football.

And the Rooney/Tevez combo was not finished for the day. Rooney made another brilliant run and Carlos hammered in the fourth goal. Talking the *Sun* through the third goal, Rooney said: 'Playing with Carlos is brilliant. He is a very clever player, very intelligent and we both work well together. I know how Carlos plays – just in behind the opposition's midfield. When Carlos plays, I know I will have to stay higher up the field and be the centre forward. The best way to play football is pass and move, and as soon as Carlos gave me the ball, I could see him starting his run out of the corner of my eye. He got on the end of my back-heel and I am delighted for him to have scored twice in this game.'

Then it was off to the Emirates for United's biggest test so far: Arsenal. Arsenal coach Arsène Wenger had talked about 'the game stopping the world' in the days before the clash. The build-up to the game was immense, with press coverage approaching saturation point. No Premier League game caught the imagination in the way that a Manchester United–Arsenal fixture did. This one was no exception.

The game ended in a 2-2 draw. United should have won it, but a last-minute goal from Arsenal captain William Gallas saved a point for the London side. Wayne Rooney put United in front just on half-time, when his shot was deflected in by Arsenal skipper William Gallas. Cesc Fabregas equalised early in the second half after Sagna seized on a loose ball in the penalty area. By his standards, Tevez had a quiet game, with most of the game being contested in a congested midfield. With 15 minutes left, Tevez was withdrawn and replaced by Louis Saha, just before Rooney missed the chance of the match when he headed sloppily wide. The introduction of Saha paid off when his superb return pass put Evra through for Ronaldo to fire his cross home. That appeared to be it, but in the 92nd minute Gallas scrappily bundled the ball into the net despite the best efforts of Van der Sar.

Julian Rigby, a freelance journalist and a die-hard Arsenal fan, witnessed the match and commented: 'Losing the game would have put United three points clear so it was a vital goal for Arsenal. The battle between Fabregas and Owen Hargreaves for midfield supremacy was absolutely engrossing. Tevez had a quiet game but was always a threat. How Arsenal could do with a workaholic forward like him. I would love to see him alongside the idiosyncratic Van Persie.'

The result left Arsenal still on top of the heap with 27

points from 11 games (eight wins and three draws). United were second, also with 27 points. The clubs had identical goal difference figures and were both on +15, but Arsenal were given top spot as they had a game in hand.

Already comparisons were being made between the holy trinity of the swinging sixties – Charlton, Best and Law – and their 21st-century counterparts Ronaldo, Rooney and Tevez. Parallels were drawn between Sir Bobby Charlton and Wayne Rooney and between George Best and Ronaldo, with the apprentice Denis Law role going to Tevez. Having had the pleasure of seeing all six in action, I would point out that comparisons between players whose careers span five decades are almost impossible to make. The game has changed so much that to compare honours gives a false impression. Ryan Giggs has won 11 Premiership medals; George Best won one title. Does that make Giggs a better player? Bobby Charlton won a World Cup winner's medal, something Rooney can only dream about. Ronaldo is arguably the greatest player in the world, and he has the trophies to prove it, but would his celestial beauty have survived the tackling of the likes of Ron Harris, Peter Storey and Tommy Smith? The Belfast Boy, George Best, came out unscathed against the most ferocious tackling ever known. Challenges that would be outlawed in the Premier League today and that would earn the players instant red cards. Regarding Carlos and the 'Lawman': could he jump as high as Denis? Before his knee injury hindered him there was no one quicker than Law in the 6-yard box at seizing on half-chances; chances that Carlos continued to spurn during his first season at United. Law was the template for strikers for generations to come. Alan Clarke's whole on-field persona at Don Revie's Leeds was a slavish copy of Law's

Carlos Tevez was a football superstar from a young age, and signed up to play for the All Boys youth club in Buenos Aires, Argentina, when he was eight years old.

Above: Carlos Tevez with his mother, Adriana Martinez, at their family home.

Below: A teenage Carlos at home in Argentina.

© *Offsid*

Tevez in action, playing for Argentina at the FIFA U17 World Championship in 2001.

Above: Carlos, playing for Boca Juniors, is sent off during a match against future club Manchester United in 2002.

© *Action Images/Darren Wals*

Below: Carlos helping his team to victory in the final of the Libertadores Cup against Brazil's Santos in July 2003.

© *Action Image*

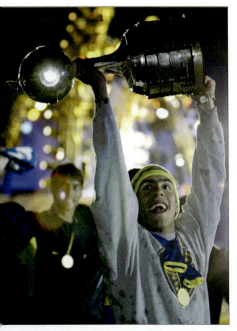

bove left: Celebrating after winning the 2003 Libertadores Cup.

bove right: Carlos holding the Intercontinental Cup, which Boca Juniors won in
*ecember 2003.

elow: Argentina's 2004 Olympic football team pose before their gold medal match
*gainst Paraguay.

© *Action Images*

Above: Carlos Tevez hugs Argentina legend and personal mentor Diego Maradona.

© *Action Imag*

Below left: Tevez celebrates scoring during the gold medal match at the Athens Olympics in 2004.

Below right: Collecting his Olympic gold medal.

© *Action Imag*

bove left: Tevez celebrates winning the South America Cup at the end of 2004.

bove right: Winning South American Player of the Year in 2004.

elow: In 2005, Carlos signed for Brazilian Club Corinthians in a deal worth over 20 million, the largest in South American football history.

© *Action Images*

Carlos with his award for the best player of the 2005 Brazilian soccer championships.

mannerisms. It goes through to Berbatov today. When Dimitar opened his account for United in Europe, his only celebration was the famous raised-arm gladiatorial salute, as patented by Denis Law circa 1964.

Individually there was no question the Busby Boys would win hands down, but collectively as a team? Now that might be a little different. The movement between Rooney and Tevez for that third goal against Middlesbrough was absolutely fantastic and was the equal of, if not superior to, anything Best, Law and Charlton conjured up between them in their pomp. Every fan of a certain age remembers Best's goal against Chelsea in the League Cup in October 1970, Charlton's volley against Spurs in the 1967 Charity Shield or Law's bicycle kick against the same team a few months later, but they were all individual goals. Compare those feats to the 15 passes that comprised Scholes's goal against Portsmouth at the start of the 2008–9 season.

The new holy trinity each claimed a goal in another four-goal romp against Dynamo Kiev in the return home match. That game brought another milestone for Carlos as he scored his first goal in the Champions League. His strike was United's second of the evening. Another one-two with the ubiquitous Rooney and a cracking right-footed drive gave United an unassailable lead. The lion-hearted striker should have made it three when clever passing between Ronaldo and Rooney carved out a good chance for him. Hardly believing his luck, he wanted to make absolutely sure and hesitated a second too long. As a result the chance was gone and the ball cleared. Two goals from Rooney and Ronaldo in the closing moments wrapped it up. Pique had opened the scoring when Carrick's header bounced off Carlos with 30 minutes gone.

The points were being accumulated rapidly now and Blackburn were rolled over 2-0 at Old Trafford on the following Sunday. Ronaldo claimed both goals, the second being manufactured for him by Tevez. The goal was created at breathtaking speed and came just 2 minutes after Ronaldo opened the scoring with a header from Giggs's cross. Straight from the kick-off Nemanja Vidic cleared up field after breaking up a Blackburn raid. Their midfielder Brett Emerton failed to deal with it and the quicksilver Saha pounced to race up field. He passed to Carlos, who very quickly crossed into the box with the outside of his left foot. The ball was as succulent as a Christmas turkey dinner; it curled round a defender and fell to Ronaldo, who controlled it instantly before slipping the ball under the onrushing Brad Friedel. The big American was the most under-rated keeper in the business and his subsequent move to Aston Villa had a lot to do with their rapid improvement. At that moment, though, he was helpless, totally bamboozled by the flight of Tevez's pass and the control of Ronaldo. Sir Alex described the second goal as 'marvellous'.

The Red express train came off the rails in their next fixture, a 0-1 loss to lowly Bolton at a freezing Reebok Stadium. It was the end of United's 10-match unbeaten run and one of the shock results that season. That United performance must rank as their worst of the season. Nicholas Anelka scored the winner after 11 minutes. He was to join Chelsea in the upcoming January window and would play a dramatic part in the end-of-season finale.

Carlos was the only one of the 'trinity' playing that day, with Ronaldo joining Rooney on the injured list. He had played for Argentina in the week but seemed immune to jet lag. There was nothing wrong with his energy levels or work rate – it was a wonder he still had his socks at the end of the game – but a bad miss by him in the second half cost them dearly. The *Guardian*'s report made out that United had been intimidated by the Bolton bully boys' tactics, and made a sardonic quip about the fact that the United strike force of Saha and Tevez had worn woolly gloves. The point was that Carlos was born on another continent and felt the cold of a harsh English winter. For physical toughness, Carlos could more than hold his own with the steely likes of Bryan Robson, Mark Hughes and Roy Keane, who were also name-checked in the piece.

Tevez redeemed his poor showing at the Reebok by scoring the equaliser against Sporting Lisbon in the Group F Champions League home leg. United trailed to a 21st-minute goal from Sporting defender Abel, whose shot had deceived stand-in United keeper Tomasz Kuszczak. That was about the only thing of note to have occurred in the first half as United struggled to impose themselves on Ronaldo's old club. Sir Alex, infuriated at the display, brought Tevez and Giggs on for the under-performing Fletcher and Nani.

Eighteen minutes into the second half, United equalised when Evra broke down the wing and crossed for Saha. A few minutes earlier, the French international missed a golden chance and the crowd were singling him out for a great deal of abuse, but he deftly turned the ball into the path of Ronaldo. For once the great man fluffed his shot and it arced across the box to the oncoming Tevez. Strangely he failed to connect with it properly and his half-hit shot spun off left-back Marian Had and veered into the net.

That seemed to be it – the crowd started streaming home early, it was a bitterly cold Manchester night and the game had been about as enjoyable as an hour of root canal work.

Two minutes into injury time, however, and the Danish referee Bo Larsen awarded a free kick outside the box. In a stunning display of skill, Ronaldo smashed in a marvellous shot that swerved into the net. It was a vital goal because it clinched the group for United. All group winners avoided each other and the return leg of the next fixture would be played at Old Trafford.

The Ronaldo roadshow continued as he picked up another brace against Fulham in a 2-0 victory at Old Trafford. Tevez was not far behind as he put in another excellent performance and collected an 8/10 score in the *Manchester Evening News* ratings. He was unlucky not to score himself, but things were looking good for the team. The crowd gave him a tremendous round of applause when, late in the game with United cruising to victory, he put in a lung-bursting 40-yard run to challenge Fulham's Simon Davies and break up an attack.

Next up in the shooting gallery were the hapless Derby County, who had had an appalling season. Bookmakers were giving odds of 25-1 for them to win at Old Trafford. In the end, Derby won just one match in the whole campaign, managing to accumulate just 11 points and scoring 20 goals. One of those goals came at Old Trafford, their first away from home of the season. United, however, rattled in four without breaking into a sweat and Carlos helped himself to two of those. Giggs opened the scoring with his 100th goal for United. Then Carlos made it two after a clever move by Ronaldo, who shaped up to take one of his faultless free kicks. Instead, he flicked a pass into the heart of the penalty area. Derby tried to clear, but the ball bobbled to Carlos; he swung at it, missed, and then scored with his second attempt. A joke goal really, but they all counted. On the hour he scored again. Wes Brown burst forward and his low cross was collected by Carlos, who side-stepped a Derby defender before cracking home. Derby pulled a goal back before United were awarded a penalty when Mears brought down Ronaldo. This presented Carlos with a great chance to grab his first hat-trick for his new team. Instead, Ronaldo refused to hand over the ball and took the kick to keep his amazing scoring run going.

Carlos was now realising just what was involved in playing for Manchester United. At West Ham, particularly in the final phase of that infamous season, he was the undisputed star of the show. He had scored twice against Bolton in one of the vital end-of-season games; had the opportunity to take a penalty in the closing stages occurred, there would be no question that he would have been given the chance. On Planet Football, that is how it worked. But at Old Trafford, players like Wayne Rooney and Cristiano Ronaldo did not pass as much as Carlos's buddies at Upton Park. So Tevez missed out on his hat-trick but the *Guardian* named him as their man of the match as his personal stock rose by the game.

Carlos did not travel to the Italian capital to participate in the final Champions League group clash with Roma. Only two of the team involved in the demolition of Derby played. Sir Alex was shuffling his cards, with one eye on the showdown with Liverpool that was set for the following weekend. United drew 1-1 in Rome. Pique, who later joined Barcelona, headed them in front before Mancini, who later joined Inter, equalised. It was a fine performance by the re-shuffled line-up against a battle-hardened Italian side that included the legend that was Totti in the team.

The Liverpool–United game kicked off at Sunday lunchtime. United were in the same black strip that they had worn at the Emirates. One of the key clashes discussed before the game was the Jamie Carragher–Tevez contest. It was a clash that Carlos won on points, running 'Carra' almost into the pitch and scoring the only goal of a tense game. Fernando Torres, who had started the season so impressively for Liverpool, should have put them in front when Van der Sar flapped at a Stevie Gerrard free kick. Presented with an open goal, the Spanish hot-shot headed wide. It was the only chance he had all game as he was brilliantly marked out of the game by Rio Ferdinand.

Javier Mascherano was in the Liverpool midfield, the first time he had played against his old friend Carlos. His presence in the team had improved Liverpool considerably but that afternoon even a player of his quality was outshone by Owen Hargreaves. The former Bayern Munich star showed exactly why, on his day and fully fit, he was the best holding midfield player in Europe.

Carlos scored just on half-time; Giggs swung over a corner, Rooney lost his marker Alvaro Arbeloa and drove the ball goalwards, and Carlos stabbed at it and turned the ball into the net for the most vital goal he had so far scored for United. Possibly the goal he had scored against them for West Ham may have had more historical importance but that effort earned United 3 priceless points and set them up to retain the title.

CHAPTER SIX
STAIRWAY
TO HEAVEN

The top strikers are all foreign; Adebayor, Torres, Drogba,
Berbatov, Tevez and Ronaldo. Where are the Alan Shearers,
Mark Hughes and Ian Rushes?
LOU MACARI

The vital win at Liverpool considerably boosted United's hopes of retaining the title. Their next opponents were Rafael Benitez's neighbours Everton, who visited Old Trafford on a chilly Sunday afternoon two days before Christmas. United won a very hard-fought encounter 2-1, with Cristiano Ronaldo scoring both goals. Carlos had a hand in the first with a square pass to the magician from Madeira, whose left-footed curling drive flew into the net. Everton hit back to equalise soon afterwards when Tim Cahill, probably the most underrated attacking midfielder in the Premier League, out-jumped Patrice Evra to score.

The dynamic duo of Rooney and Tevez tried hard to spark something, but found the going very hard against the solid Toffees' defensive partnership of Joseph Yobo and Phil Jagielka. The latter had a particularly impressive game against the freewheeling United strike force; he had been transferred to Everton when Sheffield United were relegated. The departure of such a talented defender and the reduced fee received for him, because of their loss of status, was one of the costs factored into Sheffield's claim against West Ham. Perhaps Jagielka had even more of a reason for putting in some strong challenges on the Argentinean sharp-shooter.

For a long time it looked as if Everton would come away with a draw, particularly when Howard went full-length. This was to keep out Carlos's low drive after he had pirouetted through 360 degrees to hammer in a shot. In the closing minutes, Ronaldo won the match with a penalty after a needless foul on Ryan Giggs. Carlos just managed to achieve a 6/10 rating in *The Times* for his performance in the match.

Sir Alex, who had taken to sporting a strange beanie hat for away games, gave Carlos a little Christmas break. The squad was rotated for the Boxing Day slaughtering of Roy Keane's Sunderland. The Black Cats were reduced to pussy cats as United rattled in another four goals. Carlos watched proceedings from the bench, huddled up against the freezing Northeast winds. Rooney, Ronaldo and Carlos's deputy Louis Saha shared the goals among them. Saha's brace of goals were a reminder of the force that he could have been in the team. Sir Alex was always disappointed that Saha never attained the heights his talent should have taken him to. Injury deprived him of the chance to repay his boss's faith in him. When asked to name the most two-footed player in the squad, Sir Alex always plumped for Louis.

The Parisian striker reminded him of Ian Storey-Moore, who joined United from Nottingham Forrest in the early 1970s. A powerful, brilliant goalscorer, Ian was forced out of the game by an ankle injury. He played just 41 games for United. Carlos thanked God every day for so far avoiding the sort of injuries that could cut a promising career tragically short.

An incredible topsy-turvy year for Carlos ended with a visit to where it all started for him in English football – Upton Park, his spiritual home. West Ham away was always a tricky fixture for United, as Sir Alex knew to his cost. Carlos was looking forward to going back there, but even he was pleasantly surprised at the amazing reception he received from the home fans. No other former player returning to Upton Park could have been welcomed with such an emotional outburst of love and affection. Almost as one, the crowd rose to their feet and serenaded him with chants of 'There's only one Carlos Tevez'.

Carlos responded by making the famous cross-armed gesture to mimic the West Ham crest. The special bond between the West Ham crowd and the Argentinean would never be broken. Frank Lampard had similarly been given his start at West Ham, but that relationship was soured by the England international's remarks and attitude when he left. The Hammers fans had given him the sobriquet of 'Fat Frank', which seemed to follow him around the grounds. Lampard could never understand the dynamics of the special relationship certain crowds enjoyed with their favourite players and pleaded in the press for more respect. The fact was that some players seemed to alienate crowds, while the likes of Tevez and Zola, who later managed West Ham, earned their respect.

United took an early lead in the match, with Ronaldo scoring his obligatory goal when he headed in a great cross by Giggs. In all, he opened the scoring 15 times that season. Only twice did they fail to go on to win the match. That day proved to be one of them. Ronaldo had a great chance to put the game beyond West Ham's reach in the second half when they were awarded a penalty kick. He had already scored three times from the spot, but this time put it wide for the first time that season. For once he seemed rattled by the air of hostility directed against him.

Carlos had a difficult afternoon too; he found it hard to get into the rhythm of the game and struggled to make any impact. After 64 minutes he was replaced by Anderson and watched the reminder of the match from the dug-out. It did not go well. Rio's brother Anton Ferdinand came on for Scott Parker shortly before Carlos left the field. The 22-year-old had just recovered from a hamstring injury and was slowly emerging from the shadow of his sibling.

Anton mugged United when he stole behind Darren Fletcher to nod in Mark Noble's corner with 13 minutes left. Rio looked furiously at his defenders while his brother danced with delight. Carlos hadn't seen celebrations like it at Upton Park since he scored against Bolton at the height of the relegation battle. United, who had been so commanding, were rattled by the equaliser and pressed the self-destruct button as the Hammers launched a late aerial offensive. They lost both composure and discipline as they gave away a series of corners and free kicks around the box. From one of them the other West Ham centre-back Matthew Upson soared to head in the winner.

Sir Alex was furious; he looked about as happy as Hitler on VE night. He was already something of a grumpy old man that Christmas because of the bad publicity the club had attracted with the players' now-infamous Christmas party. Jonny Evans had an allegation of rape made against him and the tabloids wrote it up like some debauched jolly. The CPS later dropped the case and Evans was cleared. It was the third time in a row that the Hammers had beaten United and the fact that both their goals had come from set-pieces irked Sir Alex even more.

After the match Carlos talked to the *Daily Mail* about his first few months at Old Trafford: 'I am at Manchester United because of Sir Alex Ferguson. He has total confidence in me and he was key to my arrival here. I suffered an awful lot in order to leave West Ham but now I am very satisfied with what I did. It was painful and people talked about my reputation, but it has been worth it. Ferguson is like a master to me, like a teacher. He is always giving me advice and helping my football get to the right level the next level. That is so valuable because when I first came to England at West Ham there was nobody there to do that. Even the best players need help.'

Carlos scored on New Year's Day against Birmingham City to earn 3 vital points and give the club a great start to 2008. It was also the occasion when he created an image that was to make him even more famous. Carlos put the dummy in his mouth after scoring the goal, which he dedicated to his daughter Florencia. It certainly was an extraordinary moment. Carlos had sold numerous dummies to opponents in games but this was the first time that he had put a dummy on himself. There were plenty of suckers in the game but now he was joining them.

The first-half goal was another spectacle involving a neat overhead kick from Carlos and an amazing back-heel from Ronaldo. It was his tenth goal of the season and he could have had more as he twice crashed shots against the post. With Rooney still missing, Tevez was United's best attacker, rocketing shots at the bone-crushing Birmingham defence, time after time. Twenty minutes from time he sustained an ankle injury which kept him out of the next fixture, an FA Cup tie against Aston Villa. Two of the backroom staff took him to the dressing room; the crowd were even more subdued after seeing one of their favourite players injured.

Carlos Queiroz, the assistant coach, was quickly on the scene to assess the extent of the damage. This was an advantage because Queiroz was multi-lingual and conversed with Carlos in his native Spanish. He was a great believer that if a player was injured or emotionally upset for any reason, then chatting him in his own language helped to comfort him.

Thankfully the injury Tevez sustained against Birmingham was not as serous as it looked at the time. Apart from severe bruising, no long-term damage was suffered. Carlos was tougher than most, which also helped on the road to recovery. Sir Alex's grumpy mood continued, however, as he blasted the United crowd for the lack of atmosphere at the Birmingham game. His gripe was that they were far too quiet and compared it to a funeral.

This seemed a bit harsh. Some of it could be put down to the cold weather, the mediocrity of the game and post-Christmas blues. New Year's Day is always a bit of a downer anyway; Christmas is well and truly over and many fans probably had hangovers from the previous night's celebrations. The prospect of returning to work and facing up to the aftermath of Christmas indulgence may also have put the fans in a bad mood.

In early 2008, the Premier League battle had turned into a three-horse race. Realistically, it was a two-horse race between United and Chelsea, with Arsenal, despite their capability and talent, a poor third. Such was the superiority of the big three all the other teams in the Premier League were being outclassed and the chance of any of them pulling off a shock win at Old Trafford was almost zero. The element of surprise had gone, so consequently the atmosphere at many of the games between the top three and the lower clubs was stilted to the point of boredom. That is one of the reasons why the fans loved Carlos, though – even in a boring game he would give his utmost.

Carlos sat the Aston Villa game out. United were playing Villa in the third round of the FA Cup, but in those days the competition lacked the kudos it had commanded in the past. Sitting a few seats away from Tevez was Fabio Capello, the brand new England coach, checking out the form of the Old Trafford England contingent. The Don looked across at Carlos, who nodded back. When in charge of Real Madrid Fabio had compiled a dossier on Tevez, who the Spanish giants had coveted since he had first broken through in South American football. Capello saw Ronaldo score his 19th goal of the season and a cameo wonder goal from the jewel in his recently-acquired England crown, Wayne Rooney.

Carlos was back for the next match, which turned out to be a 6-0 dismemberment of Newcastle. That result saw the Champions go back to the head of the table. Sam Allardyce had been surprisingly sacked by the Geordies three days before the game, and United took full advantage of the situation. The first half was scoreless – Tevez would have scored but for a great interception by the Newcastle defender Cacapa. Ronaldo scored after 49 minutes to trigger the Newcastle collapse with a trademark free kick. Carlos slammed in the second after 54 minutes, when Giggs had gained possession in the penalty area and set him up. Then Carlos turned goal-maker when he snapped up a loose ball in midfield and threaded through a wonder pass for Ronaldo to scamper through for his second, and United's third, goal. A three-goal burst in the last 5 minutes doubled

United's tally for the game and hammered out a warning to rivals of their intentions for the remainder of the season. Rio Ferdinand blazed in the fourth before Ronaldo completed his first hat-trick in United's colours. Carlos, wound as tightly as a clock spring, completed the rout 2 minutes from time when he zoomed away from a challenge and crashed in a shot. It hit the bar with a thundering smack and dropped down; referee Rob Styles awarded a goal.

Whether or not the ball crossed the line is open to conjecture, but it was entirely academic as the Geordies already trailed by five goals. For former United player Alan Smith, however, this was the final straw. The burly striker started abusing the referee and was sent off. A broken leg in an FA Cup game against Liverpool had effectively ended his career at Old Trafford. Obviously returning there was a very emotional experience for him, and the recent loss of Sam Allardyce had exacerbated the situation.

For Carlos a second goal was the icing on the cake, along with an 8/10 star rating for his performance in the *Manchester Evening News*. Ronaldo snatched the match ball from the referee and went home with it. What was now sure was that Tevez had settled in after missing the pre-season training. Carlos was fit and flying, a palpable star. Fitness equals form in the Premier League.

Reading had held United in the first match of the season and they gave them another hard game at the Madejski Stadium on 19 January. Former United legend Steve Coppell picked an attacking side who might have stolen an early lead. Carlos was the pick of the United forwards in the first half with another tireless display. As, the game wore on, though, the pace dropped and United had more of the play. It was not until 77 minutes had elapsed that the deadly duo of Rooney and Tevez finally broke the deadlock. Carlos's centre from the left was deftly touched home by Rooney, but a few moments later Carlos was replaced by Fletcher as Sir Alex wanted to flood the midfield with bodies and snuff out any late threat by Reading. Coppell's team tried to salvage it, but Ronaldo went through in the dying seconds to give the scoreline some respectability.

There was no respite for Carlos and his chums as they flew to Saudi Arabia for a five-day training camp and a testimonial game. The January jaunts were becoming a regular fixture in the team's packed calendar. On the debit side was the 6,000-mile trip; on the credit side, the exorbitant purse they picked up. Barcelona and Real Madrid had been approached first and declined the trip, but in the hard-nosed business of modern football the lure of an all-expenses-paid package was irresistible to United. Some critics thought this a gamble, with a treble up for grabs.

Carlos never bridled at the grinding routine and the unrealistic expectations of the media. The real fans knew that nobody could keep up the Herculean pace that had been set in recent seasons. That was who he played for; not the sponsors or the journalists.

The trip was a success, with United fielding a strong side of superstars and hardy perennials. They tactfully played at a languid pace, though, and lost the testimonial, going down 2-3 in Riyadh. The frantic schedule saw them take the dawn red-eye back to Manchester the following Thursday. En route they had to divert to Cairo to refuel. This took longer than expected and eventually they arrived back in Manchester after 13 hours' travelling. Ahead, Tottenham waited for them in the fourth round of the FA Cup, but luckily the contest was set for a Sunday, which gave the team an extra 24 hours to recover.

After nearly 40 minutes of the cup game United trailed to a Robbie Keane slide-in. It should have been more, but for Wayne Rooney clearing a header from the Bulgarian Dimitar Berbatov off the goal line. Then the Spurs centre-back Dawson made an error that let in Tevez for the equaliser. Rooney sent in a cross for Giggs, but his header was mis-headed by Dawson to the right of the box. Giggs darted ahead of the Spurs back Lee Young-Pyo and squared it to Carlos. Such was his perception that he had read the situation perfectly and arrived to instinctively divert the ball into the net with his left foot. It was a real opportunist's goal at a vital moment, and boosted by his goal Carlos scintillated in the second half.

Dawson gave a penalty away after 69 minutes when he used his elbow to knock away a bouncing-through ball from the threatening Rooney. Dawson walked as Ronaldo prepared to take the kick. The previous month Ronaldo had missed a vital penalty at West Ham, but this time he made no mistake as he sent the Spurs goalie Radek Cerny the wrong way. With 9 minutes left, Carlos was subbed by Anderson. The young Brazilian midfielder was in dynamic form. Already Tevez had already done enough to have been made Man of the Match in the *Guardian*. It had been a hard week, travelling halfway around the world and back, then running his heart out in a vital Cup match and scoring the equaliser.

As he had done at Reading the previous week, an event that seemed an awful long time ago, Ronaldo made the game safe when he thumped in a low drive under Cerny. Carlos modestly talked to the *Daily Mail* about Ronaldo's form: 'Today Cristiano is the best player in the Premier League.

'He has the characteristics to be the No.1 in the world. Ronaldo is the key to United. He is sensational, our leader on the field.'

Three days later Portsmouth visited Old Trafford in the Premier League and were beaten 2-0. Carlos was rotated to give him some rest after his exertions the previous week. He came on for the last 17 minutes to replace his co-conspirator Rooney. Thanks to two further goals by Cristiano, the game was already over as a contest The second goal after 12 minutes was described as the greatest free kick in the history of the Premier League. The kick was awarded just outside the box and he blasted it over the wall. It then dipped and swerved into the top corner; that trick of bending the ball and yet hitting it with tremendous power had been perfected by him in recent months.

Then it was back to London for a return match with Tottenham. The Cup game was closer than the 3-1 score line suggested and Spurs then managed by Ramos were a difficult proposition. Sir Alex changed the team and almost lost, as they found it hard going against a fiery Tottenham side. The match was a curiosity in that Berbatov scored for the team in white shirts and the red-shirted Carlos equalised in the dying seconds.

Little did the pair realise that in a few months time they would be locked into a battle for a place in the most star-studded attack in Europe. When interviewed in *Shoot* magazine, Carlos mentioned that the injury time goal against Spurs was one of the highlights of his first season at Old Trafford. Sir Alex was enraged at referee Mark Clattenburg for allowing Berbatov's goal as Jenas appeared to foul anchorman Owen Hargreaves when setting up the goal. Berbatov, his thinning hair brushed back on his perfectly round skull, was a constant threat. The game was very tough and seven United players were booked. Maybe the jet lag had finally caught up with them because the team looked a bit lethargic. They appeared to be heading for a shock defeat until gutsy Carlos's equaliser in injury time. It was really vital and one of the most significant moments of that epic season. A defeat at Tottenham would have reopened the title race and who knows what effect this would have had on United's psyche. The goal was scrappy; Nani's corner fell kindly for Carlos, who tackled the luckless Dawson and the ball ended up in the back of the net. The sweetness was coming back from a seemingly hopeless position. Some papers put it down as an own goal but the services of the dubious goals committee were not required.

Carlos was officially credited with the goal; it was the most valuable one he had scored so far since he had been in Manchester. The goal he scored, before he put the dummy in his mouth, had won them 3 points against Birmingham, but the 1 point gleaned in the slanting rain at White Hart Lane was priceless. Carlos was so strong mentally even though the agonising seconds were ticking away. Nothing had gone right for him in the game yet he was still composed and focussed enough to put the chance away.

The following Sunday, Manchester City completed their double over United by beating them 2-1 at Old Trafford in the most poignant derby match ever played between them. Carlos had learnt all about the dreadful air crash in Munich half a century before, which had killed 23 of the 44 passengers aboard. The history behind Sir Matt Busby's team was explained to him by his team-mates as part of the vast tapestry of a club that has bred legend, nostalgia, lore and love like no other in the world. The grainy black-and-white footage of the crash brought a lump to the throats of fans of all ages.

In his first season with the club Carlos had worn a variety

of shirts, mainly the first choice red with the AIG sponsorship logo and also the black with red trimming. Had he not been injured for the trip to Villa Park, he would have had the opportunity of wearing the white shirt with blue trimming. For the game on Sunday, 10 February against the team in sky blue, however, United were given special permission to wear a nostalgic shirt, which was a copy of the kit worn by the Busby Babes in the tragic season of 1957–58. The shirt was devoid of any reference to sponsors or the players' names. It was a complete one-off and would never be worn again. In fact, a good pub quiz question would be: 'In what match did Manchester United employ three players, each with a number 12 on their backs?' The answer would be that 2008 City derby, when subs Ji-Sung Park (who replaced Nani on 65 minutes), Owen Hargreaves (Anderson, 73 minutes) and Carrick (O'Shea, also 73 minutes) were all on the field. All the substitutes wore number 12 on their shirts because in the 1950s, no substitutes were allowed. Tevez wore the number 9 shirt; the number worn by Tommy Taylor and later, Bobby Charlton.

The game was played on a beautiful bright spring afternoon in a curious atmosphere, drenched in nostalgia. The only adverts were in the programme; there were none on the boards around the pitch. The minute's silence had been respected by every single person in the 75,970 crowd. Sir Alex had been worried that there might have been a problem, but as Carlos and his team-mates stood on the pitch with their heads bowed, you literally could hear a pin drop. In his strange odyssey through English football, Carlos had never encountered anything so poignant. There were 23 mascots; one for each of the Munich dead.

Rooney missed the game through suspension; it would have been good to see what he looked like in the 1950s kit.

Carlos looked smart, and it was a historic moment for him. City had their names and numbers on their shirts, but as a mark of respect, their shirts carried no sponsorship logo. They went ahead after Darius Vassell tapped home a rebound. Almost immediately, Carlos almost equalised when he shot on the turn, but City keeper Joe Hart made a great flying save. Earlier, the City Captain Richard Dunne made a brilliant tackle on Carlos as he shaped to score. The timing of the tackle was immaculate and it saved a certain goal. Dunne had a marvellous game, hoofing everything that moved. Micah Richards, who had played so well against Carlos at Eastlands in August, gave Dunne wonderful support.

After 44 minutes, new signing Benjani put City two goals ahead. There was an element of luck about it as the ball hit his shoulder, which deceived Edwin van der Sar. The second half was a complete anti-climax as City sat back on their lead and waited for United to come on to them, but the attacks never really materialised. Carlos did enough again to be voted Man of the Match by the *Manchester Evening News* and nobody received a higher rating in the United team in the *Sun*.

Slowly the game died on its feet as City ran the clock down. Their five-man midfield strangled the game and their austere defence picked off Carlos's spasmodic raids. The melancholy atmosphere really got to the crowd and they slipped away slowly, long before the end, like mourners at a funeral; but that is what it was, really. In a completely unreal atmosphere one of the United number 12s (shall we call him 12b) Michael Carrick, slotted in a goal. It was purely academic, because for once nobody really cared about the final score. The elegy to Manchester's most famous team was over.

The post-Munich blues were banished in the next match, however, as United thrashed Arsenal 4-0 in the fifth round of the FA Cup. The two sides have a rich history against each other in the competition, with the 1978 FA Cup final rightly considered to be one of the greatest finals of them all. 2-0 down and with only a few minutes remaining, United clawed themselves back to 2-2 with goals from Sammy McIlroy and Gordon McQueen before a last-ditch goal by Alan Sunderland broke the Reds' hearts. The Cup Finals of that era was like Christmas Day for the fans: it was the only domestic live game shown on TV.

In 2005, Arsenal scrambled a shoot-out victory after the game finished goalless. It was the last time Arsène Wenger had won a major trophy, with Chelsea and United dividing up the spoils of war in the following seasons. Some experts saw that game as the time when the team's paths diverged. At Old Trafford, Sir Alex began to concentrate less on home-grown players and more on buying in talent, while Wenger was the opposite. He now concentrated on bringing on younger talent – either home-grown or purchased cheaply – and eschewed the big-money transfers and influx of foreign superstars, something that hallmarked Chelsea in the early days of the Abramovich era.

Carlos was a prime example of the conspicuous consumption of Ferguson. He was only being leased by the club, already transfer fees in the region of £30m were being bandied about. He sat on the bench for the Arsenal game, but he was in good company with the likes of Paul Scholes and Louis Saha also named as substitutes. Wenger had fielded a team of youngsters and fringe players, and United effortlessly crushed them 4-0 with Rooney, again playing as the lone striker, having another terrific game. Sir Alex was experimenting with the line-up all the time and the lone striker tactic was just coming into vogue. Rooney had come in for some criticism from Sir Alex, who was anxious to see him play further up front and score more goals.

The 4-0 beating seemed to crush Arsenal, and their Premier League campaign lost momentum. Sir Alex knew the psychological damage a savage beating could do to a team's self-belief. If he had been a chess player he would have been a grand master. During the match Nani controlled the ball with his head, knee and instep to dispossess the Arsenal defender Justin Hoyte. To many it was a beautiful expression of individual skill, but Arsène Wenger interpreted this as a taunt. The mind games were to continue in the coming months as Sir Alex waged war against his adversaries.

Carlos struck a late equaliser against Lyon on 20 February in the first Champions League knockout stage at the Stade Gerland. It was an absolutely vital strike as it gave United the crucial away goal. Lyon were seen as one of the easier opponents when the draw was made, which was surprising as they had won their domestic title six years running. The French champions made a mockery of the claim by giving a spirited performance that night. Strangely enough, Carlos nearly didn't make the trip as he was held up in traffic on his way to Manchester Airport. The plane carrying the team to France was delayed for 30 minutes, which added to Ferguson's ire.

The young Karim Benzema put Lyon ahead to increase his fast-rising profile. Fast-forward a year and the 21-year-old was strongly linked with a move to Manchester as a possible replacement for a disenfranchised Carlos. Alerted by the conjecture over Tevez's future, Lyon had slapped a staggering £88m (100m) price tag on their exciting prospect. The score remained at 1-0 until 3 minutes from time, with United looking like French toast. Then, after a tremendous scrimmage in the goal mouth, Carlos scored. Paul Scholes had started the match, but Carlos came off the bench to replace him. Lyon was his that night. Among the team was a growing belief that United had a real opportunity of winning the Champions League for the first time since that incredible night in Barcelona in 1999.

Ryan Giggs talked to *Sport* magazine about the match: 'Team spirit is important. We saw that when Tevez scored late on at Lyon in the quarter-finals. That would have been a difficult game going back to Old Trafford 1-0 down – it would have been completely different, but at 1-1 we knew all we had to do was win at Old Trafford. Late goals are important because they knock the stuffing out of teams. At that point, you start to think; "Is it our year?" It was.'

Newcastle away was the next Premier League fixture, and United picked up where they left off and hammered them 5-1. Kevin Keegan was back in charge for a short, but turbulent period and could only watch as his team was smashed to pieces. For the second time in less than two months the Reds' strike force ran riot. Carlos played in the match, but did not score; Ronaldo and Rooney scored two apiece, with Ferdinand netting the other. Across the country, the odds of United retaining their Premier League title were slashed by bookmakers.

At Craven Cottage on 1 March, Carlos was on the field for 69 minutes against Fulham before he was replaced by Ronaldo. Sir Alex opted to start with Ronaldo and Rooney on the bench, while ex-Fulham striker Louis Saha partnered Carlos up front against his old club. On a bright spring afternoon, United strolled to a 3-0 victory, with Tevez having a hand in the first two goals. After 15 minutes, a busy Carlos, buzzing outside the box, was fouled on the edge of the D by the colossal Norwegian defender Brede Hangeland. Owen Hargreaves took full advantage with a textbook free kick that flew into the net. Despite the problems with his knee condition, Hargreaves was making his presence felt. A wonderful dead-ball striker, the fans only saw glimpses of his expertise. Canadian-born Hargreaves could play more roles than Eddie Murphy.

Just before the half-time break, Carlos exchanged passes with Nani and then found Paul Scholes, whose precise cross was headed home by the leaping Ji-Sung Park. Pictures of the goal show Carlos waiting behind the little Korean, waiting for any rebound. United took their foot off the gas and cruised the second half. Like all great sides, they could play in bursts, as and when it suited them. The Fulham defence must have been relieved when they saw their chief tormentor Tevez leaving the field, wiping his mouth on his cuff. There was no respite, though, as the unnerving sight of Ronaldo and Rooney entering the fray threw Fulham into further panic. So much so that within 2 minutes they conceded a messy own goal by Davis. The win left United just a point behind Arsenal.

Then it was Lyon again in the return leg at Old Trafford. Carlos was named as a sub; his omission from the starting line-up was a surprise to many. Rooney played in the lone striker role again. Sir Alex was saving his squad, with the pressure rising as the games came thick and fast. In a nervy, jerky match Ronaldo scored his 30th goal of the season from 30 starts to propel United into the quarter-finals. To counter the threat of Karim Benzema, Sir Alex had employed a five-man midfield whose brief was to cut off the supply of passes to him. With 20 minutes left, Carlos came on for Anderson might have clinched the game shortly afterwards, but he squandered the chance. The French champions could have taken the game into extra time when their sub Keita hit the post from 25 yards, but in the end it was United's 10th consecutive home victory in Europe, which equalled Juventus's record from 1997.

The following Saturday lunchtime the nerves and uncertainty that had been shown in the second half of the European game appeared again. In a shock result, United crashed out of the FA Cup to Portsmouth. That result signalled the end of their quest for the treble and their attempts to emulate the achievements of the legendary 1999 team. In the decade since they had clinched the treble at the Nou Camp, the game had moved on and the chances of any team scooping all the trophies now seemed remote. Sir Alex had two priorities that season: to retain their domestic title (thus curbing the rise of Chelsea) and, his own holy grail, becoming champions of Europe once again.

At the time the defeat to Portsmouth seemed a shock, but Harry Redknapp's men went on to lift the trophy. For an all-too-brief time it all came together for Portsmouth. Their midfield that day included two players who would subsequently move to top European teams. Lassana Diarra joined Real Madrid and Sulley Muntari was signed by Inter Milan. It was Sulley who scored the only goal of that FA Cup victory over United, from the penalty spot after Tomasz Kuszczak had brought down Milan Baros. The Polish keeper was sent off and Rio Ferdinand replaced him between the posts to try and save the penalty. Rooney pleaded for the gloves but was overruled by his captain.

United had 65% of the game but just could not put the ball into the net against a frugal Pompey defence. Carlos played for 68 minutes before being replaced by Anderson. He galloped around but could create little, and missed a good chance from close in. United's exit from the competition meant that the semi-finals were contested by Cardiff City, Barnsley, West Bromwich Albion and Portsmouth. This seemed to be an indictment of the diminished importance of the FA Cup to the big four. When quizzed by the press about the impact of their dismissal from the cup, Sir Alex made these sentient remarks to the *Sun*: 'It has to have an impact. The impact is we are going to do something about it. There is a determination and energy from our team that will show itself now.' How prophetic those words would prove to be.

United's run-in to the double commenced with a narrow win over doomed Derby County at Pride Park. A solitary goal from Ronaldo, steering in Rooney's cross 14 minutes from the end, clinched the win. Carlos took no part in the proceedings and his vigour was badly missed. United were expected to nuke Derby on their own ground, but sometimes those games are the trickiest. On 19 March, 75,476 fans watched Carlos play for the full 90 minutes against Bolton at Old Trafford on a marrow-chilling evening. The match was over in the first 20 minutes, with both goals coming from Ronaldo. Cristiano was revelling in the fact that he was wearing the captain's armband for the first time.

Carlos had an excellent game and contributed to the first goal by winning the corner from which it was scored. The number 32 was unlucky that he did not score himself; he had taken a return pass from Saha on his chest and knocked the ball past Bolton keeper Ali Al Habsi. Ricardo Gardener, the Bolton defender, saved a certain goal when he kicked the ball off the line.

From the resultant corner, Ronaldo smashed the ball into the roof of the net after the Bolton defence failed to clear. His second goal was straight out of the Ronaldo bumper book of out-of-this-world free kicks. Savagely hit, rising sharply and then plummeting into the net. Carlos and the other 75,476 rubbed their eyes in disbelief.

Liverpool were the next visitors to Old Trafford in another match fundamental to their title ambitions. Their striker Fernando Torres was in prolific form, having scored nine goals in six games. There had always been comparisons between Torres and Tevez. Carlos talked to the *Sun* ahead of the lunchtime kick-off: 'Torres is on fire, and scoring goals. But don't forget Cristiano Ronaldo – he is also scoring. I think United have the advantage with him.'

Ronaldo did indeed score, nodding in United's second goal after 79 minutes in a sparkling United performance. Carlos had come on for Anderson 5 minutes earlier. Sir Alex employed Rooney as the lone assassin in front of a five-man midfield. Rooney had managed 13 goals so far that season; 20 fewer than Ronaldo. Carlos scored 11 in the Premier League, 3 in Europe and one FA Cup goal.

Wes Brown had put United ahead after 34 minutes and Nani scored the third with a tremendous shot after walking past Stevie Gerrard. The game will be remembered most, though, for the extraordinary sending-off of Carlos's buddy Javier Mascherano following a histrionic outburst against referee Steve Bennett after he had booked Torres. Reduced to 10 men, Liverpool were no match for United, who completely dominated the game. Carlos had a great chance to score when he was put through against Pepe Reina, but the Liverpool keeper made a superb stop to deny him. The manner of United's win and the all-round strength of the side gave them great confidence for the challenges ahead.

The Aston Villa brat-pack were overrun 4-0 at Old Trafford, in United's third successive home game, the following Saturday evening. At times the football United played was breathtaking. The goals were scored among the 'holy trinity', Carlos, Ronaldo and Rooney, with the latter helping himself to two. It was hard to know who was the biggest star that rain-lashed night with such a proliferation of talent on show. Ronaldo scored the first goal with an impudent back-heel, then made the other three. Carlos scored the second. The little Argentinean started the move and finished it with a rare header. Pictures of the goal show Carlos jumping and connecting with his eyes shut!

Comparisons were being made between Ferguson's team and the great Brazil sides – the millionaire Manchester megastars against the Samba Boys. Rooney was compared to Pelé. In his early days the United striker was seen as being the next Pelé – if anyone could ever live up to that great legend. In 91 internationals Pelé scored 77 goals, an average of 0.85 per game. In 180 games for United, Rooney had notched 74 goals, averaging 0.41 per game. Carlos was compared to Romario, another small guy who used his low centre of gravity to score 56 goals in just 74 games, yielding an average of 0.76. Carlos, who at 5' 7" was an inch taller than Romario, had now scored 16 goals in 38 games, giving him an average of 0.41.

Chelsea were still relentlessly pursuing United in the Premier League, and in the Champions League United faced a daunting clash against Roma. But Carlos was in top form and ready for the battle ahead. Expectation hung in the air, and he had to deliver.

CHAPTER SEVEN

THE WIRE

Carlos Tevez reminds me of Eric Cantona in the way that he has a knack of rising to the occasion with a goal just when it's needed.
SIR ALEX FERGUSON

They are able because they think they are able.
VIRGIL

Carlos and the other United superheroes travelled to Rome for the quarter-finals of the European Champions League. It was a tricky fixture because they had already played them twice in the group stages – Rooney's goal clinched it at Old Trafford in October and then the teams played out a meaningless 1-1 draw in Rome after they had both qualified. Carlos only saw 6 minutes of action in the Olympic Stadium as Sir Alex packed the team with midfielders.

Ronaldo headed United ahead after 39 minutes from a Paul Scholes' cross. The Serie A side posed considerable problems down the flanks, but the introduction of Owen Hargreaves tightened things up. Rooney took advantage of an error by the Roma keeper Doni to grab a second goal. One of the biggest roars of the evening came from the 4,000 travelling fans when Carlos replaced Rooney in the 84th minute. In the last few moments he ran around frantically to relieve the pressure on his tiring team-mates. They were now just three games away from the final.

Ronaldo's performance came in for praise from Ferguson, who described his strike as a 'true centre forward's goal'. The Italians were not so impressed with him, however. David Pizarro, the Chilean International defender, spoke in the *Guardian* of his antics on the pitch: 'He is a great champion, but he is also very arrogant. He does spiteful things on the pitch; this is the ugliest thing for any player.' Just as Wenger had accused Nani of showboating during Arsenal's 4-0 FA Cup defeat, their opponents from Rome were disturbed by the behaviour of the United stars. But it had always been the same – George Best delighted in bouncing the ball off the shins of Ron Harris when he tried to intimidate him. Gordon Hill was another United hero who enjoyed going back to nutmeg an opponent after beating him. Around that time, reports resurfaced of Real Madrid's desire to take Ronaldo to Spain. Bernd Schuster, then the Madrid coach, was already telling the media that, 'Ronaldo has already overtaken Kaka as the world's best player.'

From the glory that was Rome, Carlos next found himself in Middlesbrough starting the match in the Riverside Stadium. Despite being early April, it was an arctic afternoon on Humberside. The game started smoothly, with Ronaldo scoring his obligatory goal after 10 minutes when he turned in Carrick's pass. But two smartly-taken goals from Alfonso Alves turned the game on its head and rocked United's bid for the title. The Brazilian Alves had been purchased from Heerenveen for a record £12m and was yet to score. Carlos knew all too well the problems of a South American adjusting to the high-tempo, aggressive Premier

League. At the time of writing, Alves had yet to make his mark for Middlesbrough but that afternoon his goals in the 35th and 56th minute were adroitly taken.

Rio Ferdinand was injured trying to block the second goal and the world's most expensive defender eventually limped off. Nemanja Vidic had been hurt in Rome and was missing from the team. As the snow swirled around, Sir Alex gambled big time. The loss of three points at the Riverside could have cost United dearly. Carlos had started brightly, but with nearly 65 minutes gone he was visibly tiring as he tried to get to grips with the blizzard. Sir Alex replaced him with Ji-Sung Park and brought on Owen Hargreaves for John O'Shea. Park rejuvenated the midfield and Hargreaves went to cover Wes Brown, who had been given a torrid time by Stewart Downing. A quarter of an hour from time Ronaldo put in Park, whose perfect pass was walloped into the net by Rooney. The loss of two points at the Riverside had enabled Chelsea to move within three points of United. Sir Alex was already talking about goal difference being a decisive factor. One thing was certain – would go to the wire.

Europe beckoned next with the return of Roma; United held a two-goal advantage over the Giallorossi, but the injuries were piling up. Ferdinand was back, but Vidic, Rooney and Ronaldo took no part. Following the hoo-ha in Rome, Sir Alex did not want to risk Cristiano against the tough-tackling Roma defence, who were still smarting from their 'showboating' treatment. They wanted revenge and with a crucial Premiership game against Arsenal looming, Sir Alex left him out for his own protection. Carlos played, though, and scored the only goal of the game to take United to the semi-finals. The Argentinean had a magnificent match, working tirelessly for his side with seemingly undiminished energy.

Roma fought hard and could have gone ahead when Wes Brown brought down their classy winger Mancini. Norwegian referee Tom Henning Ovrebo (who would of course later be involved in the controversial 2009 Champions League semi-final between Chelsea and Barcelona) awarded a penalty and up stepped Daniele De Rossi to take the kick. Di Rossi had scored at Old Trafford the previous season, but this time he smashed it straight over the bar. That was Roma's last chance of salvaging the tie. Twenty minutes from time Carlos intercepted a ball on the halfway line and passed to Owen Hargreaves. Playing in a more attacking role that night, Hargreaves curled over a perfect cross and Carlos dived full-length to head home. It made the tie absolutely safe and put United into the semi-finals for a clash with Barcelona.

It was a fine goal and Carlos celebrated by revealing a red T-shirt underneath his United shirt, which had a birthday greeting to his younger brother Ricardo Ariel. It was a marvellous night; Eric Cantona was at the match. He had recently been interviewed by *Sport* magazine and was asked how he felt when he heard the fans singing his name 11 years after he had retired from the game. 'I remember them. [smiles]. When I hear this…I feel like I am on the pitch. Many years ago. I am standing there and I can hear them. I hope it will be like this for many years. Because I like it.' The only cheer louder than the Cantona chants was when United captain Gary Neville came on for the first time in 13 months after an ankle ligament injury.

Carlos played the last 35 minutes against Arsenal the following Sunday afternoon. A narrow 2-1 victory effectively knocked Arsenal out of the title race and set United up to win the League. Arsenal narrowly shaded the first half and when Emmanuel Adebayor bundled the ball into the net early in the second half, Arsène Wenger could make a case for the title going back to London. The champions were on the ropes but they came out fighting like they had so many times before. United stormed back and after 53 minutes William Gallas handled Carrick's pass and another penalty was awarded.

Ronaldo coolly converted it by putting the ball to the right of the keeper. Neat, but the crowd sighed when it was ordered to be re-taken as Park had encroached in the box. Now the pressure was on. Jens Lehmann was in goal that day, deputising for the injured Manuel Almunia. The tension racked up a few more notches when the German international was booked for trying to distract the United winger, but Ronaldo showed why he was voted the best player in the world by holding his nerve and driving the ball to the right of Lehmann and into the net.

For the second time in three decisive fixtures, Sir Alex spun the wheel of fortune. Park had been picked because of his work rate, as a counter to Hleb, who had controlled the game for periods. Now it was time to attack. Tevez replaced the South Korean and Anderson came on for Scholes. As he passed him on the touchline, Carlos had a special word for Park, who had become a very close friend over the months. The introduction of the Argentinean galvanised United and they poured down on the Arsenal goal. Here was a man who wanted the ball. A draw would have meant that if Chelsea won the remainder of their games they would have re-claimed the title that Abramovich had purchased for them.

Owen Hargreaves had other ideas. At Craven Cottage a

few weeks earlier he had displayed his prowess at free kicks by opening the scoring with a cracker. The problem was that with Ronaldo – and to a lesser extent Giggs – In front of him, the chances were scarce. That day there was no hesitation, though, and after 72 minutes he curled in a delicious free kick following a foul on Patrice Evra. Once again Lehmann was powerless to stop it. Effectively that kick won the Premier League for United, but there would still be some twists and turns before the trophy was finally placed in Rio Ferdinand's hands.

Arsenal had 54% of the play and 15 shots to United's 13. For Tevez's team to be outplayed at home was a rarity, and it was certainly the first occasion this had happened since he joined them. The Manchester derby loss was a one-off and the Cup defeat to Pompey was a fluke, but Arsenal had, particularly in the first half, outclassed the champions. The United captain Rio Ferdinand spoke to *The Times* about the match: 'We did it the hard way. There's not many times we have been a goal down at home and had to come back, but we showed grit and determination and a great team ethic.'

Carlos had scored some highly important goals in his first year at Old Trafford. Each one seemed to grow in significance as the season wore on. His first-ever goal in the red shirt was taking on increasing value as it set up the victory over Chelsea. The West London side had lost only once in the League under Avram Grant and showed no sign of buckling under the pressure. Tevez's goal at Tottenham saved a point and kept United on course for the title, but perhaps the next goal he was to score for the Reds was of even greater substance.

It came 2 minutes from the end of the Saturday evening

match against Blackburn Rovers. Blackburn had gone in front when ex-Bayern Munich striker Roque Santa Cruz scored after 20 minutes. The goal had an element of good fortune about it, when Vidic's intended clearance ricocheted off Ferdinand and fell invitingly for Santa Cruz to rifle past Kuszczak. Christmas came early for Santa that year.

From that point on, it was Brad Friedel versus Tevez and Co. Pick of a fine bunch was an incredible close-range stop from a Carlos thunderbolt. Another wonder save came from a fierce Ronaldo header that looked a certain goal. Near the end of the grinding pressure, Friedel deprived John O'Shea of a fine chance. Sir Alex was down on the touchline and took off his hat, rubbing his forearm across his hairline after that one. There was still time, though, for Paul Scholes's flick to be headed in by the never-say-die Carlos.

At last Friedel was beaten and United kept themselves ahead of Chelsea. The 36-year-old ex-Liverpool keeper was desolate, beating the pitch with his right fist. Nani somersaulted in delight while Carlos flung his arms high in the air, body bobbing up and down like a rubber ball. It looked like the mob of players who swarmed to congratulate Carlos, led by Vidic, were only there to keep him from bouncing over the stand.

Carlos could almost taste the Premier League winner's medal but there was an even more prestigious one in Europe to be secured. Now he found himself in the starting line-up as United took on Barcelona in the Nou Camp. The game ended 0-0, nothing approaching the drama of that astounding night when the Baby-Faced Assassin executed the German high command.

That night was another chess match of a game, with both sides ultimately cancelling each other out. There was too much at stake for either team to open up; this was the real deal. It might be interesting to recall the line-ups:

UNITED	BARCELONA
Van der Sar	Valdes
Hargreaves	Zambrotta
Ferdinand	Marquez
Brown	Milito
Evra	Abidal
Ronaldo	Xavi
Carrick	Toure
Scholes	Yaya
Park	Deco
Rooney	Messi
Tevez	Eto'o

The versatility of Hargreaves was again a tremendous boost for United. With Vidic going down with a stomach bug, the team was shuffled to include Owen at right-back with Brown filling in for the Serb. Messi was playing against his fellow countryman Carlos; they shared a room while on international duty. The tiny 20-year-old nicknamed 'The Flea' had a quiet personality as opposed to the outgoing United star. Messi had a nickname for Carlos – he called him the 'Little Bull'. This was always a source of amusement to Tevez.

Deco was in the Barcelona starting side, but he was replaced by Thierry Henry after 62 minutes. His career at Barcelona was coming to an end after a poor season and a few months later he linked up with the former boss of his international side, Luis Felipe Scolari.

United had a brilliant chance of putting their super-soft

leather boots on the windpipe of Barcelona as early as the third minute, when they were awarded a penalty. The grass looked incandescent with heat and sheen as the Barcelona centre-half Gabriel Milito blocked a Ronaldo header with his arm, and the referee had no hesitation in pointing to the spot. The Barcelona team then engaged in a lengthy protest about the decision. Up stepped Ronaldo, though, who 10 days before had outwitted Jens Lehmann, one of the shrewdest and most experienced keepers in Europe. Tonight Ronaldo decided to steer the ball into the corner, rather than blaze it home. In the Nou Camp, watched by a crowd of 95,949, his side-footed shot missed the target and flew past the post.

The rest of the match was hand-to-hand combat as both sides fought for midfield supremacy. Messi had a fine match and set up a good chance for Samuel Eto'o that was hacked clear by Scholes. United set up their twin impenetrable banks of four to deny the Catalans any clear-cut chances that their superior possession deserved.

United had few chances. Tevez was used to this midfield in-fighting and ran hard to try and stretch the Barcelona defence, but they stuck doggedly to their task. Often there was nobody ahead of him in attack, and when he turned back into midfield he was swamped. United's old nemesis Thierry Henry, whose last appearance against them ended with him scoring a winner at the Emirates, forced a fine save from Van der Sar. Despite the late flurry of pressure from the home side, though, United grabbed a great 0-0 draw, which left them with one foot in the Moscow final.

It was back to the wire the following Saturday, when United unluckily went down 1-2 to Chelsea at Stamford

Bridge. The result put Chelsea level on points with them at the top of the table with just two matches left to play in the Premier League. This was the first time in the season that Chelsea were level, but United had the edge, thanks to their vastly superior goal difference. Throughout the season they had gone at sides and although the bulk of the goals had been scored by Ronaldo, Tevez's contribution could never be underestimated. He watched the Chelsea game from the bench as Sir Alex shuffled his pack again. Ronaldo was sitting next to Carlos until he replaced Rooney. Rooney had brushed aside John Terry to score the Reds' equaliser after 56 minutes, but Michael Ballack scored from a hotly-disputed penalty 4 minutes from time to win the points. Michael Essien's cross struck Carrick on the arm near the edge of the box and referee Alan Wiley awarded the kick, which incensed Sir Alex.

A nasty, unpleasant, niggly, queasy game was followed by a nasty, unpleasant, niggly, queasy brawl. Tevez, along with Mike Phelan and Gary Neville, gave a statement to support the rumour that the Chelsea groundsman Sam Bethell had made racist comments in Patrice Evra's direction. The following season Evra was fined for improper conduct and banned for four important games. Chelsea defended their groundsman and the charges were dropped. Like Russell Crowe in *Gladiator*, United were to have their revenge.

The knight from Govan had picked the team at Chelsea with one eye on the second leg of United's Champions League tie against Barcelona, which would follow just three days later. The stakes were so high that it seemed like whoever took the biggest gamble would win the pot. Ferguson had correctly gambled that even if they dropped points at Chelsea, they still had enough in the tank to win the Premier League. Tevez was deliberately rested at Chelsea to keep him fresh for the Barcelona game. A special game plan had been devised for him, and his job would be to pressure the Barcelona back four as much as possible, denying them any space at all to build from the back. It worked like a dream, with Carlos playing like a terrier, tracking back, harrying, tackling, hustling and hounding.

Paul Scholes, now 33 years of age, turned back the clock and scored the only goal of the game after 14 minutes, cracking in a superb volley. That moment was almost the crowning glory of Scholes's exemplary career for United and England. Scholes had already accumulated 18 major honours. Tevez spoke of him to *Shoot* magazine: 'Most people are amazed by Cristiano Ronaldo and Rooney, but living day after day with all my team-mates I have to say that Ryan Giggs and Paul Scholes are just incredible! Those two players just blow me away. When it comes to big matches, they play like they do in training or like they do when they are kids in the street. They bring such calmness and peace that I just can't believe it.'

Barcelona, with Messi having another great game, dominated the rest of the match but the United defence held firm. Owen Hargreaves at right-back had a storming match, linking up with Carlos to relieve the pressure. The atmosphere that night was incredible; the crowd were behind United throughout the match and drove them on. Carlos heard the rumble from the supporters – it was of a magnitude the like of which he had never heard since coming to Manchester. A territorial roar that boosted the team; that's what separates a football crowd from any other. Ronaldo told the *Manchester United 2009 Annual*: 'The supporters were fantastic. They sang for the whole game and gave the players motivation to get this great result.'

So United made it through to Moscow, to the European Champions League final. Their opponents would be Chelsea, who had narrowly overcome Liverpool in their semi-final. Sir Alex's troops had been engaged in a civil war against the West London side in the League, but now the whole of Europe was up for grabs. First, though, there was the Premiership to be retained and the domestic challenge from Chelsea to be overcome.

Two games remained; one at home to Carlos's old team West Ham and then an away trip to the JJB Stadium to take on a durable Wigan side. There was no margin for error. The West Ham game was a Saturday lunchtime clash. Sir Alex ordered all-out attack, wanting his players to go for the jugular and finish it as soon as possible. United responded by scoring three goals in the first 25 minutes to extinguish any hopes West Ham had of causing an upset. The circumstances were different from the previous season; the Hammers were safe from relegation.

Ronaldo scored the first two to drive a stake into the heart of the monster that had beaten them on their last three meetings. The first was a brilliant run that left Lucas Neill in rags, followed by cracking drive into the net. The Old Trafford crowd carried on from where they left off in the Barcelona game by building an incredible atmosphere and roaring on their heroes. An early goal settled the nerves and gave them the taste of blood. If the first goal was a textbook exercise in ball control, the second was more fortunate. Owen Hargreaves's overlap scissored through the EastEnders' rear guard and his perfect far-post cross was deflected home by Cristiano Ronaldo.

The third goal of the game was scored by Carlos and was a magnificent effort. It was the best goal of the match, and it brought the Premiership trophy almost home. Ronaldo set it up with a great pass to Tevez, who side-stepped a challenge before unleashing a tremendous drive that whistled over Green's head and into the net. It was a superb goal. The game was effectively now over as a contest and the title shifted a little closer back to Manchester.

The United fans were delighted to see another vintage goal from their hero. The tremendous reception he got from them in the last home game of the season was more than a tribute; it was a thank you. They had watched him run his heart out all season, his efforts culminating in the endeavour he had shown in the Barcelona game. Almost on cue the West Ham fans joined in with their own homage to the little Argentinean. This must have been one of the rarest moments in the Premier League; two sets of opposing fans joining together to make their own tribute to a unique player.

Soon after this mass appreciation of Carlos, a West Ham player was also treated to a joint tribute by the crowd. It was a sunny afternoon and United were moving inexorably towards the Premier League, so what the hell? This time it was Dean Ashton, who hooked in a spectacular overhead kick to receive the accolades. Hammers fans clapped because this was a sign that their hero was shrugging off the long-term injuries which had blighted his career. The United fans joined in to pay tribute to a whole-hearted player who was a credit to his sport and one they knew Sir Alex had been keeping tabs on for some time. In his exciting season at West Ham Tevez never had a chance to play alongside Ashton, and this was to be one of the few regrets he had about his time there.

The mood of bonhomie ended in the second half, though, when ex-Hammer Michael Carrick went through for United's fourth goal. Carlos continued to be a threat against his former employers and was given the Man of the Match award. The game ended 4-1 and was watched by a huge crowd of 76,013 – the largest of the season in the Theatre of Dreams. They had come to pay their respects and offer thanks for the fabulous entertainment that United had provided all season. United were now just one game away from the title.

To their credit, Chelsea never gave up their pursuit and before kick-off on the last day of the season, they were level on points. If United slipped up at Wigan and Chelsea won against Bolton, then the title would go back to London. It really had gone all the way to the wire. The last time United won the title on the last day of the season was in the fabulous 1999 treble season, when they secured their first trophy of the three with a 2-1 win over Spurs. David Beckham and Andy Cole were the scorers that day.

Carlos started the match and finished it. It was only fitting that he did, as a reward for his unstinting work rate and string of valuable goals. The Blackburn goal was still very much in their thoughts. It might have all been so different had he had not grabbed the equaliser. United won a hard-fought game 2-0; Ronaldo settled their jangling nerves with yet another penalty. Referee Steve Bennett awarded a debatable-looking kick when Rooney went down after minimal contact from Emmerson Boyce. Memories of recent misses would have daunted a lesser player, but Ronaldo was nerveless and converted the kick that virtually won United the title.

The game was still tense, as news started to drift through

that Andriy Shevchenko had scored for Chelsea (his last goal for the club in an unhappy spell in London). As always, Carlos was lively and playing with amazing technical assurance. The game had begun in brilliant sunshine but then a thunderstorm erupted with heavy rain. The going on Wigan's notorious pitch changed, in racing parlance, from 'good' to 'soft'. There was no greater judge of horse flesh in soccer than Sir Alex and he was not too bad at judging footballers either. The soft going was perfect for Ryan Giggs, with his superb balance, and after 68 minutes Ferguson introduced him for Ji-Sung Park. Only Carlos had run harder than Park but now, as always, Sir Alex decided another goal was needed. Giggs secured the title 10 minutes from time. Rooney slid the ball through a huge gap in the home defence and the Cardiff-born winger slipped the ball past the onrushing Chris Kirkland. It gave United and Giggs, who had played in every season since the Premier League's inception, a 10th Premiership title in 16 seasons.

Bolton's Matthew Taylor scored a late equaliser at Stamford Bridge; Chelsea had heard the news of Giggs's clincher and lost concentration. In the end United won the title by two clear points and a superior goal difference of 19 goals. Carlos had managed 34 appearances (3 as a substitute) and had scored 14 Premier League goals. You could say that the two points that proved to be the difference between the two titans were the ones Tevez salvaged with his last-minute goals at Tottenham and Blackburn. On the other hand, Sir Alex thought the last-minute goal Emile Heskey scored for Wigan at Chelsea had cost Avram Grant's team the title. At that stage they were five points behind with four games to play. He told the *Guardian*: 'I think the two points they dropped against Wigan probably won the title for us. It ebbed and flowed a bit. Arsenal looked like they would win it for a long period, but they dropped a few points after losing to us in the FA Cup and that made a difference. But we dropped points at Middlesbrough and Blackburn, and that allowed Chelsea back in it.'

Carlos's goal at Blackburn was the most decisive of the season by any player in the Premier League; his right-foot strike past the previously unbeatable Brad Friedel was decisive. Carlos was involved in every key match in the campaign. Firstly, he had scored his first goal for United in the 2-0 victory over Chelsea in September 2007. Avram Grant inherited a demoralised team who were five points off the pace, and did well to trim United's lead and ensure that Chelsea put up a spirited fight to the end. The jury would always be out on Grant, but he conducted himself with great dignity throughout and seemed a genuinely nice personality.

Secondly, Carlos had scored the winner at Liverpool in December – his first goal away from Old Trafford. Against the other big four teams United obtained thirteen points out of a possible eighteen, with three points dropped at Chelsea and two dropped at the Emirates.

Thirdly, Tevez scored twice in the 6-0 lambasting of Newcastle. The 11 goals, rattled in against the Magpies in the highest home-and-away wins of the season, formed the core of the difference in goals scored between the sides.

Fourthly, Carlos's points-saving equalisers at Tottenham and Blackburn, both scored away from home it should be noted, proved vital as Chelsea closed the gap at the top of the table.

In the 24 games that Tevez, Ronaldo and Rooney played together United only lost once, and that was the bizarre FA Cup defeat to Portsmouth. The 'holy trinity' accumulated 79 goals between them: Ronaldo 42, Carlos 19 and Rooney 18.

The point could be made that Carlos won the Premier League for United with this input. At Upton Park he won matches for West Ham almost single-handedly; the situation was different at Old Trafford. Ronaldo dominated the season with his amazing goal haul. Rooney, by virtue of his Englishness, was always the darling of the media. In the *Guardian* ratings of the season, both players were given a score of eight. Only Ronaldo finished above Tevez and Rooney.

Carlos had won his first title in England and could not be more pleased. In the photographs of the team celebrations he had a huge Argentina flag draped around his shoulders, and a baseball cap on his head. In his first season at the club he already had won the top domestic prize. He spoke of his feelings to the Argentinean newspaper *Ole*: 'I am happy, I am very happy. It has been more than two years since I last won the title [in Brazil with Corinthians] and I was getting used to that. This is a special title because of that. Winning again is good, especially if it is such an important title. Winning a title in Europe is not easy. One of the first I did after winning the title was to call my uncle to tell him; I had him in my mind. He is suffering from cancer and I told him this title and the one coming up was for him. He was very happy and made me happy too.'

Now all thoughts shifted to the Luzhniki Stadium and the European Champions League final. One of Sir Alex's mantras was: 'Today's the day. Tomorrow's the big day'. After Scholes's goal had knocked his team out of Europe, Frank Rijkaard, the head coach of Barcelona, spoke about English football: 'The level of English teams is high. It is very difficult to beat them because they are very strong.

They are very organised and all get behind the ball. They defend as though their lives depend on it, and they are very successful. But I do feel English teams have a lot more to give. I just feel it is a great pity it is not the most beautiful kind of football to watch.'

Barcelona had failed to score in both games against United. The narrow win at Old Trafford was the fifth consecutive game in the knockout stages that they had failed to concede a goal. On their way to Moscow United had scored 19 goals (Carlos scoring 4 of them) and let in just 5. Compare this to the 1999 team, who blasted in 29 goals on their way to glory. The attacking brilliance of Carlos, Ronaldo and Rooney had consistently grabbed the headlines but the bedrock of their success was the armour-plated defence. The difference between the two sides was that while Chelsea were a defensive team, United were a team with a great defence.

The two dominant forces in the Premier League, and now Europe, fought a grim battle for European football's biggest prize. United eventually won 6-5 on penalties – it was a fabulous and historic triumph but it had been a harrowing, exhausting, emotional rollercoaster of a ride.

A sizeable chunk of rainforest must have been consumed in the amount of newspaper coverage in the build-up to the match. Don Howe, the former England coach, was one of the shrewdest judges in the game. A lifetime's experience in the game at all levels from England international to coach at Arsenal and Leeds, his view of Carlos in the *Daily Telegraph's* pre-match analysis was: 'The Argentinean striker seems to have the happy knack of turning up in the right place at the right time to secure crucial goals.'

One of the key battles took place through the centre of

the pitch between the partnerships of Carlos Tevez and Wayne Rooney, and John Terry and Ricardo Carvalho.

Carlos spoke to the *Daily Telegraph* about the game. He was of the view that Chelsea's disappointment at missing out on the Premier League on the last day of the season would be carried with them onto the field. 'We are a better side than Chelsea; that is a psychological problem for them. They may say the Premier League is another matter but we are convinced that winning it will have an impact in what happens in the final. We are favourites and everyone knows it, and we are not worried by Chelsea. We are confident and focused but, for them, it is more difficult. This is more than a final for them their whole season rests on the outcome of this game and I am convinced that they have some problems in that team.'

Playing in the Manchester derby game that formed a tribute to the 50th anniversary of the Munich air disaster had had a profound effect on Carlos. He knew what winning the Champions League for the second time under his command meant to Sir Alex – even more so in that special year for the club. Carlos went on to say: 'The manager is very happy that we have won the League, but we know how serious he is about the competition and how much he wants to win it. He has spoken to us about the Munich disaster and what it means to the club, and we all agreed that it would be fantastic to commemorate the 50th anniversary by winning the trophy and dedicating it to the people who died.'

Five of the survivors of the crash watched the game in Moscow and were introduced to Carlos. They were Harry Gregg, Bill Foulkes, the late Albert Scanlon, Kenny Morgans and Sir Bobby Charlton. Five thousand riot police were on duty inside the stadium, many of them veterans of the war in Chechnya. One hundred million people were watching the game on television throughout the world; 14.6 million were watching it on ITV1 in the UK alone. The WAGs were watching too – Cheryl Cole, Carly Zucker, Coleen McLoughlin and Carlos's lady Vanessa Mansillo. This was the biggest game of the season; the two superpowers of English football clashing head on in the historic city. It was the US dollars of Malcolm Glazer versus the Russian roubles of Roman Abramovich. Red versus Blue. Tevez versus Terry. North versus South.

The United fans' instant dislike of the Abramovich-era Chelsea side was based on three factors. Firstly, they felt that the excessive wealth of Chelsea led them to expect to win – whatever the rules said and whatever damage was done to their rivals. Secondly, it was suggested the Premier League could not be contested fairly while such extremes of wealth existed. Thirdly, the United fans thought that Chelsea were vulgar. They believed that Chelsea had wasted money on players such as Juan Sebastian Veron, Adrian Mutu and Andriy Shevchenko, who had failed to deliver. They also thought that players like Frank Lampard, Ashley and Joe Cole and John Terry lived in luxury, engaging in the most conspicuous consumption since the Gilded Age of the late 19th century.

So, this was not just a football match: it was about globalisation, the multiculturalism of the modern game and finance. Carlos started the game. Of the 12 Champions League matches leading up to the final, he had played in 11. Michael Carrick was the only other player to have played in that many games. Hargreaves was switched to play on the right flank; it proved to be a tactical masterstroke from Sir Alex. Playing in the same role that had won him a Champions League medal for Bayern Munich in 2001, he gave Ashley Cole a torrid time, while still finding opportunities to track back to assist Wes Brown.

It had rained all day in Moscow and the pitch was soaking wet. Ronaldo headed United in front after 26 minutes; his first goal against Chelsea. Wes Brown interchanged with Scholes before sending over a cross to the far post. Rooney ran towards the near post while Tevez ventured into the centre. Their movement dragged the Chelsea centre-backs with them, and Ronaldo soared above the static Michael Essien to head a fabulous goal. Cristiano's footwork was perfect – the winger placed himself in a perfect position to thump the ball home. Essien was Chelsea's best player, but was wasted as a makeshift right-back. Never as quick or as nimble as Ashley Cole, Ronaldo frequently beat Essien in the first half.

Ten minutes later Carlos had a wonderful chance to double United's lead. Ricardo Carvalho had gone down the left and beaten Rio Ferdinand by the corner flag. Rooney chased back and retrieved the ball, and then effortlessly beat his old nemesis Carvalho. Wayne Rooney had grown up under the tutelage of Sir Alex Ferguson and quickly learnt how to soak up punishment without losing his composure. He was no longer the belligerent 20-year-old who had pressed his studs into Carvalho's groin in the 2006 World Cup. The other significant party in that notorious Portugal quarter-final, Ronaldo, waited on the other side of the field. Rooney cruised down the left, head up, and then hit a breathtaking 60-yard cross-field pass over the head of Essien to Ronaldo. Ashley Cole tried to close him down, but he was too late and Ronaldo crossed perfectly for Carlos. The United striker had eluded John Terry and met the ball.

A stooping Tevez should have scored but his diving header was aimed straight at Petr Cech. If he had directed it either side of the big keeper (as deftly as he had placed his header against Roma in the quarter-finals), it would have been a certain goal. Nevertheless it was a truly wonderful reflex stop by Cech from such close range. The rebound broke to Carrick, 18 yards out, who hit his shot straight at Cech's throat. Carlos should have scored, but Michael Carrick's miss was bad. Cech was no longer the same keeper following a succession of horrific injuries, but he was still one of the finest shot-stoppers in the world. Recently he had taken to wearing a ghastly all-orange kit. The reasoning was that this emphasised his huge physical stature and made him even more imposing and threatening to opposing forwards.

Three minutes before the break, Tevez missed another chance. Rooney lured Carvalho out to the left-back position and beat him with a wonderfully calculated cross that took Claude Makelele out of the game and left Cech stranded. Carlos stretched to reach it, to slice it over the line, but if anything he had reacted a millisecond too late. He did make contact, but without force – the ball bobbled and then spun agonisingly away from him. That chance should have sealed it.

But it was not to be, as Chelsea clawed their way back into the game and United were never to dominate it again. In first-half stoppage time Essien, in desperation more than anything, whacked in a shot from 35 yards. The ball hit Vidic, ping-ponged off Rio's back, rotated and then bounced twice into the path of Frank Lampard. The Chelsea midfielder had built a lucrative career on marauding runs into the box, time and time again. There was nobody in the game more adept at dealing with the ball in those positions. For once he did not hit it so cleanly and Van der Sar could have saved it, but he slipped and Chelsea were level.

The Chelsea midfield dominated the second half and United were at times swamped. Paul Scholes had watched the 1999 Champions League final in his suit, thanks to a sending-off for a two-footed foul in the semi-final against Juventus. Sir Alex stated that Scholes would be the first name on the team sheet for Moscow. That decision almost cost him the Champions League, though, as the brilliant midfielder ran out of steam. The fact that he had a broken nose following a clash with Makelele did not help his game. Eventually he was replaced by another legend from the class of '92 – Ryan Giggs. Owen Hargreaves, who had a fine game on the right flank, was switched inside to help out as Lampard and Ballack pushed up.

Over 30,000 United fans had laid siege to the gates of Moscow; now they roared their heroes back into the game. 'Attack, Attack, Attack,' they chanted as the rain lashed down. On the hour Carlos was almost in when Ashley Cole headed the ball into his stomach, but he was to slip on the sodden pitch before he could take advantage. Makelele gave Hargreaves a whack, but when he tried it on Carlos, he was left writhing on the pitch. The street kid from Fort Apache was playing in the biggest game of his English career and nobody was going to intimidate him. Whoever tried it on, had to go down. Makelele received treatment for an injury to his face and it was to be the last game that the ex-Real Madrid man would play for Chelsea.

Michael Ballack, a former team-mate of Owen Hargreaves at Bayern Munich, was the next to clash with the Argentinean and the United fans hooted at the German's histrionics. In the last 10 minutes of normal time Carlos found some space in the penalty area, but snatched at his shot and it flew wide. He then sent a cross towards Rooney, but Terry cleared. Neither side wanted to lose it now as the game headed for extra time. The last action of normal time came when Carvalho intercepted Ronaldo's intended pass to the threatening Carlos. The duel between Carvalho and Tevez was fascinating; the Portuguese defender loved to intercept, to snaffle the ball from the toes of his opponent. Against a stocky, raging bull of a player like Carlos this was a high-risk strategy. Carvalho was probably the most ruthless, but highly skilled defender in the world. William Gallas, his former team-mate, was probably faster, but not as mean. Carvalho was very reminiscent of the great Argentinean defender Passarella. Perhaps that is why Carlos had such a tear-up with him.

Both sides could have won it in extra time, but United finished the stronger as they found another gear. Giggs had the best chance to score when he headed Evra's cross towards the net, but John Terry cleared off the line. Carlos was still buzzing after nearly two hours; he was the fittest player on the field. The game had kicked off at 10.45 Moscow time and was now into the next day. With 113 minutes gone, Nani (on for the shattered Rooney) set off down the right, but Carlos could not reach his return cross driven low into the box. Gaps were appearing all over the pitch.

Two minutes later Carlos got into another row with Chelsea defenders, which ended with players from both sides getting into an argument. In vain Chelsea players

waited for Carlos to return the ball to them from a throw-
in; he booted it away and flashed them a smile before being
booked by Lubos Michel, the Slovakian referee. Then
Didier Drogba walked after slapping Nemanja Vidic. He
was only the second player to be red-carded in a European
Champions League final; the other culprit was Jens Lehman
against Barcelona in 2006. But United could not take
advantage of their numerical superiority. Nani sent over a
cross but it was too high for Carlos. That was the last
meaningful action of the game, as cramp set in and the pitch
was littered with exhausted players, like troops returning
from the front. United and Chelsea were tied in a knot,
totally deadlocked. So now it was down to penalties…

And guess who stepped up to take the first penalty in the
most important shoot-out in the modern English game?
That's right: Carlos Tevez.

The first kick of a shoot-out is always the most
important. If you miss it, the implications are too much to
consider. Sir Alex had no hesitation in letting the little
Argentinean take it. It was the first penalty he had taken
for United, so no pressure! And he was up against a
goalkeeper who was considered to be the best in the world.
Carlos's finals' jinx had to be broken. Twice a runner-up in
the Copa America, he vowed he would not be a loser with
Manchester United.

In the incessant rain he stepped up and sent Cech the
wrong way. Carlos turned, giving a war-whoop of joy. He
would always have that moment – scoring a penalty in the
Champions League final. It will probably still be etched in
his mind when he is an old man; that moment when the
ball went in.

Now, it was Ballack's turn. With the calm of an officer at

a firing squad, the Chelsea star blasted the ball high into the top right-hand corner. Van der Sar was near it, but not near enough: 1-1.

Michael Carrick was next up. The ex-West Ham and Tottenham midfielder had had a fine season and he wasn't going to do anything to spoil it now: 2-1.

Juliano Belletti had been brought on near the end for the bruised Makelele, specifically for the task of taking a penalty. That is exactly what he did, zinging it nonchalantly home. The score was 2-2.

Now it was Ronaldo, who would later be named the Greatest Player on the Planet. Carlos watched from the halfway line with the other players, staring flat at the goal. He had done his best; now all he could do was look on like the rest of the world. Ronaldo had always been fascinated by the stop-start penalties that Pelé had patented. In a friendly once against Sheffield Wednesday at Hillsborough Pelé, playing for Santos, had taken the first penalty of its type to be seen in England. This was decades before Ronaldo was even born. Pat Nevin tried it in a League Cup game against Manchester City in November 1984, but made a hash of it. Ronaldo did the same that night. All he had to do was score, but just as at Barca, he messed up. His jerky run lacked momentum and his half-hit shot to the right of Cech was easily saved. Then Lampard slotted home Chelsea's third. Edwin van der Sar almost blocked the penalty by getting a hand to it, but it was hit too hard and United were now behind 3-2. The fans and players could hardly bear to watch.

Owen Hargreaves stepped up for his kick; the pressure on him was unbearable. If he missed now, it would be all over. Hargreaves was second only to Tevez as the most underrated star of United's astounding season. His injury problems clouded the terrific impact he had made to the cause. He could literally play anywhere and had chipped in with vital goals and match-winning assists. Now, he needed to score a vital penalty. Hargreaves did not let United down – his penalty was the best of the evening, beautifully struck up in the corner. Cech flew across the goal but it was already hitting the back of the net. United were still in it, but every Red heart sank when Ashley Cole made it 4-3. Nani levelled for United, but now Chelsea only had to convert their last penalty to take the Champions League trophy back to London.

John Terry strode up to the spot. Didier Drogba would have taken the penalty, had he not been dismissed. Inexplicably, Andriy Shevchenko, once the deadliest finisher in Europe, sat on the bench. Few would have bet against him in that situation, especially in Russia. Terry wanted the glory; his decisive kick would have guaranteed him immortality in the Chelsea hall of fame, but it was not too be. He was seen by many as the most overrated player ever to captain his country; now it was time to stand up and be counted. In the scrimmage with Didier Drogba earlier in the match, Terry had appeared to spit at Carlos. Television pictures showed a spat between the two, with Carlos walking, away wiping his neck. Terry denied spitting and told the *London Lite*: 'There was some pushing and shoving I admit that, but no spitting, that is not my style. No way would I spit at another player.' UEFA spokesman William Gilliard said: 'We must wait for the report from the referee and the UEFA delegate.' Always the diplomat, Carlos tried to play down the fracas: 'I do not understand the attitude of Terry. He told me that I was not a sportsman because I would not put the ball out. For me, this is a forgotten subject now.' UEFA seemed to forget it too because nothing further was heard after the match.

But in an event that many United fans saw as karma for the alleged spitting incident, Terry missed the kick. He claimed that he slipped at the crucial moment, but this was open to interpretation. Many felt that he had slipped after the kick was taken. In any event, the ball hit the outside of the post and it was still 4-4.

That moment ensured that John Terry's name would be forever woven into the folklore of Manchester United. Ronaldo, Rooney and Tevez had etched their names into it by different means. John Terry was already highly unpopular with the United fans but this incident turned him into a figure of derision. When Terry's name was read out at Old Trafford the next time he played there, it was greeted with tremendous cheers. The most amusing of the banners and placards made by fans to compound his misery was a spoof on the *Mr Men* series of children's books – a new character called Mr Penalty (missed a penalty) with a drawing of Terry.

Back in Russia, the ultimate prize was up for grabs now. Anderson scored for the Reds and Kalou for the Blues to make it 5 each. Then it was Giggs's turn, and every bit of his vast experience and huge heart was behind the kick that he thumped home. It was fitting that he scored that goal in the match that saw him beat Sir Bobby Charlton's all-time appearance record for United in his 759th outing. United edged in front now – 6-5. Next on the hit list was Nicolas Anelka, whose last goal against United had been the winner for Bolton back in November. Carlos watched him shape up to shoot. He looked absolutely terrified and made his intentions clear to Holland's most capped player, Edwin Van der Sar, who dived to his right and saved easily.

United had won their third European Cup.

It had been a ridiculously close contest – United had 56% of the possession and 52% of the territory. An iconic image from the final was of the United team parading the cup with Carlos wearing his shirt the wrong way round. He also had the Argentina flag tied around his neck; perhaps it was the same one that he had sported at Wigan, 10 days before. Maybe he had taken it to with him Moscow as some sort of lucky charm. Also draped around his neck, of course, was his winner's medal. A picture almost as amusing showed him biting on his medal, as it was some foil-covered chocolate.

Carlos earned a 6/10 rating in the *Sun*. The *Guardian* gave him 7/10, while the *Daily Telegraph* awarded him a 6. He told the *Manchester United Annual*: 'It has been a long time since I felt like this – it's a huge emotion in my heart. In Argentina, *Ole* (nothing to do with Solskjaer) wrote: 'Tevez struggled to make an impact with football, although he was not anonymous and fought for the whole match. Reviewing Tevez's interventions, his clashes with opponents clearly outnumbered his chances to cause damage through skill and power. His team's play did not help. Manchester, especially in the second half and the first extra period did not produce much.'

Carlos told the *Daily Mail*: 'When I was a child, I never thought I would be now lifting the Cup, but dreams usually come true and I am very, very happy. I came from a couple of finals I lost to Brazil in the Copa America and Once Caldas in the Libertadores. This time I had to win it.'

CHAPTER EIGHT

THAT DIFFICULT SECOND SEASON SYNDROME

He's got a winning mentality. He wants to be the best, he wants to win, he wants to score goals. If he's on the bench, he wants to come on and do well. He's not one to sit down and sulk and ask, "Why didn't I start?"
OLE GUNNAR SOLSKJAER, LEGENDARY 'BABY-FACED ASSASSIN',
NOW A COACH AT OLD TRAFFORD

After the euphoria of that amazing night in Moscow died down, Carlos was left with two of the most prized honours in world football – the Premier League and Champions League winner's medals. An amazing haul and a fitting monument to his Herculean efforts.

Season 2008–9 started with reports that Tevez's long-term future at Old Trafford seemed far from certain. Wayne Rooney was desperate for United to secure the permanent transfer of the player that had scored 19 goals in that epic season. The England striker told the *Manchester Evening News*: 'It's crucial that we get him signed and I am sure that will happen.'

The first rumblings of the credit crunch that was to devastate the world economy were starting to echo around the banking institutions that summer. Meanwhile, Sir Alex was stepping up his hunt for the Spurs striker Dimitar Berbatov, who was involved in a bitter struggle with his club.

United Chief Executive David Gill stated in July 2008 that a permanent deal for Tevez would be concluded in the autumn. However, Sir Alex confused the situation when he suggested that the deal would be done at the end of the season.

A British record fee of £32m was apparently agreed to make Tevez a permanent signing, which would surpass the £30m Chelsea paid for Ukrainian striker Andriy Shevchenko.

After his fabulous first season Carlos was established as a favourite with the fans and expectations were high. In the music business there is a saying about bands facing the pressure when following up their successful debut album – 'second album syndrome', they call it. In the same manner footballers always face a difficult time when they play in their second season, especially after setting such high standards. The younger the player, the greater the pressure. Tevez was no longer in the first flush of youth and had already gleaned a wealth of experience in top-class games. It was going to be an interesting season for the United buccaneer.

The Argentinean started like an express train. United's first competitive match in England was their Community Shield tie against Portsmouth. By a strange quirk of fate, United had played the Cup winners a few weeks earlier in a friendly match in Abuja, Nigeria. Carlos missed a penalty kick very early in that match. The penalty was given after England defender Glen Johnson brought down Fraizer Campbell. In his first attempt, Tevez converted the kick easily. The referee ordered a retake though, when Chris Eagles encroached in the box. This time, Carlos nearly brought down the crossbar when he smashed the kick against the underside of the bar with David James just an onlooker.

Both Eagles and Tevez made amends for their errors, though, when they scored early in the second half. The

THAT DIFFICULT SECOND SEASON SYNDROME

promising youngster Eagles was shortly to join Burnley as his chances at United were severely limited by the world-class talent in front of him at the club. Carlos showed a glimpse of that talent when he powered into the box before unleashing a terrific shot past the England goalkeeper David James.

Another English international, Jermaine Defoe, cut the deficit for Harry Redknapp's side in the last minute. When they met again at Wembley a few weeks later, United were again the winners.

Before that, the Reds had played Espanyol in a testimonial for their former striker Ole Gunnar Solskjaer. Carlos was lucky to stay on the pitch after a flare-up. United finally overcame a belligerent Espanyol side to win 1-0. The game was almost a solemn occasion as it marked the end of the Norwegian legend's glittering United career. He had been an immensely popular player, who stood for unfashionable qualities like humility, honesty, sincerity and integrity. Combined with the deadliest finishing ability since Denis Law, Solskjaer had cemented his status as one of the greatest players ever to grace the Old Trafford pitch. Solskjaer had donated a huge amount of the game's proceeds to a children's charity he had set up in Africa, and fans were delighted with the news that he would be staying on at United to become the reserve team coach.

Tevez was voted Man of the Match in the Community Shield. Clearly he had been United's best player in the pre-season games. He was on top form, displaying phenomenal energy by chasing every ball, firing in shots from all angles and generally running around like the Duracell bunny.

Played on one of the few hot days of a poor summer, the game ended 0-0 after 90 minutes, but United won 3-1 on penalties. The Reds were making a habit of winning those big games in shoot-outs. Portsmouth assistant manager and former United striker Joe Jordan lamented his side's wayward shooting as they missed a succession of spot kicks. Their left-back, Hermann Hreidarsson, accused Carlos of stamping on him in a deliberate manner after a fracas. The United forward crumpled in a heap following a 75th-minute challenge by Hreidarsson. Referee Peter Watson denied United a blatant penalty, which snapped Carlos out of his usual sunny disposition. Instantly grabbing the defender by the throat, he only narrowly escaped punishment. Hreidarsson insisted he had only grabbed Tevez to stop him stomping on him.

Sir Alex was quick to praise Tevez's performance against Portsmouth and told the *Guardian*: 'Carlos came to us a year ago, straight after the Copa America. His fitness now is light years ahead of where it was then and we are expecting big things from him. The great thing about Tevez is that he has a heart to play the game. He is not intimidated at all; he fights for every ball and is a real handful. The decision to make him Man of the Match was fully justified; it was a superb performance. He was a constant thorn to Portsmouth and it was just a pity he did not get a goal.'

The summer had been dominated by the seemingly endless saga of Ronaldo's on/off move to Real Madrid. With an ankle injury ruling Cristiano out for the start of the season, and Rooney starting with a hangover from England's non-appearance in the European Championships, the focus switched to Tevez. The media saw him as the focal point of United's attacking force in the coming season. Things did not work out like that, though.

The first setback happened when Carlos missed the first Premier League match of the season when he had to fly back to Argentina following a family bereavement. United drew their opening match against Newcastle 1-1, a disappointing result as it was to turn out. Shorn of their megastars, United's critical need for strike power was apparent. An unmarked Obafemi Martins put the Geordies ahead from a corner, but within 2 minutes Darren Fletcher equalised. Newcastle coach Kevin Keegan was delighted with his team's performance but the euphoria of holding the double Champions was shortly to dissipate. Yet again the Geordie messiah walked out following internal wrangles and the team slid down into the bottom half of the table.

Jonas Guitierrez was an Argentinean team-mate of Carlos, who had recently joined Newcastle from Real Mallorca. He was disappointed that he did not get to play against his fellow countryman after warning his colleagues of the constant threat that the man known as 'The Lion' posed. Jonas was born in Buenos Aires and was another product of their ferocious street football. The fast-paced defender's nickname was 'Spiderman' after he celebrated scoring for Real Mallorca by pulling on a Spiderman mask and firing imaginary webs into the crowd. Guitierrez was another tremendous player from South America with a vaudeville personality.

Carlos was back in the side when – surprise, surprise – United played Portsmouth yet again. This fixture was played on the August Bank Holiday Monday at Fratton Park. An away win here was vital, because Chelsea and Liverpool had both won their opening fixtures and United faced an 18-day break from Premiership action. The reason for this was that first, they were involved in the European Super Cup final, and then came the international breaks. Such were the quirks of their fixture list for season 2008–9.

In the opening months of the season they faced tough away fixtures against the other members of the big four. United had to travel to Liverpool, Chelsea and Arsenal, followed by their December sojourn to Japan for the Club World Championship tournament. Some pundits were already writing off the champions' chances of retaining their title, predicting they would crash and burn in the opening weeks.

A fine team performance at Portsmouth dispelled some of the doubts. Once again, Darren Fletcher was the scorer of what proved to be the only goal of the game. Carlos was instrumental in setting up the goal with a superb pass inside the Portsmouth right-back Glen Johnson to Patrice Evra. The Frenchman accelerated away and crossed for Fletcher to flick into the net off the defender Sylvain Distin. A scrappy finish, but a marvellous build-up, with Carlos's pass the pick of the 13 that comprised the kaleidoscopic move.

United easily defended their lead against Portsmouth's robotics and Anderson might have increased it with after another dazzling interchange of passes between Tevez and Rooney, Tevez earned a seven-star rating in *The Times* for his whole-hearted performance against the team that had proved a 'bogey' side to United in recent seasons.

On the Thursday they flew out to Monaco for their Super Cup clash with UEFA Cup winners Zenit St Petersburg. The Russian side were seen as one of the up-and-coming forces in the European game and had beaten Glasgow Rangers to win the trophy. Their squad boasted the inclusion of Andrei Arshavin, one of the stars of Euro 2008. Arshavin had been courted by Spurs all summer, who had hoped to fund the move with the transfer of Dimitar Berbatov. Roman Abramovich even sailed into town to lend his support to his fellow countrymen.

Earlier in the year Lewis Hamilton had won the Monaco Grand Prix on his way to securing his first Formula One world title. For periods in the match Carlos had torn around the Stade Louis XI like Lewis's McLaren racer. He was the exception, though – many of his team-mates badly misfired as the Reds missed out on the chance of having their name engraved on the trophy. Only Tevez's indefatigable will to win kept United in the game as the Russians took a 2-0 lead. Pavel Pogrebnyak's agile far-post header just on half-time put them deservedly ahead and on the hour the Portugal international midfielder Danny made it 2.

The United defence was at fault for both the goals, while all the attack could muster was a superb solo run by Carlos, which ended in Rooney wastefully blasting wide.

Carlos had better luck in the 73rd minute when he turned the ball into the path of Vidic, who threaded his shot home through a group of defenders. That should have set things up for a grandstand finish, but United seemed strangely subdued. The only event of note that happened in the oddly-disappointing closing stages was when Paul Scholes punched the ball into the net and was dismissed for his second yellow card. It was Scholes's third European red card in successive seasons.

All in all, it was a disappointing match for United. Sir Alex was bidding to be the first coach to win the Super Cup three times, having won it in 1983 with Aberdeen and with United in 1999. The Commander in Chief of Old Trafford had tripped over a television wire in the build-up to the match, which sort of summed things up. Only Carlos played well. The match was shown live on ITV and pundit Robbie Earle said, in his half-time round-up: 'Tevez's work rate was undeniable.' In the second half former Liverpool defender

Jim Beglin said in his commentary that, 'Tevez was playing them on his own.'

So much so, his performance helped clinch the manutd.com August Player of the Month award after he received 49% of the votes. Darren Fletcher was second in the poll, picking up 39%, but it was Carlos who had dominated the month. Former United defender David May was particularly impressed with the Argentinean's flying start to the season and told the United website: 'He's come back from the summer break more energetic than ever. He's like a breath of fresh air – his work rate's tremendous and he's really stood out. You don't associate hard work with too many centre-forwards, but we are blessed to have Carlos Tevez and Wayne Rooney, who will both work their socks off for you. He's unselfish and his interchange play, especially with Rooney, has the potential to rip defences apart.'

August was to prove a satisfactory month for Tevez, but on the last day of the month two events occurred that were to have a huge effect on his career. The first was the takeover of neighbours Manchester City by the Abu Dhabi United Group for Investment and Development. The new financial strike force to hit the Premiership was backed by the Abu Dhabi Royal Family. Among their numerous assets was Chrysler Building in New York and a 5% share in Ferrari. The oligarch Roman Abramovich's money had dominated the Premiership, but at a stroke he was reduced to pauper status by the multi-billionaires of the Abu Dhabi monarchy.

As a statement of intent City hijacked Chelsea's bid for the Brazilian superstar Robinho, and signed him for a British record fee of £32.5m. The consortium's head, Dr Sulaiman al-Fahim, pledged to splash out a further £540m on players. He told the *Metro*: 'The best players in the world average £30 million. To win the Champions League we need a minimum of 18 players at that level.'

Soon rumours were sweeping Manchester that Tevez was one of their top targets. Carlos himself thought that the audacious signing of Robinho had transformed the nouveau-riche City into genuine contenders for their title. In an interview with the *Sun* he explained: 'Robinho will greatly improve the quality of Manchester City. They will be much closer to the top this year. He's one of those great players that people want to go and watch because he has a lot of fun playing.'

It takes one to know one, Carlos. In the same interview he made the point that City had done the double over his team last season, and in the coming year they would be even harder to beat. Tevez was a great admirer of the brilliant City defender Micah Richards, who he complimented as being his best marker in the last season.

Across town another big-money transfer deal was done, with United purchasing Dimitar Berbatov from Tottenham for £31m. It was the conclusion of a transfer saga that had dragged on all summer. Berbatov's agent Emil Danchev admitted that United had come sniffing and had made an offer in July. Spurs chairman Daniel Levy branded Sir Alex as being both 'arrogant' and 'hypocritical' and reported United to the Premier League. The following month Berbatov was snapped signing a Manchester United shirt and this triggered another row.

Years previously Paul Ince, while still playing for West Ham, had posed in a United shirt; an action that still led to him being booed at Upton Park when he returned as manager of Blackburn. The bad feeling continued to fester between United and Spurs. Levy was furious when he heard on transfer deadline day that Berbatov was in Manchester – and having talks with United without his permission. Then Manchester City tried to upset United's applecart, starting an improbable bidding war by offering an astonishing £34m for Berbatov. Spurs accepted the offer, but Berbatov had his heart set on a move to the Manchester side that played in red and refused City's advances.

Sir Alex sweetened the deal by including his promising striker Fraizer Campbell in the package, allowing him to go to White Hart Lane on a year's loan. At 11.45pm, a quarter of an hour before the window was slammed shut, Berbatov finally signed for United. Sir Alex was delighted at what he considered was a key signing; some clubs were collecting expensive players like trinkets, but not him. Berbatov was the last of a dying breed – a clinical finisher, a poacher with preternatural cool. The type of player that many considered United had missed since the retirement of Ole Gunnar Solskjaer.

The Norwegian had played against Berbatov when he starred for Bayer Leverkusen in the 2001–2 Champions League semi-finals. The German side had knocked United out of the competition and the Bulgarian striker left a lasting impression on Ole and his manager. Solskjaer, happily installed as reserve team coach, told MUTV: 'I think he's the right one. His performances for Spurs have been great. I knew he was a good player when he played against us for Bayer Leverkusen. We're delighted we've got him.'

The 6ft 2in striker was very quick and very good in the air, but his reluctance to conform to expectations and his all-consuming desire for goals were even bigger assets. Ryan Giggs told the *London Lite* newspaper: 'Berbatov is a Manchester United-type player. He has that physique and stature because he is over six foot, so he offers something a little bit different to Wayne Rooney or Carlos Tevez. For a big man, he has a superb touch. But he also has a big personality, the personality you need to be a success at Manchester United.'

Sir Alex saw Berbatov as the fulcrum of the attack, with Rooney and Tevez supplying the movement. The plan was to push Rooney closer to goal, with Carlos dropping deeper. Berbatov's ability to hold the ball up would enable him to put Rooney and the Argentinean in for chances. The slick inter-changing of the pair had been an integral part of United's double success. David May had referred to it when Tevez won the August Player of the Month award. How would it work with a third component involved in the mix? Was Tevez's new role at Old Trafford now just to do the running for Berbatov? Nobody knew it at the time, but the arrival of Berbatov signalled the beginning of the end of Tevez's career at United.

The United fans saw a dream start to the Tevez/Rooney/Berbatov triumvirate when they travelled to Anfield for a vital Premiership fixture the following Saturday lunchtime. In the two previous seasons, United had snatched vital wins at the home of their bitter rivals. Carlos's winner there in 2007–8 had set them up for the title. Rafael Benitez, the Liverpool boss, had yet to record a win over United.

evez started the game after returning early from the Argentine having received a red card. Within 3 minutes, Berbatov had set up Tevez for his first goal of the season. In the opening minute, the Bulgarian had appeals for a penalty turned down when his snap shot hit Jamie Carragher. A neat turn from the debutant, a few minutes later, deceived Carragher and a perfectly weighted pass was played back to Carlos, who scored with a curling drive beyond Pepe Reina.

It was his first goal of the season and should have paved the way for another famous victory. Tevez was wearing the new lily-white away kit with the controversial blue trim. The kit had made its debut in a friendly against Aberdeen, but the first showcasing of it in the Premier League was at Anfield.

After scoring the goal Tevez kissed a new tattoo inscribed on his arm. The media tried to decipher the tattoo, which appeared to be of the late actor Patrick Swayze, star of the classic *Dirty Dancing* movie. Exactly why Carlos chose to have such a tattoo was unclear.

Liverpool had not even scored against United in the Premier League for nearly five years and looked outclassed for the opening 25 minutes. Then fate gifted them a highly fortunate equaliser. Xabi Alonso's weak shot sliced off Patrick Evra and was inexplicably turned into an own goal as Edwin van der Sar could only deflect it against Wes Brown and the rebound flew into the net. It was a complete fluke, but it put Liverpool firmly back in the game. United seemed deflated by the bizarre incident.

In the second half of this frantic North-West derby Liverpool wrestled the midfield from United. Owen Hargreaves was pitched into the fray after 66 minutes to replace the ineffective Scholes. The continued absence of the Calgary-born holding midfielder had raised questions about his long-term future. His long-standing problem with tendonitis had flared up again and his presence was greatly missed in the team. Sir Alex had hoped to deploy him against Zenit, but his overall fitness level was of huge concern to him.

It was another brilliant midfield holding player who dominated the game, though Carlos's compadre Javier Mascherano. Driving down the right, the ex-West Ham player drew Vidic and Giggs towards the by-line. The ball broke to Kuyt, who turned back to Ryan Babel. Clipping the ball on the bounce, the Dutchman turned it high into the net for the winner.

United's attack had fizzled out and the service to Tevez dried up. Berbatov's prominent game deteriorated into a replica of his Tottenham away performances, standing hands-on-hips, detached from the action. The fallibility of United that day, the decimation of their midfield and their weak attack, came as a shock to both players and fans. Javier Mascherano, rightly named as the Man of the Match, savoured the moment, then spoke to *FourFourTwo* magazine of his friendship with his fellow Argentina international: 'I have a good relationship with Carlos. He is playing for Manchester United and me for Liverpool, but it does not matter because we are friends. I am happy for him that he has done well, that he has won the Champions League. When we play against each other, of course I want to win, to beat him. But he is my friend and I am happy for him when he is successful. He had the chance to win the Champions League, and when he was in Argentina he won the Libertadores Cup. So he has many winners' medals now.'

Liverpool were cock-a-hoop at beating United for the first time in nine Premier League matches. Sir Alex was furious at what he described as 'Conference team defending', which had led to United conceding two soft goals. Liverpool were now six points ahead of the current champions and the next Premier League fixture involved a trip to Stamford Bridge against another of their biggest rivals. Chelsea were unbeaten in 84 Premier League home games in a run stretching back four years; even before Jose Mourinho had taken over. But before that, there was the matter of a home Champions League fixture against Villarreal.

The Group E fixture took on added interest with the much-anticipated comeback from ankle surgery of Ronaldo as a second-half substitute. Ronaldo spent the entire summer believing he would end up in the white of Real Madrid. The saga ended, for the moment, with Sir Alex having to fly to Portugal to meet the superstar and emphasise that he would not be sold, no matter what price Madrid were willing to pay. There were even reports of the final fee being in the region of £75m. Carlos Tevez was of the view that the return of the former Sporting Lisbon player would kick-start United's season into life after a lacklustre start. He told the *Metro*: 'Cristiano is a massive player for us. It is like having an extra player when he is there. He is such a danger to our opponents and it will be a big boost to have him back.'

Tevez took the chance to talk about his contract position. Since the arrival of the former Tottenham striker, the future for Carlos seemed a little less clear: 'From the first moment I came here, I would have loved to sign a long-term contract. It would be wonderful if the chairman put a long-term contract in front of me. I would sign it without a doubt.'

Perhaps uncertainties were starting to creep into his play around then, as the faintest of insecurities flickered across his mind about his long-term future at the club he loved. AIG, the team's sponsors, had been bailed out by the US government and things were starting to look a little uncertain across the world of football. The score in the Villarreal match was a disappointing 0-0, which ended United's sequence of a dozen straight home wins. It was their third consecutive goalless match with Villarreal, an emerging force on the Spanish scene who had finished second in La Liga the previous season. They represented United's toughest test in a group also comprised of Celtic and the Danish side Aalborg.

With Berbatov sidelined with a knee injury, Carlos started the match alongside Rooney. It was a dull first half, mainly enlivened by his ceaseless running. Tevez provided one of the few moments of excitement when he blazed in an angled drive that the Villarreal keeper Diego Lopez palmed away. On the hour, the prodigal Ronaldo returned to the fold, replacing Ji-Sung Park. There had been much speculation as to how the fundamentalists among the Old Trafford faithful would react to the renegade Cristiano after his summer flirtation with the Spanish giants. There was no problem, though, as the crowd rose to give him a great ovation. A couple of body swerves and a step-over later, it was as if he had never been away. United looked a different side with him in it. Shortly before his introduction, Villarreal had almost gone in front when Franco back-heeled Angel Lopez's cross against the inside of the post.

Carlos had a good chance to clinch the match 20 minutes from time in a breakaway attack. Rooney over-hit his cross, though, forcing Tevez to lose a vital split-second in controlling the ball. Tevez would have liked to have hit a first-time shot, but the extra time needed enabled the defender Rodriguez to scramble the shot off the line after it had beaten the keeper. That signalled the end of Tevez's contribution to the match as he was later replaced by Ryan Giggs.

The drawn match showed how hard the task of defending their Champions League trophy would be. In the previous four years, each of the winners – AC Milan, Barcelona, Liverpool and Porto – did not make it past the last 16 of the knockout round the following season. United still looked tired; how much the efforts of winning the trophy in Moscow that May night had taken out of them remained to be seen.

Their opponents that night, Chelsea, waited for them in another lunchtime Premier League kick-off. Conspiracy theorists were already saying how hard United's fixtures in the first half of the season were, and how congested things would get later on. The knives were already out for United, with questions raised over the purchase of Berbatov, the fitness of Hargreaves, the loss of the tactical ability of Carlos Queiroz. Chelsea, with Luiz Felipe Scolari in charge, had hit the ground running and seemed to have put their disappointment at twice losing out to United behind them. Scolari had Chelsea playing a better brand of football – they were unbeaten and a victory over Sir Alex's men would have given the Reds a nine-point deficit to make up. Many in the game were of the opinion that such a lead would have proved unassailable at that stage of the season.

The pre-match war between the sides was stoked up by a couple of incidents. In his Friday press conference Luiz Felipe Scolari joked that, 'Maybe next season Cristiano is with me.' Big Phil could not conceal his dream of working with Ronaldo again; he had been his manager for five years when he was in Portugal. But with Abramovich hitting the financial brake at Stamford Bridge as a consequence of the global downturn, such a move seemed unlikely.

A more serious issue, though, was the fact that the FA were looking at Sir Alex's comments over John Terry being allowed to play against United in the match, despite the Chelsea captain being sent off at Eastlands the previous weekend. The United boss claimed that the appeal verdict was influenced by Keith Hackett, the head of the Professional Game Match Officials Board. The Scot told the *London Lite*: 'From what I had heard Keith Hackett has told the referee [Mark Halsey] to rescind the red card and he would not do it. If it had been a Manchester United player, Keith Hackett wouldn't have done this.'

The case had raised a number of issues over the lack of mobility in Terry's game – the Brazilian striker Jo had left him for dead, only for Terry to stick out a leg and then grab him around the waist. Most United fans couldn't less if Terry played or not; after gifting the Champions League trophy to them, they had rewritten their 'Viva Ronaldo' song to namecheck him. A thank you to the Chelsea defender for presenting the Champions League to them on a plate.

Carlos did not feature in the Chelsea match at all. Sir Alex had a hard decision to make; his options being to leave Tevez out and disappoint either Ronaldo, about to be voted the Best Player in the World, or record, signing Berbatov. He was facing his biggest selection problem since the treble-winning season, when he had four top-class strikers at his disposal.

United found some of their best form of the season and all but smashed Chelsea's home record. Ironically, it was eventually to fall to a goal by Xabi Alonso of Liverpool a few weeks later. United dominated early proceedings and took a first-half lead through Ji-Sung Park. They clung to it until late in the game, when a reckless challenge by Rooney on Ashley Cole led to a free kick. John Obi Mikel floated the ball over for substitute Salomon Kalou to head home.

Sir Alex was disappointed that after taking the initiative his team had not gone in for the kill and put the game beyond Chelsea's reach. Berbatov had shown some neat touches and held the line well in the first half, but as the game wore, on he became an increasingly isolated figure. Hargreaves' playing in what was to be his last match of the season for United, had a fine game.

In the latter stages of the game, with an increasingly desperate Chelsea pushing up, it would have been a good idea to introduce Tevez, brooding on the bench, into the action. It was an encouraging performance after the poor start, but the fact was United should have taken all three points. The addition of Tevez might have made, the difference.

On the way to Euston to catch the train home, the United team coach was attacked by a group of men. A stone was thrown and a window cracked. A man was arrested and the players, already drained by the exertions at Stamford Bridge, were stunned. Carlos told the *Daily Mail*: 'As for what happened on the bus, that was unfortunate and scary, but it can happen anywhere.' The United superstar had seen it all before: having grown up in the slums, he was unperturbed by events but the incident spoke volumes about the hostility that still existed towards the Premier League champions. West Ham fans had attacked the United coach two years previously when Carlos was playing for them.

The next match was against Middlesbrough in the Carling Cup. Sir Alex fielded his usual Carling cocktail of battle-hardened veterans and promising youngsters. Carlos was on the bench, but replaced Ronaldo on the hour. The rampaging winger had continued his rehabilitation by opening the scoring with a header from a pinpoint Giggs' corner. A sloppy header by Vidic let in Johnson to equalise for Boro shortly after the break, but goals from Giggs and a neat vignette from Nani put United through to the next round to play QPR.

Once again Tevez's presence livened up United, but he was unable to score the goal his effort deserved. The sight of the world-class player on the field must have inspired the gung-ho 17-year-old Danny Welbeck, who was having a run out that night. The raw youngster showed some neat touches in the game and playing alongside Tevez could only have boosted his confidence even further. Just observing the Argentinean's clever positioning must have been a real education for him.

The evening was soured by the sending-off of Boro defender Pogatetz for a reckless challenge on the highly-rated Brazilian youngster Rodrigo Possebon. At first it was feared that he had broken his leg; Carlos ran to console his team-mate and even the tough footballing soldier of fortune winced at the horrific sight of the blood-soaked injury.

Bolton came to Old Trafford the following Saturday and Carlos started the match, with Rooney on the bench. One of the most controversial incidents of the season happened in the second half when the referee Rob Styles awarded United a bitterly-disputed penalty. Cristiano Ronaldo – who else? – cut inside the box and the Bolton defender Jlloyd Samuel appeared to win the ball cleanly. Styles immediately blew the whistle for a penalty, which Ronaldo crisply converted. The Bolton captain Kevin Nolan told the *Guardian*: 'Ronaldo was on the floor saying, "I didn't want a penalty." Carlos Tevez was going, "It's not a penalty." There were 20 players in and around the box and every one of them knew it wasn't a penalty. But the other guy was wearing black and somehow he thought it was.'

Encouraged by what Nolan called 'a free goal', United poured forward. Carlos was subbed for Rooney, who ran about like a man possessed before he curled in a second goal. Rooney had recently played well for England in the World Cup qualifying games and there were signs that he was finding his best form after a subdued start to the new season.

Carlos had been misfiring in recent games; as always, the

effort and the tracking back was there, but the final pass was going astray and the goal threat had diminished. The Tevez/Rooney/Berbatov combination was still in its formative stages and Sir Alex was already rotating the trio depending on their form and fitness levels. The problem in games like Bolton was that in midfield there was nobody equipped to spread the ball. Carrick had broken his foot in the Liverpool match and Hargreaves had succumbed to tendonitis. Tevez had tried individually to break down the Bolton defence but when Rooney replaced him, he attempted to spread the ball around quickly.

Manchester City were linked with a sensational attempt to lure Carlos across town in the January transfer window. The Sunday tabloids were running stories that the mega-rich City owners could smash the bond between Sir Alex and Tevez by offering him a staggering deal to play at Eastlands. The continued uncertainty surrounding his future at Old Trafford was leading to intense speculation about where he would be playing. Bookmakers Paddy Power offered 1-4 that he would still be on the books at Old Trafford on 1 February, when the transfer window was shut.

Kia Joorabchian, Tevez's agent, was an advisor to the Abu Dhabi United Group, so there was a direct link to the heart of the Manchester City boardroom. Joorabchian had been a key figure in the deal that brought Robinho from Madrid and gazumped Chelsea. It seemed that City were cranking up their media machine in an attempt to intimidate the rest of the Premiership and destabilise their local neighbours.

The United roadshow's next port of call was to the Northern tip of Denmark and the Energi Nord Arena for their Champions League match against Aalborg. It was the biggest game in the history of the Danish champions and they were overawed by the superstars from the Premier League. Rooney started ahead of Tevez. United won 3-0, with Berbatov getting off the mark with two goals. The finish for his first United goal was superb, struck as if it was a training ground exercise but with tremendous power. Berbatov was obviously in love with his own mythology: would Old Trafford be so willing to be smitten?

Carlos came on for Rooney for the last half hour. He bundled a shot in over the line but it was disallowed for a foul. United wore their blue strip that evening. The retro-style kit was a homage to the colours that they wore in the 1968 European Cup final. Reaction to the kit among the fans was mixed as some factions did not like to see their favourites in that particular colour, but for that season United now had the range of the red, white and blue strips which had come to prominence in the eighties.

United were back in their traditional colours on the weekend when they travelled to Blackburn, now managed by former United midfielder Paul Ince. The past conflicts between Sir Alex and the ex-England international were well documented, but now a mutual respect had grown between them. Tevez did not start this match either; Berbatov was partnered with Giggs playing in the middle. The Welsh wizard played behind their new striker, with Ronaldo wide on the right and Rooney at wide left. Ferguson had assured Wayne at the start of the season that he would play him in his favourite position, but with the veteran Giggs now in the twilight of his career, he was eking out what was left of his marvellous talent by using him in that role.

Sir Alex replaced Giggs with Carlos on 66 minutes; by that time United were two up through Wes Brown and Wayne Rooney. For the next 10 minutes the soaking crowd were treated to the sight of the most famous 'fab four' since those lads from down the road on Merseyside sang their songs. Wayne Rooney, Carlos Tevez, Dimitar Berbatov and Cristiano Ronaldo played together for the first time in the Premier League. The little Argentinean occupied less conspicuous space on the landscape of the Premier League than Ronaldo or Rooney, but his contribution to winning the double in 2008 had been immeasurable. If Cristiano was the avatar of the modern game, then Wayne was an embodiment of its maverick image. Tevez was the team's alchemist and Berbatov was the poacher.

Rooney soon went off to be replaced by Park, and despite some hard running and rapid interchanging by Carlos, the score remained unaltered. The big question remained – could the four play together as a unit? Particularly, where would Carlos fit into the equation and could he maintain the momentum when he most needed it?

CHAPTER NINE
THE TEARS OF AUTUMN

*I'm not as effective in the penalty area anymore. That is something
I have lost and I have to get that back. I used to score better
goals, but something strange has happened. I think it has to
do with the fact that the person up front has to do a lot more
for the team than just score goals.*

CARLOS TEVEZ

A startling confession there by Carlos. He made that remark while on international duty in Argentina. The press revealed that he had had a heart-searching talk with the then coach of the national side, Alfio 'Coco' Basile. The article appeared in the *Daily Mail* in mid-October and the English press jumped on it, turning it into a beef with Sir Alex and claiming that Carlos was risking the wrath of the United boss by talking in this manner.

Carlos missed the 4-0 thrashing of West Bromwich Albion at Old Trafford on 18 October as he only returned from international duty late on the Friday afternoon. He was given a complete break from football and was not even in the squad. Rooney opened the scoring against the Baggies to take his tally for the season to seven to Carlos's solitary effort at Anfield. Sir Alex admitted to the *Manchester Evening News* that he was going through 'torment' trying to integrate three world-class talents into two striking berths.

'It's my torment! It is very difficult trying to gauge whether I can play the three of them together. I have been thinking about it for a couple of weeks now. It is possible, with one of them playing in behind. Making the choice is a very difficult thing to do because they are all terrific players.'

These words were spoken before his team took on Scottish giants Celtic. Managed by former folk hero Gordon Strachan, they had an abysmal away record in Europe with a solitary draw and 17 losses out of 18 games. Their dismal run continued when United bulldozed them aside with an easy 3-0 victory, their 50th Champions League win at home. Carlos was consigned to the bench and the man who replaced him, Dimitar Berbatov, opened the scoring. The goal looked suspiciously offside. The same player added a second after Ronaldo's free kick had been blocked. Two typical poacher's goals – what United had lacked an opportunist, what he was bought for.

Tevez replaced him on the hour and set up the third goal for Rooney with a superb pass. Former Scottish international Pat Nevin was covering the game for Radio 5 Live and he made a point of how desperate Tevez was to make an impression in the limited time that was left. Like the goal at Portsmouth, it was part of an exquisite build-up which had started with Van der Sar's rolled-out clearance and involved a maze of consecutive passes.

Tevez spoke in depth to the *Sun* about his partner Rooney. 'There was all this nonsense about how myself and Wayne couldn't play together but we showed everyone. We have a perfect, intuitive understanding on the pitch, plus we get on brilliantly as pals. Give Wayne half a metre of space and he'll pull out a brilliant goal. Wayne does amazing things, even when he has next to no space. As soon as I played with him, I copied his movement and explosiveness away from defenders, as there is less time or space when you play for United.'

Another lunchtime game followed at Everton. Needless to say Carlos failed to start yet again. It was a disappointing match played out in the pouring autumn rain. Fletcher put United ahead midway through the first half when he glided into the box to fire home. Only two fine saves from ex-United keeper Tim Howard kept the Merseyside team in the match. In the second half United's grip on the match weakened and Everton's new signing Marouane Fellaini headed a deserved equaliser. Carlos replaced Fletcher with 12 minutes to go, but he had negligible impact as their goal threat sputtered out. To lose two points while in a winning position against a mediocre side like Everton was the sort of display that costs champions their crown.

Sir Alex probably should have introduced Tevez into the action much earlier by replacing one of the ineffective midfielders. Deploying him and Rooney wide while letting Ronaldo sit behind Berbatov may have made all the difference.

Ronaldo had a particularly disappointing match and was singled out in the press for his apparent lack of interest in proceedings. He more than made up for it a few nights later, though, scoring both goals in an easy stroll against Carlos's old team from the East End. Tevez started a game for only the second time in nine matches, and Rooney was rotated to make way for the player that had been such a focal point of the recent history of West Ham.

Possibly the occasion of playing against the side that he had such affection for got to him. The added pressure of literally playing for his place in the team and the fact that he must have been reminded of the impending litigation surrounding the Sheffield United case could not have helped. Be that as it may, he looked a shadow of the player that had worn the claret and blue a season and a bit before. The forensic eye for detail and cobra-like reflexes seemed to be missing.

Ronaldo was presented with the Golden Boot award before the match for being the top goalscorer in Europe, and after 14 minutes he spun to shoot home Nani's centre. On the half-hour Ronaldo slid in number two after an astonishing piece of skill by Berbatov, showing razor-sharp form that night. It was the best piece of skill seen so far that season. The Bulgarian seemed hemmed in on the byline by West Ham defender James Collins. With a skip and a pirouette that would have impressed the judges on *Strictly Come Dancing*, he produced a Houdini-type escape and turned the ball into the path of Ronaldo to thrash in the second.

West Ham fan Russell Brand was in the middle of a huge media storm at the time about messages left on the answerphone of *Fawlty Towers* legend Andrew Sachs. The comic still found time away from the maelstrom to watch the match and wrote in his *Guardian* column: 'Berbatov demonstrated a talent bordering on the mystic; time appeared to bend as he flew Icarus-like down the flank, over the by-line, trapping the ball before floating in a perfect cross to the equally touched Ronaldo.'

Carlos was denied a penalty after a vigorous challenge from Hereia Ilung, but he failed to shine against the team he had kept in the Premier League. Perhaps they knew his game too well; other defenders had been studying his play and this was another reason why he was finding it harder that season. By his own exacting standards his game was becoming increasingly neurotic. The situation was garnering a lot of publicity and attention.

Sir Alex assured Carlos that he remained an integral member of the squad and had a part to play in the later stages of the season, when he thought the action would really hot up. In an interview with the *Guardian,* the ex-Glasgow docker discussed the current situation regarding his Argentinean striker. 'On Wednesday I wanted to see how the combination of Tevez and Berbatov worked together, but I think Carlos was so wound up to do well that they became two separate parts. Obviously there is always that language barrier with Carlos. I have had a couple of discussions and it is quite straightforward. He wants to play and that is great. I have reminded him how we operate, the same with Rooney. He understands but it does not mean to say he is happy. It's going to be that way; there will be no change in policy. He is happy here, the players love him, the fans love him, there is absolutely no reason because he has been left out a couple of games why that should be a negative part of the negotiations to get him here full-time.'

Possibly he was trying to placate Tevez, as once again he did not start in the seven-goal thriller against Hull the following Saturday. A few years previously, the thought of Hull scoring three times at Old Trafford in a Premier League game would have been unthinkable. In the match programme, Sir Alex described the ascent of Hull as the success story of the decade. Determined to crush the new boys' spirit, Ronaldo scored the first from another assist by Berbatov, but Hull fought back to equalise. Then Carrick and Ronaldo both scored to give United a comfortable half-time lead. When Vidic stabbed home the fourth on the hour it looked like Hull were heading for a heavy defeat.

Carlos came on shortly afterwards but Hull had not read the script and drew United into an increasingly physical battle. Rooney's volcanic temper erupted again and he was involved in an ugly skirmish with Boateng as the Tigers clawed their way back into the game. Substitute Mendy pulled a goal back and then won the penalty kick conceded by Ferdinand, from which Hull scored their third. This was converted by Geovanni (who had now scored against United for three separate clubs; Benfica and Manchester City were the others). In the end even Tevez was back helping out as Hull pushed hard for the equaliser. This was a game in which Owen Hargreaves's combative qualities were sorely missed as the United defence looked unconvincing. It was the first time they had conceded three goals at home since Mourinho's quick-buck Chelsea had won 3-1 three years previously.

Ex-Liverpool midfielder Jan Molby was covering the match for Radio 5 Live and when asked about the selection quandary, he ventured that, 'There would be plenty of chances for Tevez later in the season.'

The return leg with Celtic was the next fixture that Carlos played in. Celtic were a different proposition at home at Celtic Park from the team with the appalling record in Europe. Carlos played for 71 minutes before being replaced by Rooney; he looked distinctly unimpressed by the switch. Gordon Strachan had admitted before the game that his team could not hope to match United but the Bhoys, roared on by their fanatical crowd, put up a spirited performance. They took an early lead through Scott McDonald and that was how it stayed until late in the game when Giggs headed an equaliser. In the dying seconds the blue-shirted Berbatov spurned a gift of a chance when from eight yards out he slashed wildly at Ronaldo's cross and put it well wide.

A famous visitor had come to see Carlos at the Carrington training ground the day before United travelled to Arsenal. Recently appointed as the new Argentina coach, Diego Maradona had a mere six months' coaching experience with Deportivo Mandiyu and Racing Club. The ex-West Ham duo of Tevez and Javier Mascherano were seen as vital components of the new team he was trying to create. Diego's appointment received tremendous coverage in the press. There was even a suggestion that England should find a role for Gazza – the reasoning being that players respect and idolise certain heroes despite their problems.

This was true of the United players; a few years earlier Maradona had popped into the Chelsea training ground at Cobham and reduced the multi-millionaires to a bunch of star-struck school kids. Maradona had a similar effect at Carrington; the Old Trafford team had met so many celebrities and superstars over the years that they had grown blasé about it all. This guy was a different class though; arguably still the biggest football name on the planet. People would give an argument about Pelé and Johan Cruyff, but Diego came from a different generation. Maradona would always maintain that if he had not had a 20-year cocaine addiction Pelé would not be mentioned in the same breath as him. Another United legend, George Best, the only player from the British Isles who belonged in that glittering clique, memorably made a remark in the same context: 'If I had been born ugly, you would never have heard of Pelé.'

Tevez and Maradona had a mutual appreciation society going. The 48-year-old World Cup winner once declared that 'Tevez is like a son to me'. Carlos wanted no special treatment from his idol. In an interview with Radio La Red, he stated: 'It is going to be difficult. Diego should think more with his head and less with his heart that he is now the head coach. I don't think it will be easy because I know his temperament. It is hard to handle the squad as we are all stars in our clubs. It's awkward that he has Riquelme, Messi and Tevez to stay focused.

We could not have a better motivation than having Diego as a coach. I think he'll want to come onto the pitch with us. I know him very well and I am sure it will be that way. I am very happy for him. It's going to be funny. I hope I can get a seat close to him on the bus. I am imagining myself training under him in March.'

Interesting how Carlos talks about himself in the third person. How many great players are guilty of this? Ronaldo slipped into this mode when he talked about collecting the Ballon D'Or award for 2008. Eric Cantona was another fine example of this mode of behaviour. In the 1994 FA Cup final Dennis Wise tried to psyche him out when he stepped up to take a penalty. Eric, before effortlessly slotting home the kick, snapped to Wise, 'Cantona does not miss penalties.'

After his talks with Carlos, the legend of the 1986 World Cup and his assistant Carlos Bilardo met the rest of the team. Usually the training ground was full of lively banter and jolly japes. A few weeks earlier Patrice Evra had put a mouse down the back of Gary Neville, to mass hilarity. That day, though, there was a respectful silence amongst the players – as if a senior statesman or the Pope had descended upon them. The training matches were highly competitive with so many world-class players battling for a place in the team. Sir Alex noticed an added frisson around the training that morning.

Rio Ferdinand was celebrating his 30th birthday and received a marvellous gift when Diego presented him with a signed shirt. A staggeringly rich young man by anybody's standards, Rio would never have to resort to putting the garment on eBay. The ex-Hammer was absolutely made up at meeting his favourite player of all time and the main reason why he started to play football.

The bloggers had their fun at the expense of Diego; certain figures in the media like ex England International Terry Butcher could never forgive the hand ball incident though it happened a lifetime ago. The most amusing was a United fan who made reference to Tevez's 'mother' visiting him. With his big hair, earring and strange fur-hooded parka, Maradona looked a bizarre figure.

Rumours buzzed around that Maradona had told Carlos that he would not pick him for Argentina if he was not a first choice in the United team. This was another pressure on him, and a vital reason why he had to regain his place in the team.

The Diego phenomenon continued – he also went to Liverpool to see Javier Mascherano and there was a constant stream of their star players wanting to greet him. Rafael Benitez held a meeting with Diego in his office but it was punctuated by players knocking on the door trying to meet the new Argentina boss. Jamie Carragher even took his family along to shake the hand of the 'hand of God' player.

The Arsenal game on 8 November was named the 'lunch crunch' by the media. Once again questions were asked about the timing of the fixture. Tevez and co. had been at Celtic Park on the Wednesday night; now it was Saturday lunchtime. The previous season, only a goal by William Gallas in the dying seconds had scrambled a point for the home team. There was never much to choose between the sides. In the 36 occasions Wenger and Ferguson had clashed in all competitions, each side had won thirteen times with ten draws.

Sir Alex had recently attended a dinner with Arsène Wenger and had ventured that his team's clashes with the North London side carried more meaning than those with the team in blue across the other side of the capital. He added that Arsenal versus United equated one team's history against that of the other.

The fixture was probably the biggest draw in football. Few teams derived greater pleasure from upsetting the form book than Arsenal. The previous week they had lost to Stoke City and the bookies were giving 9-4 for an Arsenal victory over United. That was the best price ever for an Emirates home win, and those who took it were rewarded as two Samir Nasri goals condemned United to their second away defeat of the season.

Tevez was on the bench and could only watch as Rooney, head shaved closer than Travis Bickle in *Taxi Driver*, squandered two early chances. In a magnificent game of attacking football, United created 21 goal attempts – one more than against Celtic – yet once again failed to win. Berbatov showed some wonderful touches but faded as the game wore on; his half-clearance led to Arsenal's opening goal. Ronaldo missed a golden chance shortly after midfielder Nasri put Arsenal two goals ahead. Carlos replaced Rooney as the reds strikers were constantly squeezed for space. The Arsenal three-man central midfield of Diaby, Denilson and Cesc Fábregas choked the life out of United's supply line to the forwards.

Throughout the match Rooney and Berbatov had

switched from flank to centre, from centre to flank. The Arsenal back four stood firm, though, refusing to be flustered and continuing to frustrate the United strike force. Nobody was more frustrated than Rooney, and his last action before being replaced by Tevez was a speculative shot that miscued for a throw-in. United laid siege to the Arsenal goal in the closing minutes and young starlet Rafael Da Silva set up a grandstand finish with a beautifully-struck goal. It was the sixth consecutive match that Arsenal had conceded a last-minute goal, but they hung on for a famous victory. It was a bad result for Tevez's team; they had not beaten Arsenal away since 2005, when they still played at Highbury.

The quest for a hat-trick of consecutive Premier League titles was now in jeopardy. Sir Alex had set them a target of 85 points but after the Emirates result they were stuck on 21 points and only one of them had been gleaned from their away trips to the other members of the big four. Remarks like 'playground stuff' were bandied around by Sir Alex after the match. He agreed that it was great football for the fans, but he was disappointed by the result. The olive branch between him and Wenger had been stripped bare of its leaves over the years, but the spirit of the match had been excellent.

The next mid-week game was the Carling Cup match against QPR, who were now jointly owned by three of the richest men in the world: Lakshmi Mittal, Flavio Briatore and Bernie Ecclestone. Carlos started the match in a team that showed eight changes from the Arsenal clash. Some saw it as an indication of how far his stock had fallen of late for him to be picked for a match like that. The team could be said to be C-list, while A-listers Rooney and Ronaldo were hobnobbing with Ecclestone and his cronies in the stand. The little guy Tevez was never one who shirked from a fight, though, and he knew that the more games he played in, the more chance he had of recapturing his best form and forcing his way back into the reckoning.

It was Rangers' first visit to the Theatre of Dreams for 13 years. It was almost 22 years to the day since the team from Loftus Road had provided the opposition in Sir Alex's first home game in charge of United. John Sievbaek scored United's winner that day. The last team to include a player to score a hat-trick in the league against United there was QPR, in an astonishing 4-1 victory in 1992. To Carlos Tevez though, in the last years of the first decade of the 21st century, they were unfamiliar opponents in a strange kit.

Since winning the Carling Cup in 2005 against Wigan, United had had a poor record in the competition. An embarrassing defeat at the hands of Southend and the previous season's loss at home to Coventry still rankled. United were determined to put that behind them against another team from the Championship. The game was played in continuous rain and United started slowly. The first action of note was when ex-Tottenham keeper Radek Cerny made a fine save from Carlos's dipping shot after 15 minutes. Apart from another near miss from Carlos, turning O'Shea's cross just wide, that was about the sum total of the action in the first half. Poor fare to put in front of the Formula 1 billionaires.

There was little improvement in the second half except for Park hitting the post around the hour mark. The buzzing Carlos sent in another venomous drive from close range, which Cerny did well to tip over the bar. With the game shuffling towards extra time, the England under-19 starlet

Danny Welbeck was introduced for Rodrigo Possebon. The Brazilian was now happily recovered from the dreadful tackle he had suffered in the previous round of the competition. Welbeck had an immediate impact when after 75 minutes he was cut down by the Hoops' full-back Peter Ramage and a penalty was awarded. Up stepped Carlos to take the spot kick. It was a crucial moment for him; he had not scored for two months and United needed to avoid any further problems in what was proving to be a tricky season. If his confidence had been dented anyway by recent events, he showed no sign of it in taking the kick.

The fans were treated to a moment of Tevez magic when he produced a theatrical run up to his penalty. Tucking one foot behind the other, his jerky stop-start run sent Cerny diving to the ground. A simple tap to the other corner was enough to score the solitary goal of the evening.

Tevez was delighted to have scored the winner and the relief showed on his face. A caller on Danny Baker's *606* phone-in show on Radio 5 extolled the virtues of the penalty and DJ Danny called for footage of the kick. The speculation over Tevez's future died down briefly, but it intensified again when reports appeared in the press suggesting that Real Madrid were keen to sign him.

Ruud Van Nistelrooy, holder of the Champions League record for the most goals in a season, had joined Madrid from United, but the Dutch striker had been ruled out for the rest of the season following a major knee injury. Reports were rife that Tevez would be signing in the January window as his replacement. The Spanish football websites were full of speculation that he would soon be playing for Real. They stated that Ferguson and Tevez had not spoken about Real's interest, but in their view the club's treatment of him meant that he would not be in Manchester much longer.

The relationship between the two clubs had reached a new low in May 2008 when the Madrid president Ramon Calderon branded Sir Alex senile. Calderon had been incensed by what he saw as Ferguson's risible comments about Madrid's connections in the past with the Spanish dictator Franco. Madrid would have loved to have acquired Carlos in retaliation for their thwarted attempts to lure Ronaldo to Spain in the summer. Strong rumours also linked Tevez's fellow countryman Hernan Crespo with a move to the Bernabeu. Like Carlos at United, Crespo had fallen down the pecking order since the all-conquering Mourinho took over in Milan. Both men had a burning ambition to break Batistuta's record as the all-time top scorer for Argentina.

Rooney missed the next home game against Stoke through illness, a chest infection ruling him out. Carlos started the match and had a fine game as United thrashed Stoke 5-0. Although Tevez did not score himself, he had a hand in two of the goals and his general play underpinned a fine team performance. After just 3 minutes, a clumsy foul on him outside the box enabled Ronaldo to score the first with a rocketing free kick. It was his 100th goal for the Reds in 208 starts, plus 45 appearances as a substitute; a truly amazing record. Ronaldo set up number two by running towards the Stoke defence at a surreal pace. Like most teams, they had no option but to retreat. Cristiano flicked a sideways pass to Carrick, who slammed home the second.

The scurrying Carlos carved out the third goal for Berbatov. Linking well with Dimitar, Carlos back-heeled superbly for the ex-Spurs striker to swivel and slot in the third. Just a glimpse of what could have been a burgeoning relationship between the two men with a total transfer value of nearly £65 million. With 15 minutes to go, Sir Alex took the tiring Tevez off and replaced him with the debutant Angolan striker Manucho. Another sub, Danny Welbeck, who had won Tevez the penalty in the previous game, entered the fray and blasted in his first goal for the club. It was a great shot that almost lifted the goal out of the ground. The unyielding bombardment of the Stoke goal continued and Ronaldo wrapped things up with another free kick to complete their biggest win of the season. Sir Alex was pleased with the result; it was 50 years to the day that he had scored his first goal in the big time for Queens Park against Stranraer.

Tevez had put in another energetic display against a tough tackling side that had recently beaten Arsenal. He needed some goals though as tangible proof of his efforts. The *Manchester Evening News* had given him seven out of ten for his efforts, but he still seemed troubled by the situation.

Diego Maradona talked to the *Sun* about his surrogate 'son': 'Tevez is worried about not being in United's first choice team. He's got a challenge ahead of him to win a place among lots of extremely good players, including Wayne Rooney and Dimitar Berbatov. But I saw him and told him the best way of showing his ability is to win the arm-wrestle against all the other players. Then he'll give himself a good chance with the Argentine team. I believe in his ability and I know he features in Sir Alex Ferguson's plans.'

The midweek internationals were next on the agenda but Carlos did not feature for Argentina as he was serving a suspension. Berbatov's Bulgaria were taking on Nemanja Vidic's Serbia and in the match Dimitar picked up a hamstring injury which ruled him out of the next Saturday evening clash away to Aston Villa. It was not a great day for him as Serbia won 6-1. The drain on resources caused by the dictates of the midweek international games was another reason for maintaining a large squad. Coupled with the sheer slog of the competitions, it put tremendous strain on clubs.

Tevez partnered Rooney up front on a raw early winter's night in Birmingham. The stats were in United's favour; they had won their last 11 games against Villa in the Premier League. You had to go back to 1995 for the last time Villa had beaten United – the victory that had triggered Alan Hansen's infamous 'You'll win nothing with kids' quip.

On this occasion the game ended goalless; the first time in 49 league games that United had played out a 0-0 draw. All evening Tevez and Rooney worked hard but they offered little threat. Their best moment came when a wonderful ball from Rooney put Tevez into the box, but as he shaped to shoot, he was bundled over by Villa midfielder Gareth Barry. No penalty was given. The white-shirted Carlos, playing in black gloves, had a wild shot that was well wide and later Rooney missed a gilt-edged chance from close in.

Sir Alex had called for his strikers to be more ruthless; away from home they had managed only seven goals. Carlos was not attacking sides enough; his only strike away from home was his effort at Liverpool. Worryingly for Sir Alex, all Ronaldo's Premier League goals had been scored at the Theatre of Dreams. Tevez's fantastic work rate, covering every inch of the pitch, was masking the fact that he was not really hurting defences. Villa pressed United throughout the match. They were desperate to break into the elite big four and had targeted Arsenal's spot in

Above left: Tevez posing for publicity photos before Argentina's 2006 World Cup campaign in Germany.

Above right: Showing off his skills with the ball during a training session.

Below: In action against Holland in the 2006 World Cup.

© *Action Images*

Tevez signs with West Ham – unaware of the controversy this move would ultimately create.

Above: Tevez and fellow signing Javier Mascherano pose with team manager Alan Pardew on 5 September 2006.

Below: Tevez, Mascherano and Marlon Harewood share a joke during training.

bove and *below left*: Tevez in action for West Ham against Palermo.

© *Action Images/Scott Heavey/Tony O'Brien*

elow right: West Ham United chairman Eggert Magnusson at the FA Premier League quiry into the Tevez affair.

© *Action Images/Steven Paston*

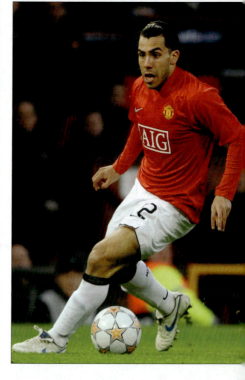

Above: Putting the transfer saga behind him, Carlos poses with his new boss, Manchester United manager Sir Alex Ferguson, and other new signing, Anderson, in 2007.

© *Action Images/Jason Cairndu*

Below left: Playing with his daughter, Florencia, at a hotel pool in July 2007.

Below right: In action for Manchester United.

© *Action Imag*

Carlos celebrates winning
the European Cup with
Manchester United in 2008.

Above: Carlos is met by hordes of fans as he arrives at Eastlands to be unveiled as a City player.

Below: The infamous 'Welcome to Manchester' poster.

© *Action Imag*

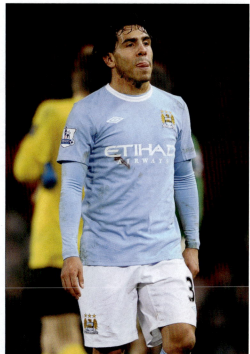
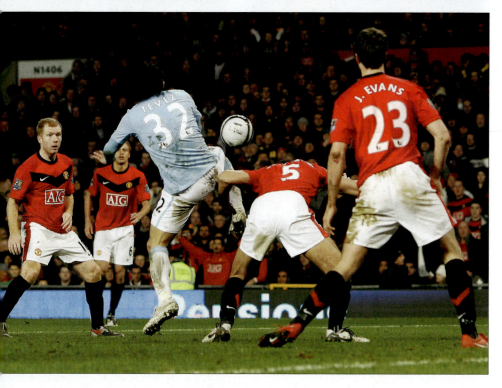

above left: Tevez shows off his new sky blue shirt.

above right: City's star striker in action.

below: Tevez scores against Manchester United in the Carling Cup semi-final second leg.

© *Action Images*

Silencing his critics: Carlos Tevez shows where his loyalties lie with his famous rebuke
Gary Neville.

© Action Ima

particular. After 71 minutes Tevez was replaced by Nani as the game slowly died on its feet. The performance Carlos gave in this bruising encounter earned him 6/10 in *The Times* ratings, but in the present set-up he was little more than a peripheral figure.

Villarreal held United to their fourth consecutive goal-less draw a few nights later in El Madrigal. The game in Birmingham a few nights before had been Villa for real; now it was Villarreal! The Spanish side kept their unbeaten home record in the competition and United stretched their record to 18 Champions League games without loss. Only United, Liverpool, Barcelona, Ajax and Inter Milan had won the trophy without losing a game.

Carlos only saw 4 minutes of action, replacing Michael Carrick after 86 minutes. Once again it was impossible for him to make any impact in such a limited time. Ronaldo had been the subject of what Ferguson described as 'systematic fouling'. Two Villarreal players had been booked for fouls on him and then Capdevilla received a red card for a knee-high challenge. In the circumstances it would have been an idea to bring Tevez on earlier. Sir Alex's dilemma heightened as he struggled with the seemingly irreconcilable elements at his disposal. United's poor record in Spain continued. Their 2-0 win in Deportivo in 2002 was their solitary victory. Argument could be made that they had won the Champions League there in 1999. Nevertheless the holders progressed from Group E with a game to spare.

Manchester City were United's next opponents on the Sunday. Both the Mancunian giants were in uncertain form. Their managers knew that they had to win and both needed to please club owners who were anything but locals. City's best form in the season had been at home. The previous weekend they had given Arsenal their biggest spanking for years by beating them 3-0 at Eastlands. Sir Alex cranked up the propaganda war before the hostilities began in the 150th Mancunian derby by saying that there was 'plenty of talk' from City earlier in the season. The reverberations of this were to be felt later on in the season.

Berbatov won his fitness battle over the hamstring injury and started in his first game against City since snubbing them on deadline day. Tevez sat the whole game out, which must have added to his increasing frustration. Rooney had promised that United would prove that they were 'the kings of Manchester' and he kept his word by scoring the only goal of a dull encounter. Michael Carrick had set him up for the winner with a rasping left-footed shot that City keeper Joe Hart could only palm out for the juggernaut Rooney to clip home. It was his 100th goal in club football and Sir Alex was delighted at the type of goal it was, comparing it to Andy Cole's opportunism. Cole had recently been in the press advising Carlos not to make the same mistake as he had done by quitting the club.

By coincidence Ronaldo had been sent off for a lunge against Cole in the 1-3 defeat to City in January 2006, and he was sent off for a second time in this Manchester derby when he inexplicably handballed a corner in the City penalty box. This earned him a second booking for unsporting behaviour and a red card. With 20 minutes left, City pushed up on United's ten men to try and salvage the game.

Chris Waddle, the former England winger, was commentating on the game for Radio 5 and suggested that Tevez should be brought on to 'do some running'. City were enjoying a numerical advantage and Waddle thought that the introduction of Tevez would relieve the pressure on the monolithic United defence. The advice went unheeded; Berbatov dropped deeper before being substituted. Instead of Tevez coming on, though, it was Ryan Giggs. United held on for a vital three points.

The next day Ronaldo collected the Ballon D'Or – the first United player to win it since George Best 40 years before. Meanwhile, the man who had won the South American equivalent of the award, Carlos Tevez, wondered what the future held for him. It was now clear that Berbatov and Rooney were the number one choice as strikers and the uncertainty about his transfer only added to his worries. With the credit crunch biting even harder, the position became even more confused.

On the first Wednesday evening in December 2008, United entertained Blackburn in the Carling Cup. Since United had beaten them 2-0 in October, the pressure on coach Paul Ince increased as their string of bad results continued. Ince seemed to react badly to the immense pressure that he was under already, talking about people who 'were out to get him'.

Carlos was under great pressure too; he knew he had to do something outstanding if he was to have any chance of splitting the Berbatov/Rooney combo. Sir Alex had reconfigured the United side from the one that had finished at Eastlands, making ten changes. After 35 minutes Tevez opened the scoring – or did he? Ryan Giggs swung over a corner and Carlos, stationed at the far post, soared to meet it. At the same time so too did the Blackburn and South African midfielder Aaron Mokoena. The ball flew into the net for the first goal. Carlos celebrated like it was his goal. Footage appeared to show the stooping Mokoena heading the ball into his own net. The matter was referred to the dubious goals committee, and Tevez was awarded the goal.

Whatever the authenticity of the strike, it bolstered Carlos's confidence. It was exactly what he needed at that point to snap him out of the trough that he had been in danger of slipping into. The result was never in doubt from that moment on. Carlos made the second goal for Nani 4 minutes later. The young Brazilian collected a ball from a throw-in and interchanged passes with Carlos. The return pass from him was superb, perfectly weighted, and Nani fired past keeper Paul Robinson. Just on half, time, the England keeper made a great block from Tevez that saved a certain third goal.

The former Scotland manager Craig Brown praised the attitude of Tevez in the half-time summary of the match on Radio 5 Live: 'Tevez is an important player for Manchester United. In the circumstances there has been no petulance from him, no temperamental behaviour. Things that Sir Alex wanted to see.'

Early in the second half a more enthusiastic Blackburn pulled a goal back through substitute Benny McCarthy, who beat Ben Foster at the near post after a slip by Gary Neville. Old Trafford was a happy hunting ground for the big striker. A late header by the South African when he was playing for Porto in March 2004 had set up the goal that knocked United out of the Champions League. Jose Mourinho was their manager that night and the Portuguese side went on to lift the Champions League; you know the rest.

Stung by the goal, Tevez tore into the box to collect Giggs's pass and was hauled down by Andre Ooijer for an undeniable penalty. One of Sir Alex's pronouncements was that he was never in favour of the player who had been fouled taking the penalty kick. Carlos had disproved this theory when he scored against QPR. Once again, the Argentine ace scored from a penalty kick for United when he effortlessly rolled the ball home as Robinson went in the opposite direction. Carlos was in unstoppable form, displaying the energy and single-mindedness that had contributed so much to United winning the double the previous season. He was everywhere; dropping back, exchanging passes, instigating attacks and finishing them off.

Two minutes later Tevez scored again after a simply breathtaking move by United. A rapid exchange of passes involving Tevez and Anderson completely ripped the Rovers rearguard apart. Carlos's close-range finish gave Robinson no chance. Depending on the outlook it was either his first hat-trick in the Premier League or his second goal of the game. The goal and move received a terrific reception and an equal one greeted Paul Scholes when he came on as sub for Possebon after 66 minutes to enrich his first game in two months.

Carlos celebrated after scoring with the slant-eye gesture that the Spanish basketball team had displayed at the 2008 Beijing Olympics. It had caused a storm at the time, but for some reason nobody in the British media had picked up on it and a possible major incident was averted. Why Carlos did it was unclear. Possibly it was an oblique signal to Real Madrid to come and get him.

In a bizarre finish to the game, Blackburn scored twice in the closing minutes to give the somewhat false impression that it was a close contest. Benny McCarthy was at the heart of it, creating a chance for Matt Derbyshire to score before turning in the third when Derbyshire returned the favour.

The small contingent of Blackburn fans who had paid £41 for the privilege of watching their side being dismantled took time out from abusing Paul Ince to chant: 'We're gonna win 5-4'.

With memories of Hull's recent final flurry etched in their minds the United fans wondered if something sensational was going to happen. They were right, but it came from that man Tevez, who was determined the night would be his. Another tremendously powerful run took him to the edge of the box, where he managed to manoeuvre into space before lashing home a brilliant shot. It settled the argument about his first-ever hat-trick in English football. Actually it would have settled any argument about his talent, anywhere.

Sir Bobby Charlton was watching that night from the director's box. Charlton might have hit a harder shot in his goal-strewn career. A goal against Tottenham in the Charity Shield or another away to Chelsea stick in the memory, but even the great man in his pomp would have struggled to equal its sheer ferocity. 5-3! And Tevez had scored three (or possibly four...) and made the rest. The Stretford End had been taunting Ince with their chant of 'Charlie, Charlie, what's the score?' – 'Charlie' came from Sir Alex's reference to Ince as a 'big-time Charlie' at the time of his departure from Old Trafford. The baiting had started in the closing minutes of the Premier League game at Blackburn. Ince did not attend the post-match press conference as the pressure level was now intolerable. Modern football did not take long to discredit a manager; just a few bad games.

Tevez was the centre of attention though after his vibrant performance. It was a no-brainer to say that he was voted Man of the Match. He took the match ball from referee Alan Wiley as a souvenir of that wonderful night. What a collection of swag the guy from the mean streets had accumulated over the years! Back on Radio 5, Craig Brown continued to extol the virtues of Carlos: 'This boy Tevez had a wonderful night, it was a sharp committed performance.'

On TalkSport Radio host Danny Kelly was a huge fan of Carlos. After the game on his show, he fielded a stream of calls from United fans all clamouring for Tevez to start every game. Kelly made the point that for a player like Carlos it was absolutely essential that he started every game. Talking to the *Sun,* Carlos claimed four goals: 'I am very pleased to have scored four goals because it is the first time I have done that in my career. I was really looking forward to the match because I have not been playing much. But our performance showed we can play Champions League standard football in any cup competition.'

Sir Alex Ferguson heaped praise on the Man of the Match: 'Carlos produced an absolutely marvellous performance and that was great to see. It makes my job more difficult of course but it makes the club stronger. Their two late goals caused us a bit of a twitch until Carlos scored the fantastic fifth.'

Since the arrival of Berbatov from Tottenham, Carlos had struggled to maintain a regular place in the team but his superlative exhibition against Blackburn had shown what a world-class player he was. The bravura performance of technical brilliance was not enough to earn him a start in the next game against Sunderland, though.

CHAPTER TEN
CHAMPIONS
OF THE WORLD

*The goals were the best way for Carlos to respond. He is a real fighter
and he will never shy away from that. The fans know what Carlos
is about. He works hard every time. No matter what is happening,
his work rate is always phenomenal.*
JONNY EVANS

*Carlos Tevez once again looked pretty much the purest, most zealous
soul in all of football. It was no wonder the Old Trafford fans occasionally
break from their idolatry of Cristiano Ronaldo with mournful echoes
of "Don't Cry For Me Argentina".*
JAMES LAWTON

Carlos was awarded the opening goal against Blackburn
and consequently ended up with four goals in the
Carling Cup match. The freeze-frame technology confirmed
that the long haired striker had almost certainly managed to
get the last touch to Mokoena's header and guide it into the
net. It was a close call: it still looked as if Mokoena, with
Carlos coming from behind, had tried to head clear but had
lost his balance and diverted it home. Blackburn had no
objection to Tevez claiming the goal and United were
delighted that he could now boast of a four-goal haul. In
any event, the dubious goals panel had no jurisdiction
outside the Premier League.

There was no doubt that Tevez's four-goal spree had given
Sir Alex food for thought. He told the press: 'Without

193

question Carlos has given me a big selection problem and I have been doodling on my notepad over the last couple of days, trying to work out how I can fit all these players in. He gave a fantastic performance of energy, aggression and running. He is always a trier and I admire him for that, but it does not make my job any easier.'

The roar from the 75,400 crowd when Carlos entered the fray against the Black Cats was only eclipsed by the din when the eventual last-gasp winner went in. However, the jury was still out on Berbatov in the minds of most United fans: Tevez had earned his spurs in their eyes, so why couldn't Ferguson see the obvious?

Roy Keane, the hard-tackling prawn sandwich condemner, had quit the Sunderland job the day before the game. Had he stayed a little longer, it would have been the third game in a row that Sir Alex would have met a team coached by one of his former charges. In 51 matches against teams managed by former United players he had lost only five, two of those at home. United's home record against Sunderland was even more impressive: the last time the Wearsiders had tasted victory there was when they won 2-1 on the last day of the 1967–8 season. George Best had scored for the Reds; 18 days later he scored again in the European Cup final against Benfica.

To the United cognoscenti Keane the stormtrooper was of the same milieu as Best, but like Paul Ince and to a lesser extent Mark Hughes, he found that management was a different game altogether. After two years of unbridled success at Sunderland this season had gone horribly wrong and the increasingly bearded Irishman lost six of his last seven games before his walkout.

Showing 11 changes from the Blackburn game United

started slowly, lacking their usual fluency and penetration. They just had too much of the ball, too much time to create attacks; the old failing of tending to overcomplicate things with clever flicks and feints that led to breakdowns in the attacks. Alan Green was covering the match for Radio 5 Live and when Tevez came on with 30 minutes left, he made these succinct comments: 'How long will Tevez be at Old Trafford? He's too good a player not to be playing all the time. Tevez is not a fringe player but a top-class international who needs to play regularly.'

Hosting the 606 phone-in after the game, Green agreed with a caller that Tevez was 'an absolutely fabulous player' and suggested that in all the uncertainty surrounding his £32m purchase he could see him leaving the club.

By playing nine blue-shirted men across the middle a stubborn Sunderland continued to frustrate the home side, who had 71% of the play. An unchallenged Berbatov missed a golden chance when Tevez fed Carrick, whose perfect cross was sloppily headed over from six yards. Tevez had a chance 11 minutes from time when he swivelled and fired just wide after Rooney flipped the ball into his path. The crowd groaned as their hero failed to hit the target but the siege continued. In the last minute he tried to set something up with a neat back heel in the penalty area that was blocked by the ex-United defender Phil Bardsley. That looked to be about it, but Nemanja Vidic scored in extra time when Carrick's long-range deflected shot struck the frame of the goal and the big Serbian scooped in the winner.

Sir Alex had gambled in the last 10 minutes by pushing Nemanja up front and using him as an auxiliary centre-forward. It beggared the question, though, with the £90m strike force of Rooney, Tevez and Berbatov up front, surely this was an indictment of their ability? Stats indicated that in all United had 27 attempts at goal in the game and all they had to show for it was a scrappy goal from a centre-back. That had been the problem all season; their failure to convert enough of the chances they had created. It was a vital win for United with the absence caused by the trip to Japan for their participation in the Club World Cup looming. Sir Alex had given United a target of a three-point margin with the other contenders by the year end.

Carlos's head buzzed with the events of the week. It was United's title to lose, but the imbalance caused by the acquisition of Berbatov had affected him more than anyone. Sir Alex had taken Tevez aside on Friday and informed him the only reason he had not started against Sunderland was because of the effectiveness of Rooney and Berbatov in the Manchester derby. The press wrote it up as Ferguson telling him to be patient.

The debate about the merits of Tevez and Berbatov was at its height at that time, conducted in the bars and chat rooms of Reds' fans. Berbatov had only scored once in the previous eight games; in all he had six goals in 14 starts. The three-pronged spearhead of 2008–9 – Rooney, Ronaldo and Berbatov – did not look as effective as the previous season's trio that had included Tevez. Berbatov had not established himself as a clinical finisher. His four goals in Europe had been doubles against the lesser lights Celtic and Aalborg, all rather anticlimactic. In the Premier League his goals had been restricted to strikes against two of the weakest teams, West Bromwich and Stoke. Opinion was divided over Berbatov – an unorthodox player at the best of times. A lot of his subtlety of touch and perception of situations went unnoticed; it was a direct comparison between the turbulent work rate of Tevez and the vision of Berbatov. The ex-Bayer Leverkusen striker has not yet gained legendary status at Old Trafford.

By not choosing him to start the match against Sunderland, Carlos had been effectively snubbed by Sir Alex; if a player had scored four goals in one game, what else could he do? The underlining message, despite how it was dressed up by Ferguson, was that he was a rotated player now and not the focus. It must have rubbed a huge dose of salt into his already-stinging wounds. While at Chelsea, Jose Mourinho had spoken of his 'untouchables', the nucleus of the team he picked regardless of form.

At this critical juncture, the reasons for Tevez to remain at Old Trafford were as follows: Carlos was a world-class player. He had kept West Ham in the Premier League single-handedly when they looked doomed. The fact that a huge claim was about to be settled on this fact was irrefutable proof. If any further proof was needed, Carlos was a proven force at United, in both the Premier and European Champions League. The old Liverpool maxim of 'show us your medals' was further evidence, should it have been needed.

United needed several options up front for tactical reasons and also as cover for injuries, suspensions and loss of form. When they returned from their sojourn in Japan, the pundits were predicting that they would face as many as 40 games in less than five months. They were still fighting on four fronts: the Premier League, Champions League, FA Cup and Carling Cup. Despite the immense potential of the young guns like Welbeck, Manucho and Campbell, none of them were ready to step up to the plate at that moment.

Conjecture was that the actual balance outstanding on the deal was not £32m but some £10m less, and that figure had already been paid to the consortium in loan fees. With Manchester City literally having money to burn, his resale value was probably double. The reluctance to enter into a deal until the option date to sign him expired was understandable, particularly against the backdrop of rising unemployment and economic chaos.

There was always the constant threat of serious injury. At times, the stocky striker from Argentina seemed indestructible. The same reflexes that had served him so well on the mean streets of South America now looked for the scimitar-type challenges. The tackle on Possebon in the Carling clash with Middlesbrough was still on his mind. A tackle by another Boro player, Gary Smith, had broken the leg of young Ben Collett in a United reserve game in 2003. Manchester Crown Court had recently awarded starlet Ben, once tipped to be the new Beckham, a record £4.5m compensation payout for the 'horror tackle' which had shattered his right leg, and with it his glittering future.

Carlos only had to look at his friend and team-mate Owen Hargreaves for further proof of the cruelty of football. At that moment Owen was back in Canada recovering from operations on both of his knees in a desperate attempt to cure the tendonitis that threatened to destroy his brilliant career.

The fee for Tevez was a big talking point among the fans. Ronaldo still seemed on course for a transfer to Real Madrid, many thought. Cristiano insisted he was happy in Manchester, but his body language, the sadness in his handsome face and a growing distance from his team-mates seemed to tell a different story. The fee for Tevez would be probably be less than half for what United would receive from the Spanish giants for Cristiano.

Speaking of Real Madrid, they had just agreed to purchase Klass-Jan Huntelaar from Ajax as the replacement for the crocked Ruud van Nistelrooy. Huntelaar had been high on Sir Alex's wish list in the past and his move to Madrid ended speculation about Tevez joining them at least for the moment. Carlos was a firm favourite with the fans; he had won them over by never giving less than 120% in every game, whether it was a European Champions League final in Moscow or a Carling Cup fixture against a Championship side. Berbatov's listless displays at Chelsea and Liverpool were replicas of some of his pallid performances away from home at Tottenham. The man who was four times voted Bulgarian Player of the Year seemed to retreat into a cocoon when the game was going against him.

Tevez's work rate away from home was little short of amazing. His non-stop chasing, harrying and hustling of the opposition when they had the ball made him United's first line of defence in their opponents' own half. The constant closing-down of the opposition by his exertions enabled Ronaldo and Berbatov to have more freedom to operate. A problem was that his predatory skills were often overlooked because of his hard work outside the box. In the first half of the 2008–9 season the United strikers spent too much time outside of the box.

Could Ferguson have been taking advantage of Tevez's humility by his treatment of him? TV and radio sports presenter Steve Bunce was asked at the time of Berbatov's acquisition whether he saw the £30m striker as being content to play in a Solskjaer-type role. Steve reminded everyone of the size of Berbatov's ego and said that he would most certainly not. In Ferguson's eyes the 'untouchables' were Berbatov and Rooney. Tevez was quickly shunted aside when Rooney regained his form; Carlos's exploits in the previous season cut no ice with Sir Alex, who at times was managing with his heart. His loyalty to the 'old school' of Giggs, Scholes and Neville was an example of this.

On the plus side, Tevez was fully integrated into the English game. Some overseas players never overcome the speed and physicality of it. Torres at Liverpool was experiencing that difficult second-season syndrome, not helped by a succession of hamstring injuries. At the same club Robbie Keane was struggling to justify his £20m transfer from Spurs. To paraphrase financier Bunker Hunt, who once cornered the world's silver market, a billion dollars wasn't what it used to be.

The bottom line, though, was that a striker was judged by the amount of goals he scored. Work rate, the refusal to become lazy when not involved in the play, leading the line and, good passing skills all counted for nothing if the goals-to-appearances ratio was low. In the harshest light, the deficiencies in Tevez's game included his tendency to hold onto the ball too long. Close analysis of his game indicates an inability to dribble past defenders to his left; he invariably goes to his right. He has also been guilty of erratic finishing, the worst example of this coming in the 2008 Champions League final, when he missed two sitters, but his profligacy in the Aalborg game showed a more recent lack of composure. Because of his physique, he sometimes struggles to impose himself in the penalty area. Pitted against those bad points, though, are his unquestionable work rate, his commitment, his strength and his toughness – both mental and physical. Surely these far outweighed any weaknesses.

Comparisons were being made again with Andriy

Shevchenko, who Chelsea seemed content to keep on the bench. But Shevchenko's best days were behind him when he arrived in London; hopefully Carlos's still were in front of him. Sir Alex admitted that he had spent hours in his office at the Carrington training ground trying to find a combination that would harness the big four of Tevez, Ronaldo, Rooney and Berbatov. Fergie told the *Sun*: 'Each player is certainly flexible enough to play in different roles. It would make for a very attacking front line. When Tevez came on against Sunderland he brought a real energy.'

Carlos scored again in the opening moments against Aalborg in the return Champions League Group E fixture. Ryan Giggs had provided the pass, after a slick interchange with Rooney, and the little striker raced through to score. It was his first goal in the competition since he calmly scored the opening penalty in Moscow the previous May. Shortly afterwards, he had the chance to make it 2-0, but wasted a great opportunity by firing wide. It looked easier to score and a goal then would have set United up for a big haul against the outclassed Danes. Carlos had the goal in his cross-hair sight, but the miss was symptomatic of his wasteful finishing that night. As the evening wore on, he wasted chance after chance in front of the Aalborg goal. Instead of a goal-fest, a strange paralysis crept over the team.

On the half-hour the Danes amazingly equalised when Michael Jakobsen headed Anders Due's free kick past Tomas Kuszczak. Michael was a rabid Reds fan and for him to glance in a chance at Old Trafford must have given him the thrill of his life. Before the match the Danes had been taking photographs of each other on the hallowed pitch.

Aalborg was the first town in Europe to be captured by German paratroopers in World War II, but that night they stormed through the self-styled best team in the world. Just on half-time Due whipped over another cross and Curth headed the second past a flabbergasted Kuszczak with the bulky-legged John O'Shea out of position. When the whistle blew for the half-time break, Carlos trooped off, head down, his face as red as his shirt.

The petulant Rooney had conducted a running battle with the Aalborg defence all evening, but was composed enough to equalise early into the second half. The problem was that there was no real drama left in the unbalanced group and it was academic if United won, drew or even lost on the night. With a glut of fixtures stretching ahead, it was human nature for the players to take their foot off the gas, if only subconsciously.

The UEFA stats relating to Group E made interesting reading. In all, Carlos had 6 goal attempts against Aalborg. He was rewarded with 1 goal, 1 blocked and 4 misses. A better performance would have seen him surpass his tally against Blackburn. The stats for all his performances in the group stages reflect a total of 13 goal attempts. Berbatov, who missed the game with an Achilles injury, had one less attempt in his group games; 9 of these had been on target and his reward was 4 goals. Perhaps the most telling stat available, though, was that overall United had scored only 9 times in Group E from 106 attempts – the most wasteful ratio of all the 16 teams that had progressed to the knockout stages.

Carlos made back-to-back starts when he lined up at Tottenham on 13 December. Rooney's suspension ensured that the number 32 was in the opening line-up. It was only his seventh start in the Premier League that season. Bad feeling still seemed to exist between United and Spurs; a legacy of the Berbatov transfer, perhaps. Sir Alex had accused the Tottenham Hotspur chairman Daniel Levy of 'milking' the sale of Dimitar and also 'having a problem' with their acquisition of Michael Carrick.

Tevez's boss regarded that Saturday early-evening fixture against Spurs as one of the most important of the season. They would fly off to Japan after the game and he knew that to have any chance of retaining their League title, they must be in touch with the leaders after Christmas. It had been Carlos who scored the last-minute equaliser at White Hart Lane the previous season to set them up for the title. The weather in London was dreadful, pouring with rain all day; the evening was moody and rain-soaked.

Tevez's first contribution to the game was a hard, but fair tackle on the Tottenham centre-back Jonathan Woodgate, which saw the defender limp off. His next significant piece of action in the game was a strong run down the wing and a cross that flew over the bar. Mark Bright, the former Crystal Palace striker, was covering the game for Radio 5 Live and commented about Tevez's present predicament: 'The January transfer window is just around the corner, does he want to continue to sit on the bench?'

Berbatov had a poor evening; in a conspicuously below-par performance he failed to make any impact and received constant abuse from the Tottenham fans.

An agitated Sir Alex appeared on the touchline wearing an expensive dark overcoat and, rather incongruously, tracksuit bottoms and a woollen hat. He thanked Tevez for his performance and replaced him with Giggs. Immediately, the tempo of the game dropped. A shrewder option might have been to keep Carlos on the field and maybe introduce Anderson for Park. The game fizzled out unenthusiastically into a no-score bore. Spurs keeper Gomes, who had been making howlers all season, saved his side with a marvellous stop from Giggs's murderous free kick. Two precious points washed away in the North London rain. Chelsea, Arsenal and Liverpool all dropped valuable points so it could have been worse.

Straight after the frustrating game at Tottenham, United flew to Japan for the Club World Cup; they would be away for 10 days. Sir Alex welcomed the break, comparing it to the 1999 expedition to Brazil, when United came back with their batteries recharged and retained their Premier League title. A 'Mickey Mouse' competition was how some detractors described it. The new coach of the resurgent Spurs, Harry Redknapp, had been dismissive of the venture, pointing out the effects of jet lag and the time difference.

Critics were perplexed at United's decision to enter the competition, but many of their fans detected a hint of jealousy in the remarks. The only way a club could enter the competition was by winning the Champions League, and the total prize money on offer was a princely $16.5m. United were the only British team to have previously won the competition, thanks to Roy Keane's winner against Palmeiras in the Inter-Continental Cup held in Tokyo, in November 1999.

Earlier incarnations of the competition consisted of an annual clash between the champions of South America and the winners of the European equivalent competition. By 2008, the competition had been extended to include the champions of Oceania, Africa, Asia, North and Central America, and the Caribbean. This consisted of eight games spread over 10 days, but because of their Premier League requirements, United had been given a bye to the semi-finals.

England coach Fabio Capello had recently talked of the Premier League being more competitive that season. Capello had had experience of playing in the World Club championship himself in both 1993 and 1994, in his time as a player for AC Milan. He also warned United of its side effects when he told the *London Lite*: 'A lot of the big four are drawing matches because they are tired up here [in their heads].' Speaking of the fatigue, he went on to say: 'I know this very well; I went two times and it is not easy. The players will be tired.'

The ex-Real Madrid coach was right there. After an 11-hour flight, Carlos looked fatigued as he arrived at the airport; he had spent most of the time listening to his MP3 player. On the flight there had been some wealthy Japanese businessmen, who had booked their tickets especially to be flying in the company of the United posse. They were huge fans of the Premier League. The Japanese public's appetite for it remained insatiable.

The team was mobbed at the airport; Carlos was just behind Ronaldo, who waved his lime-green boots to the fans. The crowd was mainly girls, very young, some pretty, wearing United T-shirts and little leather boots. Football was big business in Japan and it was growing all the time. Sir Alex was a football visionary. He knew what appealed to the public – style, glamour, skill – the personification of the dynasty he had built at Old Trafford and was determined to keep intact and expand. That is why he had no qualms about using his best players and strongest formation in the tournament.

David Gill, the United chief executive, was convinced the competition would increase in profile in the future and told *Metro*: 'Who is to say what this competition will look like in future years' time? I am sure it will be recognised as a competition of major significance. It is a very prestigious competition that will only get bigger.'

The United team stayed in a luxury hotel in Yokohama. Carlos spent the first few days resting up, trying to acclimatise to the 9-hour time difference. They visited the stadium to do some light training and check out the facilities. It was very hi-tech and only a few years old, having been constructed for the 2002 World Cup. The team needed to recharge their batteries for the immense campaign they faced in the early months of 2009.

Expectations seemed so unreasonable that the players became superstitious about meeting them. They would spend most of their time in their hotel rooms watching huge TV screens, strolling around the harbour or eating the M&Ms they had bought at the airport. Carlos knew that they could not afford to slip up in Japan – the quality of the opposition may not have been top drawer, but United were a monumental scalp and the players were well aware that the other teams would be desperate to claim a victory over them.

The Japanese fans besieged their hotel in scenes reminiscent of the days of Beatlemania. Next door to the hotel was a conference centre, which hosted a huge press meeting, with journalists and reporters from all over the world. Such was the congestion that outside Sir Alex, still chewing gum, and Darren Fletcher, the players' representative, had to take a ride in a stretch limo to drive the few yards to the building. Carlos was a virtual prisoner in his room, being one of the most recognisable footballers in the world. The team had a whole floor to themselves.

United's opponents in the semi-finals were the Japanese team Gamba Osaka. They had finished eighth in the Japanese

J-League the previous season, but had been chosen as Asia's representatives in the tournament as they had won the AFC Champions League. They had a gifted central midfielder in Yasuhito Endo and three useful Brazilians, Mineiro, Lucas and Roni, but their defence was suspect against pace. Berbatov had travelled with the team to Japan, but a virus meant he missed the opening game. For once this left Sir Alex with no searching questions about the players required to fill the strikers' berths. Carlos started alongside Rooney with Giggs, the most decorated player in United's history, playing behind Tevez. It was his second appearance in a World Club competition, having played in Tokyo in 1999 with Gary Neville and Paul Scholes. Sir Alex rewarded his loyal foot soldiers with games in the prestigious tournament.

Carlos could hear the crowds chanting the names of the United stars. About 1,000 British fans had made the trip to the Land of the Rising Sun and could also be heard among the mammoth 67,618 crowd crammed into the Nissan stadium. It was a remarkable amount of travelling support, especially given the financial crisis that had tightened its grip on the UK economy. Carlos was full of admiration for the fans who had come so far to support them. Even the concierges outside the hotel were wearing United scarves to complement their usual formal attire of top hat and tails.

The weather in Japan was only a few degrees warmer than back home in Manchester. That helped a great deal in adjusting to their new environment; a sudden increase in temperature would have caused even more problems and could also have left them open to the risk of infection when they returned to the UK.

Giggs made the first goal when his corner was headed home by Vidic. The second goal was a reprise of the first –

another pinpoint cross by Giggs, and Ronaldo rose to nod home. Carlos was in the box for both goals, but his predatory instincts were not required. In the second half, United went into cruise control and turned on some exhibition stuff to entertain the locals. With 17 minutes left, Rooney came on for Carlos; Sir Alex wanted the Japanese fans to have a glimpse of the England star. Almost immediately, this triggered an exhilarating burst of goals. Six goals were scored in the closing stages; three from each side. Before the match United warlord Ferguson had warned Tevez and his team-mates not to take the J-League side lightly, and accurately predicted they would give the Reds a severe test.

Yamazaki pulled a goal back for the Japanese side, which briefly lifted the hopes of the home fans. United then showed why they were playing for the World Championship when they scored three goals in a devastating burst. Rooney scored twice, with a header from Fletcher sandwiched in between. The carnival was not over, though, as Endo showed why he was so highly rated by converting a textbook penalty. There was still time for Hideo Hashimoto to rattle one in as the home side made a Kamikaze attack, but United survived to win 5-3.

This set up a final against Ecuador's Liga de Quito the following Sunday. The game kicked off at 10.30am UK time. Sir Alex had requested that Carlos and his chums still operate on UK time so that when they returned home, the disruption from jet lag would be minimal. Liga had been the first team from Ecuador to win the Copa Libertadores the previous season, after winning a penalty shoot-out against Fluminese. It must have been quite a match as the scores were level at 5-5 at the end of extra time.

The crowd were desperate to see the Reds in action.

Before the final, the third-place play-off game between the vanquished Osaka and Paucha was being staged. The Japanese authorities had specifically requested the United squad did not make any public appearance while the game was on because they were afraid of the disruption it would have caused among their fervent fans. Before the match Sir Alex delivered a stirring speech to his players to rouse his troops and inspire them to a historic and pivotal victory. He emphasised the importance of the win and the psychological lift it would give to the club. So far that season, for a variety of reasons they had failed to reach the giddy heights of the previous two years, but he saw that moment as the turning point.

The starting line-up for the final was:
> Edwin van der Sar
> Rafael Da Silva
> Rio Ferdinand
> Nemanja Vidic
> Patrice Evra
> Anderson
> Michael Carrick
> Ji-Sung Park
> Wayne Rooney
> Carlos Tevez
> Cristiano Ronaldo

The Quito line-up included Damian Manso, a typical Argentinean playmaker with bags of skill, a great range of passing and a tough edge. The veteran Augustin Delgado, who had played against United for Southampton, was one of the substitutes.

The first half was a tense affair, played on a windy evening. Workaholic Tevez was involved from the start, racing into the box to challenge the Ecuadorian international keeper Jose Cevallos. The 37-year-old had an inspired evening as he made a string of fine saves to keep United at bay. The pick of these was a great catch, following a firm header from Carlos after 15 minutes. On 40 minutes the rollicking Carlos powered in a fierce shot and the agile Cevallos made a superb save by palming the ball away. Carlos was more effervescent than a vitamin C tablet dropped into a glass of iced water. The fact that he was playing against a side from South America made him buzz around even more. Quito had no intention of mixing it with United. They seemed almost content to play for a penalty shoot-out, just lying deep as United came on to them.

Early in the second half the whole complexion of the game changed when Vidic was sent off for elbowing Claudio Bieler. The exit of the big Serb Nemanja also signalled the departure of Carlos from the tournament. A forward had to be sacrificed to enable a reshuffle to be made. Clearly upset, Carlos was replaced by Jonny Evans. Sir Alex instantly reconfigured the United line-up as Evans went into Vidic's position and Park switched to the right, with Ronaldo now playing through the middle. Rooney switched to the left to patrol the area Carlos had been occupying earlier.

Reduced to ten men, United were still dangerous. Many great champions have been on the ropes but have come back to take the title; United were no different. Seventeen minutes from time, Carrick passed to Ronaldo, whose clever pass found Rooney. It was instantly dispatched by the bullet-headed striker into the back of the Quito net with a wonderful curling drive. Rooney was having a marvellous tournament; Tevez had been unlucky to be subbed, but he had two of the world's greatest forwards in front of him in the queue. Sir Alex's gamble of sacrificing Tevez in the match had worked.

Van der Sar, who had won a Club World Championship with Ajax in 1995, beating Fabio Capello's AC Milan side, made sure he won another one with two great saves from Manso. The Ecuadorian side were masters of the counter-attack and United were forced to play a very contained game. United had now clinched their stellar hat-trick of major honours: they had the domestic, European and now the world championship. Carlos joined in the celebrations as the shiny ticker-tape showered the team and Rio lifted the strangely-shaped trophy. Petrolhead Rooney won a Toyota car to join his fleet of luxury motors, which included a £112,750 Bentley (similar to Tevez's white car) and a £177,100 Aston Martin Vanquish. Comparisons were being made with Rooney's winner and Norman Whiteside's FA Cup clincher in 1985 against Everton. The Reds had gone down to ten men in that fixture too.

While they were in Japan, the draw for the next round of the European Champions League was made and United were intriguingly drawn against Jose Mourinho's Inter Milan. Already the mind games had started, with the ex-Chelsea coach dismissing Ronaldo's claims of being the best player in the world. The 'Special One' was suggesting his striker Zlatan Ibrahimovic was a better player than the winner of the Ballon d'Or.

After the celebrations in Japan, Tevez went back to his hotel room. Too tired to sleep, he watched the Arsenal versus Liverpool match, which was being transmitted live from the Emirates. Robbie Keane hit a fine equaliser as all the top sides dropped points, meaning the newly-crowned World Champions were still very much in contention for the Premier League.

Despite the tribulations of the last few months, 2008 was Tevez's *annus mirabilis*. He had gone some of the way to fulfilling the vast potential within him and had won four major honours. Now it was time to say *sayonara* to Yokohama. On the plane leaving Japan, Carlos sat at the back, watching a DVD. Perhaps he was thinking about the year that had flashed by. How many street kids from Argentina had made it that far?

A kid from another inner-city slum, Rio Ferdinand, was delighted at winning the trophy. He told the *Sun*: 'To come back as winners is a great feeling and it would be nice if this sets a trend for the next part of the season, as up until now we have been a bit inconsistent in our performance. Yet here we played like the Manchester United of the last two years. We have not really done that this season at all. A lot has been said about the tournament; It has not been well received in England but you saw our reaction when we won it.'

Back in Manchester, on Boxing Day morning United had their first-ever visit to the Britannia Stadium. The team had come back to England late on the Monday night and the players had slept all day on the Tuesday. Stoke City now awaited them; a few months ago United had beaten them out of sight, but now it was a different ball game all together. Stoke, although trapped down the bottom of the League, had gained a reputation as formidable opponents. United made six changes from the team that had played in the International Stadium. They were back to fighting strength, with Carlos retaining his starting place and

Berbatov on the bench. Rooney was desperate to play; of all the squad he seemed least affected by jet lag. There was an intimidating atmosphere inside the stadium and the first half was very tight, with space at a premium. Stoke were desperate to stay up in the big time and employed a system of two banks of four with about five yards between them. This denied Tevez and Rooney any room to operate.

Carlos showed no effects from his Japanese exploits. In fact, as the game wore on he grew stronger, seemingly genuinely invigorated by his break in the Far East. After 9 minutes he headed wide of the far post. Against a physical team like Stoke Sir Alex needed the aggressive presence of Rooney and the durability of Tevez. No other player at Old Trafford could stretch a defence like Tevez. Ever reliable, his persistence and energy gave the Stoke back four no respite. Early in the second half, he cut inside and hit in a fine shot, which the Stoke keeper Thomas Sorensen did well to tip around the post. A few minutes later, the ball landed at Richard Cresswell's feet in the middle of the penalty box. Somewhat surprised, he fired a good chance wide. Stoke defender Andy Wilkinson was sent off in the second half for his second bookable offence. As in the semi-final in Japan, Ronaldo had been singled out for severe punishment from the opposing players.

Sir Alex gambled when he took off defender John O'Shea after 64 minutes and brought on Berbatov. Ferguson had admitted that it had taken time for the players to 'understand Berba's qualities'. At times, the absence of chemistry between Berbatov and Tevez was clear. Things changed, though; Berbatov created a marvellous chance for Carlos with just 7 minutes left. Twisting and turning, he flicked over a superb pass to the far post. Tevez pounced and instantly smashed the ball into the back of the net. It was a superbly-crafted goal by Berbatov. The blue-shirted Carlos was absolutely delighted – he ran behind the goal to celebrate with the United fans, shaking a few outstretched hands along the way. It was a vital goal, scored after their excursion to Japan in a tricky fixture which was seen as a potential banana skin.

Sir Alex spoke to Sky Sports after the game about his Argentinean match-winner: 'He scores important goals and came up trumps again.' In the *Manchester Evening News* Tevez was voted the best United Player of the Match; he scooped 48% of the poll, nearly twice as much as his nearest rival Vidic, who polled 26%. Tevez's kick into the Stoke net could well have kick-started his and United's season.

CHAPTER ELEVEN
TEVESTATING!

HE is a tiger. He fights for every ball and it is great to have someone with that attitude in your team.
SIR ALEX FERGUSON

If you are first, you are first. If you are second, you are nothing.
BILL SHANKLY

I think English people love me because I do my best every weekend. I have always done my best every weekend. I have always done my best, as well as in West Ham, Corinthians or Boca shirts.
CARLOS TEVEZ

The Champions of the World, Masters of the Universe, etc., etc, played their last fixture of that amazing year at home to Middlesbrough. Carlos took no part in it, though, as he was 7,000 miles away back home in Buenos Aires. Sir Alex had given him a week off; some tabloid reports suggested he had gone home because of a 'family matter', which could have meant anything. Truth was he needed a rest; he had the full backing of the club in any event.

Sir Alex admitted that he had been about to sub Carlos for Ji-Sung Park at the Britannia Stadium just before the little striker smashed home the winner. The United boss was glad that his team were capable of 'winning ugly'. Whether or not this was a direct reference to Carlos was unclear. In his absence, Berbatov came back to prominence and in a close encounter, grabbed the winner against Boro. United had to wait until 20 minutes from time before snatching the winner. The ex-Bayer Leverkusen striker Berbatov pounced on Carrick's deflected cross to coolly fire home. In a quirky statistic, only Chelsea had scored more goals in Premier League visits to Old Trafford. Despite some threatening moments, Boro were unable to improve on their impressive scoring record and Carlos's comrades cut Liverpool's lead at the top still further.

The enigma that was Dimitar had probably his best game in the United number 9 shirt in the FA Cup game at Southampton on 4 January. The ownership of the legendary number 9 had been a sore subject for Carlos; he had harboured a special desire to wear the shirt vacated by Louis Saha when the French striker joined Everton. Instead, Berbatov had been given the shirt when he joined from Spurs.

In the FA Cup third-round match Berbatov put on a magnificent show of centre-forward play. He failed to score, but lit up a dull winter's afternoon by displaying the full range of his skills. United wore their blue kit that afternoon, as they had at Stoke; the same shirt that George Best and co-wore in their first European Cup triumph in 1968. Southampton, like Stoke, were in red-and-white stripes.

In the 1995–6 season in a fixture against the Saints, United had worn their infamous grey kit in an astonishing 3-1 defeat. Sir Alex complained that the players couldn't see each other in their grey shirts and shorts, and the team made a somewhat embarrassing costume change at half-time. The grey shirt was consigned to the dustbin of history.

Oddly enough, Southampton doubled their goal haul against United the following season when they hit 6 past them. They were a formidable team in those days, with

Matthew Le Tissier being their main asset. Times were hard now, though, and cash-strapped Southampton found themselves at the bottom of the Championship table. They had some highly promising youngsters but were lacking the nous and toughness to survive. United cruised past them; 19-year-old Danny Welbeck scored his first Cup goal to put them ahead. Further efforts from Nani and Darron Gibson turned it into a Sunday afternoon stroll against the lightweight Saints. Before the shock exit to Leeds in January 2010, the last time United had gone out of the Cup at the first hurdle was just down the road on the South Coast at Bournemouth, before Tevez or Welbeck had even been born. Welbeck's emergence raised yet another question mark over Carlos's long-term future with the club.

Meanwhile, even though he was away, Carlos was appearing frequently in the press. He issued a statement from South America via Kia Joorabchian, declaring his unswerving loyalty to United and stating that he was keen to sign a deal. The *Guardian* printed the communiqué: 'We have not started talks with Manchester United yet, though I am keen to stay. Sir Alex has told me he wants me to remain a United player and that is certainly my desire too. My contract ends in the summer and we have agreed to sit down at the appropriate time and discuss a new contract. Nothing I have heard from the club suggests it will be otherwise.'

Kia Joorabchian, who held the key to this, added: 'Manchester United have indicated they would like to sign Carlos for the long term, but we have not started negotiations yet. There is no urgency as his contract runs until the summer. Carlos has always said his intent is to stay at United and nothing has changed. The supporters have been amazing to him and he loves the club.'

The statement was in response to earlier statements and rumours that had been circulating that week. Carlos had told Radio del Plata in Buenos Aires: 'Now all clubs are on an equal footing. If a club comes to me and offers me a five-year deal, I will accept it for peace of mind. I will sign my last contract, and then I figure that I will go back to Boca [Juniors]. That could be in four or five years. I want everybody to know no offer has been made. I do not like that they are playing with our fans, who show their love to me in each match.'

Carlos went on to make some remarks about Real Madrid, which could not have sat well with Sir Alex. 'Who would not want to play for Real Madrid?' he said. He went on to tell the radio station: 'Like Manchester, they are one of the best clubs in the world and it would be a pleasure to play for them.'

A relocation to Madrid would have infuriated Sir Alex after seeing them court Cristiano Ronaldo for so long. Carlos was of the long-held view that Ronaldo should have been granted his wish to become a Galactico. When the tug-of-war between the world's biggest clubs was at its height the previous summer he had told the *Guardian*: 'It is clear he is a very important player for us but that is a personal decision which is up to him only. I understand Cristiano. Every footballer wants to pay at Real Madrid. I also think that everyone wants to play for Manchester United but, if what he seeks is something else, that should be respected.'

The papers had a field day with the story, building up the connection with Real and also suggesting that Kia Joorabchian would also be interested in doing business with Inter Milan. They tried to build a rift between the player and his manager too. The papers were full of headlines like

TEVEZ AND FERGIE AT WAR OVER NEW DEAL and FERGIE AT THE END OF HIS TEVER. Sir Alex responded by telling the *Manchester Evening News*: 'I have no idea about Tevez. The contract is due to be the end of season anyway, but obviously we tried to bring it forward and we will keep trying to do that. But it is difficult with agents sometimes. All the managers signing players this January will experience that.'

Sir Alex's reference to agents should be noted. In his autobiography, *Managing My Life*, he devoted a whole chapter to his dealings with Andrei Kanchelskis's agents and the notorious Norwegian Rune Hauge. His view then was: 'The proliferation of agents in modern football has caused many headaches and heartaches, but these wheeler-dealers do have their uses when it comes to keeping abreast of what is happening on the transfer-merry-go-round.'

The *Daily Telegraph* stated that Carlos denied he had rejected a new contract, and insisted that he had no discussions about making a permanent arrangement to stay in Manchester. 'I didn't like him [Ferguson] saying I didn't like the offer I was made because neither my agent nor me was given one.'

Kia Joorabchian told Radio 5 live Sport about the current situation: 'All Tevez said in the interview was that it was not true he has rejected an offer from United; he has not made crazy demands. He just wanted the fans and the people to know that we have not had any contract talks.' Carlos's agent refused to be drawn on Tevez's long-term future at the club. 'It is very hard to predict. It's football; Things change by the minute, by the hour. It's not a no. You never know.'

It was apparent that Carlos was unsettled, tired of playing second fiddle to Berbatov and tired of appearing in the lower-profile matches. Was Berbatov's star power going to eclipse Tevez's? The message boards were jammed with fans postings. Most were of the view that Carlos was a better player than both Rooney and Berbatov, and that he should be signed as soon as possible. In a poll conducted by the *Manchester Evening News*, 84% voted for him to stay at Old Trafford. Very few questioned the sort of money required to complete the deal.

The problem was that in 2009 the credit crunch was really starting to bite. Eight banks had been part-nationalised, Woolworths had disappeared, unemployment had reached 2m and debt levels were at a record high. It was the greatest financial crisis since the 1930s. Every part of the globe was gripped by recession. Realistically, were Manchester United going to spend £25–£30m when Carlos had openly admitted that he only wanted a 4- or 5-year contract before returning to Boca? The money men were even more prudent now as they were operating in the shadows cast by AIG. It was clear that United would not be rushed into an expensive deal for the Argentina striker.

With his whole future still in doubt, Carlos went to Derby to play in the semi-final of the Carling Cup. There was some conjecture surrounding whether he would even be in the starting line-up following his recent outbursts, but he decided to let his feet do the talking to show that he was worth the hefty fee required to land him. It didn't work out like that, though; it was a vastly disappointing evening as United turned in, possibly their worst performance of the season to go down 1-0. It was a completely different game from the Southampton Cup match, Derby being a far more physical side. Nigel Clough, son of the legendary Brian, had been appointed manager 24 hours before the game and a carnival atmosphere prevailed. Carlos's annoyance at his team's display was palpable.

Danny Welbeck lined up alongside Carlos, with Rooney and Ronaldo as insurance on the bench. Tevez put in his usual hard running, but it was a middling performance. The Argentinean took just a fraction too long on the ball, his final ball was just a fraction off, and he looked just a little too slow. The *Manchester Evening News* gave him just 5/10. Carlos's vague future at Old Trafford was discussed by the Radio 5 Live commentary team. Graham Taylor remarked that it would be 'very interesting'.

Kris Commons scored the only goal of the game after 30 minutes with a 25-yarder that simply flew into the net. The Derby striker kept his toe down and hit through the midline of the ball; a great hit. It was a shoddy goal to give away – Commons was given too much space to line up his shot. Owen Hargreaves was back home in Canada recovering from the operations on both of his knees and was sorely missed. Sir Alex had purchased him with the brief of denying teams exactly the amount of space that Derby had exploited so effectively.

Carlos had been United's talisman in that competition with his 5 goals in 4 games, but he could make no impression at Pride Park. There was no doubt that the intense speculation about his future seemed to have affected him. In the last month he had made round trips to Japan and Argentina, the emotion of his return home to see his family, the rollercoaster sensation of the battle at Stoke had all taken their toll. The underlying factor, though, was the uncertainty of it all, with his unresolved contractual situation dominating everything.

Ronaldo, Rooney and Carrick were all introduced in the

second half to try and salvage the situation. In a tactical change, Carlos was switched out to the right and Ronaldo pushed into the orthodox striker's position. Ronaldo just missed with a swerving free kick and Carlos's shot screwed high and wide over near the bar, but that was the sum total of United attacking play. The stats indicated that against QPR his team-mates had created 4 clear-cut chances for him to score. Against Derby they had created zilch and Carlos had been unable to come up with anything himself. He had spent so much time and energy chasing around that he could not play as an out-and-out striker.

In the closing minutes Robbie Savage came on as a sub for Derby. When the final whistle blew, Savage ran to get Carlos's shirt with the number 32. Robbie, along with a lad called George Switzer, was one of the only members of the famous 1992 Youth Cup-winning team not to play for the United first team.

Gordon Taylor, chief executive of the Professional Footballer's Association, joined the debate about Carlos's predicament and told the *Telegraph*: 'Third-party signings are something to be worried about. United have paid good money to get him on loan, now they are being asked to pay a huge amount to buy him. The person who owns his economic rights will make a killing and that money is not staying in the game.'

Carlos's poor showing at Derby meant that he did not get into the starting line-up for the battle against Chelsea the following Sunday. He was named among the substitutes but did not make it onto the pitch. A highly significant fact was that Tevez had only started only once in the matches against the 'big four'. At Anfield, he scored his first goal of the season against Liverpool, but he had only been included in the side because Ronaldo was still getting over his ankle injury. Carlos came on as sub during the Emirates defeat, the last time United had conceded a goal in the Premier League. Against Chelsea at the Bridge he had not featured.

United Legend Paddy Crerand was interviewed about the Tevez situation and told Radio 5 Live his views: 'Tevez should stay. If you are a local lad it is a little bit easier to be on the bench but for a foreign player to come here and not get a game, it is not so easy.'

Chelsea were given a sound thrashing 3-0, and their record of not having lost an away game in the whole of 2008 was shattered. The game showed how United had progressed from Moscow and how they were now at the epicentre of the Premier League. Chelsea, however, had gone backwards. Roman Abramovich did not attend the game. Rumours were rife that he had put the club up for sale, as reports indicated he had lost billions in the global credit crunch. Times were suddenly hard around Stamford Bridge. The tabloids even reported that the Bridge had been sold, but it later transpired that Manchester City had purchased full-back *Wayne* Bridge for £10m and a £100,000-per-week salary.

Cristiano Ronaldo was finding it tough too, driving his £193,000 Ferrari 599 GTB into a tunnel barrier at Manchester Airport a few days before the Chelsea game. It was a bad crash and the beautiful car – which he'd purchased just two days earlier – was totalled after he skidded on an oil patch. Amazingly, he walked away from the wreck without a scratch. The next day he arrived at training in a £150,000 Bentley Continental GT, identical to the one driven by his Argentinean team-mate. What would be the next set of wheels for the chaps? US President Barack

Obama had recently taken delivery of £300,000 stretch limo with bullet-proof glass, armour plating throughout, night vision cameras and tear-gas cannons. Sounds ideal for those away trips to Merseyside!

In the Chelsea game the fans were treated to flashes of the old Ronaldo. For the first time that season he started beating players on the outside. On too many occasions he had cut inside in diagonal runs, which had the effect of making a congested penalty area even more crowded. Just on the break he headed home, only to have the goal unfairly disallowed.

Rooney and Giggs had worked out an amazing trick, which worked even better than they could have hoped for. United won a corner and Wayne dribbled with the ball slowly to the corner flag. As the laws dictated, he placed it in the corner arc but then dragged the ball slightly back with the sole of his boot before walking away as though Ryan Giggs would take the corner. The gimmick, though, was that in moving the ball out of the corner arc, Rooney had actually taken the kick and the ball was already in play. Suddenly, Giggs spurted forward and crossed the ball for Ronaldo to head home. This whole incident totally mystified the assistant referee, as well as the static Chelsea defence. The official incorrectly ruled out the goal. Justice was done, though, when Giggs swung over the retaken corner and Berbatov flicked on for Vidic to head down and into the net.

Rooney scored United's second when he cheekily pushed his foot through Ashley Cole's legs to turn Evra's cross past Cech. Near the end United scored a third to underline their total superiority. This time Berbatov, playing with tremendous confidence, reacted quickest to convert Ronaldo's free kick. The Chelsea defenders glared at each other. Tevez never saw any of the action and remained on the bench throughout the duration of the match. Ronaldo flew off to Zurich after the final whistle to collect his FIFA World Player of the Year award. Had Sir Alex seen fit to unleash Carlos to run at the demoralised Chelsea back four, perhaps the thrashing would have been even more emphatic.

The match statistics were clear: it was 11-1 to United when it came to shots on target, and all the goals had come from crosses. It was clear that the Chelsea infrastructure had been severely weakened; the lifeblood of the club that had enjoyed such success in Mourinho's short reign seemed to be ebbing away. Since the Premier League began in 1992, United had acquired fewer points against Chelsea than any other side. The average was 1.24 against Chelsea, compared with 1.48 against Arsenal and 2.34 against the others.

Mourinho had been in the crowd and talked of his visit to Old Trafford to the *Daily Telegraph*: 'I was doing my homework for the Champions League. It was my first time back since I left Chelsea in September 2007. I enjoyed it very much. I was with some players from the club; I was with some players from Chelsea, with some people from the club. I was with Sir Alex. The atmosphere was, as always, very enjoyable. It's a pity that the game was not such an emotional game because 3-0 is a result that destroys a bit the emotional edge.'

Jose returned to Milan, comparing his old club to the Champions of Europe. Meanwhile Chelsea appeared to be in decline. United had outwitted and outmanoeuvred them at every turn. Sir Alex's view was that Chelsea faltered in their quest for domination because of 'short-termism' – the purchase of ready-made stars, most of them with a limited shelf-life like Ballack, Shevchenko and even Deco. On the other side, United had invested shrewdly in younger players with greater potential such as Ronaldo, Rooney and Tevez.

A wonderful example of the perceived schism between the cultures was Juan Sebastian Veron, a fellow countryman of Carlos. Veron had found himself at a crossroads in his career at Old Trafford when he was in a situation remarkably similar to that of Tevez. He told the *Daily Mail*: 'I hope Tevez stays at Manchester United because it is important for Argentine football. He will know what he has to do to resolve the situation. I hope it is all resolved for the best.'

Veron was back in Argentina and playing some of the best football of his life for his home-town team, Estudiantes de La Plata. He had started off his career at Estudiantes before moving to Tevez's team, Boca Juniors. From there he moved to Italy, where he played for Sven Goran Eriksson's Lazio. Sir Alex purchased him for £28m in July 2001, but the midfielder was weighed down by the huge fee and never showed his true fantastic potential. Abramovich bought him for half the fee after two years at Old Trafford. In a further two years his value had dropped to almost nothing and he was loaned out to Milan.

Like Carlos, Veron had an engaging personality and a bizarre taste in garishly, ritzy clothes. Both shared a passion for luxury cars. Veron's idol was another great Argentinean red, Che Guevara. The fans loved Veron and his trademark 30-yard passes were the stuff of legend. One in particular, against Deportivo La Coruna in the Champions League in April 2002, stands out. In the second half 'Seba' curled a daisy-cutting, long-distance pass with the outside of his boot between two defenders for Ole Gunnar Solskjaer to slam home. The 67,000 people present were lucky enough to witness a goal they would never forget; the smouldering

Veron could probably have been a legend of the same pedigree as the Norwegian striker. Sir Alex tried to persevere with the radical changes that Veron had brought to the club but ultimately conceded his particular brand of magic was not suited to the cut-and-thrust of the English game.

Carlos appeared on the touchline during the Chelsea game and was given a tremendous reception by the crowd. Their cheers were music to the ears of the United substitute and he milked the occasion by putting in some accelerations on the touchline to get even more applause. Chants of 'Sign him up, Fergie' began to filter down to pitch level.

Another world-famous Argentinean had witnessed the mauling of Chelsea. Maradona had gone to Old Trafford hoping to see Tevez in action. The 48-year-old had triggered a fire alarm in his opulent hotel, early on that Sunday morning by puffing on one of his trademark Havana cigars. The Chelsea team happened to be staying there as well, and they were forced to evacuate the building. Terry, the Cole boys, Anelka and the others had their sleep disturbed and then shivered in the cold as the Greater Manchester Fire Service checked out the building.

Maradona was disappointed at not seeing Carlos and was quoted in *Corriere dello Sport* as saying: 'I saw Manchester United win without Tevez. This isn't good for him. Certain episodes are certainly bringing closer his exit. Italy and Inter, in particular, would be excellent solutions. What's more, his contract is running out, which makes it easier to change team.'

Diego was anxious not to see his surrogate son's career stagnate at Old Trafford. A link-up between Carlos and the furrow-browed Zlatan Ibrahimovic was his idea of a dream strike force. Maradona was also suggesting Atletico

Madrid's Argentina superstar Sergio Aguero should join them in Milan. Sergio was in a relationship with Giannina, Maradona's daughter, who was expecting their first child in the spring. Aguero was a huge fan of Carlos and frequently praised him in the press.

The following Wednesday, United moved into second spot, leapfrogging Chelsea and cutting Liverpool's lead to just two points. This they achieved by narrowly beating an in-form Wigan, thanks to a Wayne Rooney goal. Carlos did not start the game and watched from the bench as in the first minute Ronaldo crossed for Rooney to tap in at the far post. Berbatov and Rooney had started the game following their sparkling performances against Chelsea. Tevez joined the fray after 7 minutes when goalscorer Rooney limped off with a hamstring problem. Another rapturous reception greeted him when he came onto the pitch. As always, Carlos put in another enthusiastic performance. After 25 minutes he had a great chance to score when he found himself in front of Wigan keeper Chris Kirkland. Carlos effortlessly went around the keeper, but Titus Bramble got back to make a marvellous block and deny him a certain goal.

In the second half, Wigan upped their tempo and made some serious attempts to get back into the game. The guy in the shirt with number 32 on it came in for some serious punishment from the Wigan defence. They had realised he posed the greatest threat to them. One particularly harsh challenge left him limping and doubtful about the coming visit to Bolton.

Mark Lawrenson, the ex-Liverpool defender, was summarising the game for Radio 5 Live and described Tevez as being 'streetwise and tough'. His fellow commentator Alan Green described the United striker as being, 'as hard as nails.'

An amusing incident occurred when Carlos was receiving treatment off the pitch after sustaining one of many hefty challenges. Paul Scholes won the ball in midfield, and looking to set up an attack, caught sight of Carlos's mane of dark hair on the far right. With a perfect flourish of his left foot, he hit a 30-yard pass – but the problem was that Carlos was not on the field of play and the ball went off the pitch for a Wigan throw-in.

Despite the harsh treatment he received from the Wigan defenders, Carlos was declared fit enough to participate in the away fixture against Bolton on 17 January. Always a difficult match for United – they had slipped up at the Reebok Stadium the previous season, with Nicolas Anelka's goal being the difference between the teams. All season United had been playing catch-up with Liverpool and Chelsea. Difficulties with fixtures, injuries and loss of form compounded their problems, but now they were about to reclaim their place at the head of the table.

Sir Alex was about to remove Carlos from the action in the dying minutes of the game, with the score 0-0. Danny Welbeck was already down on the touchline, ready to come on. The fourth official was about to signal for the substitution when Carlos dispossessed defender Joey O'Brien, rode a challenge from Gary Cahill and ran to the edge of the box. Keeping his balance in the treacherous conditions, he crossed a peach of a ball. Berbatov, who had struggled all game to make an impression, threw himself at the ball and flicked it past the splendid Bolton keeper, Jussi Jaaskelainen. It was enough to win the match and put United on top of the League for the first time that season.

In that evening's BBC *Match of the Day* programme host Gary Lineker eulogised about Carlos's run and cross. It had produced a killer goal of a clinical simplicity. The ex-England captain said that United did well to win a tricky game with such a classy goal: 'It was a good ball in from Tevez.'

The goal echoed the winner at Stoke. Park was about to replace Carlos at the Britannia Stadium, but he had avoided being substituted, thanks to a brilliant flash of inspiration. This time, he scored after fine work by Berbatov. At the Reebok, both men earned a 6/10 rating for their performances. A picture in the same paper showed Carlos warmly embracing Berbatov as they celebrated the crucial goal.

Despite the fact that Carlos had fallen behind Berbatov in the pecking order at Old Trafford there was not a hint of animosity between the players. The flashes of brilliance sparked by the two forwards hinted at the gestation of a partnership between the diffident Bulgarian and the slum kid from Argentina. Sir Alex spoke to the *Telegraph* about Berbatov's progress: 'I am delighted with the way things are going this season and I am especially pleased by Dimitar Berbatov's progress in settling into the team. When you pay a lot of money for a player he inevitably comes under very close scrutiny. That is what happened to Juan Sebastian Veron and Dimitar has also suffered from the impatience of people when a new guy makes a big move. At Tottenham, he orchestrated most of their play and if, at times, he has looked a bit isolated, it was because our players needed to adjust to him, just as much as he has needed to learn our ways. But he has settled very well and I have the feeling we are about to see the best of Berbatov.'

Prophetic words from the warlord of Old Trafford, as United were about to explode in the coming weeks. Tevez received no namecheck in the statement, but clearly he was one of the players who needed to 'adjust'. It is also worth noting that when Carlos joined United, he settled in more quickly than Berbatov and won the crowd over in a relatively short space of time. The Old Trafford crowd had yet to warm to the Bulgarian striker; they still liked their players to work hard. Tevez possessed the grit they prized above everything.

The win at Bolton was United's fifth consecutive win in the Premier League since they had returned from the Club World Cup in Japan. Sir Alex was anxious to kick on and put some distance between his side and the other title challengers, but first he had a couple of Cup games to contend with. Derby visited Old Trafford the following week and took a battalion of 12,000 fans with them; the largest away contingent ever to visit Old Trafford. They witnessed a simply awesome display from Tevez, which propelled United to a Carling Cup final against Tottenham Hotspur. It was Carlos's finest performance of that difficult second season so far. The tabloids knew Tevez was an important figure in the modern game and were now giving him the same coverage as huge names like Gerrard, Owen, Ronaldo, Rooney and Lampard received. It was unequivocal confirmation of his increased status. The *Sun* ran a banner headline: TEVASTATING.

Carlos was the star man in a side depleted by injury – there were six changes in the team for the Derby game – and he inspired the Reds to a hard-fought 4-2 victory over the Championship side. The Argentinean gritted his teeth and battled on; it was as if he was on a one-man mission to ensure that United won the League Cup. On previous occasions United had been to the final six times, winning just two, against Nottingham Forest in 1992 and Wigan in 2006.

Nani scored the first goal with a carbon copy of his wonderful effort against Spurs in August 2007 – the strike that had announced his arrival on the big stage at Old Trafford. O'Shea scored the second, cleverly beating the offside trap to put United 2-1 ahead on aggregate. Carlos had carved the chance out for him in one swift movement which took out two Derby defenders.

The game appeared to be over as a contest after 34 minutes when the new Brazilian discovery Rafael Da Silva snapped up the ball. This was after a short Ryan Giggs' corner had not been cleared by the Derby defence. It was turning into a teenage rampage as Rafael crossed a perfect ball into the box. Six yards out, Carlos stooped to head the ball over ex-United keeper Roy Carroll and into the net. As he celebrated, Carlos lifted his red shirt to reveal a red vest he wore underneath. On it he had scrawled a birthday greeting to his brother-in-law with a marker pen. It was his sixth goal in the Carling Cup and made him the joint top goalscorer in the competition. Goal number seven appeared to have been scored when he rolled in another just on the break, but it was disallowed for offside.

Ronaldo came on for Giggs in the second half and Sir Alex tried a combination of him and Tevez playing through the middle. The ex-Aberdeen manager was always experimenting with the flexibility of his line-up. Deftly shaking the cocktail of talents at his disposal, he knew his superstar forwards were adaptable enough to play in different roles. Sir Alex's dream was to find a system that could have incorporated the confusion of all four talented personalities into the same team without risking the midfield or defensive strength of the unit.

A dazzling 30-yard pass move ended with another Carlos

header being tipped away by Carroll for a corner. Tevez was the dominant force that night; he seemed to be everywhere. Throughout the game the crowd chanted for Fergie to sign him and also they let rip with the 'Argentina, Argentina' chant which seemed to spur him on to even more exertions. Derby clearly had not read the script, though. Their substitute Giles Barnes blazed home from the spot after Jonny Evans conceded a penalty. This led to a late flurry of goals as the rain continued to fall.

Carlos took it as an affront to his sensibilities that Derby had scored against his team and immediately charged into the box. The crowd chanted; how they enjoyed watching the little Argentine play. His ability to go through the smallest of gaps was in evidence that night. Carroll had little option but to bring Tevez down after he had gone round him and was about to side foot home. Ronaldo commandeered the penalty kick and swept it into the net. With a hunched stance, Carlos watched, hands on hips. The last time he had a sniff of a penalty was back in Moscow. The last few moments were surreal as Barnes smashed home a free kick that his namesake John would have been proud of. Carlos had two late chances to score but it finally ended 4-3 on aggregate. The *Sun* made Tevez their 'Dream Team' star man with 8/10.

For the seventh season in a row United had reached a Cup final. Tottenham Hotspur were the next team on the United hit-list when they visited on 24 January for the FA Cup fourth-round tie. Eight defenders were unavailable for a variety of reasons, but Carlos started for the third successive game in place of the crocked Rooney. Now in superb form he put in another towering performance that ensured United won 2-1 and went through to the next round.

The broadsheets wrote about the 1981 Tottenham Cup

Final victory, inspired by their superstar Argentinean players, Ossie Ardiles and Ricky Villa. Carlos was not, even born when the bearded Villa scored one of the greatest solo goals of all time. It clinched the victory over Manchester City in the replayed 100th FA Cup final. Like all superb solo goals, it defied analysis with instinct, intuition and a large dollop of luck playing as big a part in it as skill.

Villa was a childhood hero of Carlos's. Since being in England, Tevez had been given a crash course in the heritage of some of its greatest clubs. A thread of South American players ran through that history, a tradition that was being maintained by Tevez.

Spurs took a shock lead after 5 minutes when Russian striker Roman Pavlyuchenko eluded Vidic and stole in to glance a header firmly past Ben Foster. For a short while the United fans wondered if Harry Redknapp was going to pull off another Cup shock, as he had with Portsmouth last season. Carlos hit the bar after 17 minutes with a snap shot that smacked against the crossbar and flipped over into the cold Manchester evening air. Soon afterwards a glorious move involving Berbatov and Ronaldo put in Carlos for a fierce shot that the Spurs keeper saved superbly. Tevez was unstoppable that night, bustling and hustling, tackling and sprinting. The love affair with the United fans intensified. He was one of them, doing what they would do if they ever found themselves lucky enough to be wearing the red shirt. Run, work, run, work and never stop. That is why the fans could never understand and never forgive players who gave less than 100% for the Manchester United cause.

The running power of Carlos led to United's equaliser. The only way Spurs could stop him was by conceding a corner, and the goal that followed was straight out of the treble-winning season's coaching manual. Carrick whipped over a low cross to Scholes, who was standing on the edge of the D. This was Scholes's killing zone; he crashed in a shot and it deflected off Huddlestone. Carlos was standing in front of the goal and ducked out of the way as it flew past him, Spurs keeper Ben Alnwick, and into the net.

Two minutes later the game was over as Carrick, playing the best football of his career, put in Berbatov for the winner. A superb goal by anybody's standards – a sublime pass from the ex-Tottenham midfielder only bettered by Berbatov's first touch. It was ironic that Dimitar scored after receiving terrible abuse from the travelling Tottenham fans. Tevez continued to run Spurs ragged and it was a pity that Welbeck did not play a little closer to him to take advantage of the knock downs and flicks. It was Tevez's ability to close down players that earned him particular praise.

ITV were covering the game and ex-Chelsea midfielder Andy Townsend said: 'Tevez still has something to prove, closing down three, sometimes four, men. A recording of his performance should be sent to the Spurs team.' David Pleat was equally generous in his praise of Tevez. Here are some extracts from his commentary featuring his comments on Carlos: 'A very unselfish player... A champion of industry... Covers miles in a game...He takes players for a walk...He does not score enough goals, but I would keep him.'

Teddy Sheringham was also in the studio as a guest, immaculately dressed in a dark Comme des Garçons suit. Looking not a day older than when he equalised at the Nou Camp a decade before, Teddy chose the quick-footed Tevez as his Man of the Match. No one would argue with that. In the *Manchester Evening News* Tevez polled 56% of the votes for their Man of the Match. The only downside was the yellow card he received in injury time, as always he was working flat out till the final seconds.

Sir Alex was delighted with Tevez's performance in the match and told the *Manchester Evening News*: 'He has got great enthusiasm, he is a tiger; he fights for every ball and it is great to have that attitude in your team.'

You don't often hear Premier League managers praise a member of the opposition, particularly after a player has had a major part in knocking them out of the Cup. Harry Redknapp was no ordinary manager, though, and the man who was instrumental in discovering Rio Ferdinand and Michael Carrick at West Ham said of Carlos: 'If you looked for endeavour and fantastic effort we would all like to have Tevez in our team. He was an example to everyone – the way he ran and chased, how the crowd responded to him, but there are very few of those people around.'

On the following Tuesday night it was back to Premier League action against rock-bottom West Bromwich Albion. For the visit to the Hawthorns United had 12 first-team players injured, but they were still able to field a highly focused team of 11 internationals. West Brom were trounced 5-0, and Baggies fan and comedian Frank Skinner wrote an amusing article on the match in *The Times* about his visit to the match: 'There's something about Manchester United that makes me become abusive and irrational. When the fifth goal went in, I told a slightly confused man next to me that Manchester United not only represented what had gone wrong with football, but also what had gone wrong with society.'

It was their sixth straight Premier League win and the 11th game since Van der Sar had to pick the ball out of the back of the net. By the end of the game at West Brom,

United had not conceded a goal for 17 hours and 12 minutes. In that time you could have watched series five of *The Wire* or flown to Dubai and back. Petr Cech's record for successive clean sheets set up under Mourinho was now in pieces. Tevez had another immense game, scoring the second goal and charging at defenders with his quick determined runs. His goal came a minute before the break, when Park was fouled out on the wing and Giggs hit over a high cross. Erstwhile England keeper Scott Carson should have made an easy catch but he mistimed badly and the ball squirmed from his grasp. Instantly Carlos responded and lashed the ball into the net. A gift of a chance, certainly; arguably the easiest opportunity to have come his way since he joined United.

United had dominated from the start; the game kicked off 30 minutes late because of severe traffic problems on the M6 and M5, which had delayed the United fans. Berbatov gave United the lead after 22 minutes with his 11th goal of the season; Carlos was just two behind. Any hopes the Baggies might have had of at least salvaging a point disappeared when referee Rob Styles sent off full-back Paul Robinson for a challenge on Park.

The stiletto-sharp Carlos was wearing white boots to match his hairband and they were just a blur as United crushed West Brom. The brawny Vidic bludgeoned in the third when he headed home another Giggs corner. United were attacking at will and Ronaldo wrapped it up with two goals in 8 minutes: 5-0 – the biggest away score since Newcastle was exterminated at home the previous spring. Sir Alex was absolutely delighted at the performance which he described as 'ruthless'; his team had now moved three points ahead at the top of the table.

United treble-winner Andrew Cole appeared on the Radio Five *606* show and was asked if he thought Tevez would be staying at Old Trafford. He said: 'Tevez should stay at Old Trafford. He should not make the mistake I made and leave Old Trafford too early.'

Cole admitted that Berbatov was a 'class act' and made the point that he was a totally different player from Cantona, so all the comparisons between the two were irrelevant. Cole came across as amusing and laidback; he admitted that Teddy Sheringham still did not feature on his Christmas card list.

Everton visited the Theatre of Dreams for another early Saturday evening fixture. The game had been brought forward to accommodate David Moyes's men, who had a replay with Liverpool to squeeze into their engagement book. The previous season, a Ronaldo penalty won the fixture and history repeated itself as the World Player of the Year scored again from the spot. The kick was awarded for a trip on Carrick; with Ronaldo stepping up to the spot it was a formality. The two Neville brothers were United and Everton team captains and exchanged pleasantries before the game.

Carlos had another busy game; he was used as the front man. In the first half, he forced ex-United keeper Tim Howard into a fine save. A right-footed free kick by him in the second half brought another fine save from Howard. Later he shot over the top after another intricate passing movement set him up. The win put United five points clear of their nearest challengers, Chelsea – it was looking ominous for their rivals. Everything was still up for grabs. Wayne Rooney watched the match from the warmth of the directors' box. He was about to resume training, so where did that leave Carlos?

CHAPTER TWELVE

NOT QUITE A FAIRYTALE ENDING

Tevez is a great player and I like him very much. He is a bit like me but perhaps more of a striker than I was.
GIANFRANCO ZOLA

What's posterity ever done for me?
GROUCHO MARX

Carlos Tevez should sit on the bench with no one.
MARADONA

Nice praise there from Gianfranco. The Premier League managerial merry-go-round was in full swing in early 2009 and Luis Felipe Scolari was soon on his way, sacked by Roman Abramovich after a disappointing run of results for Chelsea. Guus Hiddink replaced him, their fourth coach in 17 months – or was it their 17th coach in four months? Sir Alex mused in the press about patience.

Carlos appeared in the opening line-up at Upton Park on 28 February, alongside Dimitar Berbatov. Those West Ham boys would have been so disappointed had their hero had not played, and once again Carlos received a reception from the locals comparable to Lindebergh's ticker tape reception at New York after the first transatlantic solo flight.

Carlos stood in the centre of the pitch as all four sides of the ground paid homage to him. If you could have bottled what he had, it would have sold out. People were talking in terms of United scooping all five honours – the Club World Cup, Carling Cup, Premier League, Champions League and the FA Cup.

United broke their dystopian sequence at Upton Park by winning 1-0, thanks to a superb second-half goal by Ryan Giggs. It was similar to the goal that Hungary scored against England when they thrashed them 6-3 in 1953. Giggs scored with his right foot. It meant that he maintained his wonderful record of scoring in every season since the Premier League had started, all 17 of them. Gary Speed of Leeds and Everton had kept alongside him in the scoring stakes, but now even he was no longer playing in the top flight, which meant that Ryan was the undisputed champion. The stats kept flowing; it was the 13th game in a row that United had not let in a goal and their fifth 1-0 victory away from home.

Carlos had a similar game at Upton Park for United as he had the previous season. He was industrious and showed enough classy touches to have the locals recall his past exploits; he never really hurt West Ham, though. Perhaps he couldn't bring himself to do that at Upton Park. So he did not add to the tally of goals that he had scored there in a West Ham shirt. Fans on the online message boards debated whether he looked better in a white headband than a black one. The commentator on Radio 5 Live said that he looked like a washerwoman with the white headband on. Still, the United war party did enough to take the three points. Before he was subbed, the last piece of significant action involved Tevez participating in a high-speed passing exchange which left the crowd cheering wildly and Zola nodding in agreement. The white-shirted Tevez left the field to another rousing reception from the home fans and a congratulatory pat on the back from Sir Alex.

For the second time in recent weeks, Jose Mourinho took a chance to check out United. As a testament to his appeal there were more cameras pointing at him than at the players of either side. Mourinho looked even smarter than in his Chelsea days now that he did his shopping on the Via Montenapolene.

Carlos spoke to the *Daily Mail* about his feelings regarding West Ham: 'I gave my all for West Ham, I scored some important goals and as I discovered when I went back there, it is still appreciated by the fans. They don't blame me for anything that happened. As far as I am concerned why should it be the Carlos Tevez affair? It is West Ham's affair. This is not my problem and it was not my fault. I did nothing wrong. I came to England to play football, and for West Ham and Manchester United I have tried to do that to the best of my ability. If West Ham have not submitted the documents correctly, that is down to them. It was nothing I did, but I have found myself caught in the middle of it.'

The strength of the United squad was such that some pundits were saying it was the greatest collection of players ever gathered at Old Trafford. Two fantastic teams could be fielded by the same club and the following line-ups were detailed:

A TEAM	B TEAM
Foster	Van Der Sar
Rafael	Neville
Ferdinand	Brown
Evans	Vidic
Evra	O'Shea
Park	Carrick

Fletcher	Scholes
Gibson	Anderson
Nani	Tevez
Ronaldo	Berbatov
Giggs	Rooney

The permutations were endless; the B team included the trio of Tevez, Rooney and Berbatov, which Sir Alex had not really used as a viable attack. Owen Hargreaves, twice a Champions League winner and voted the England team's Best Player in 2006, was not even considered because of his dual knee operations. Sir Alex Ferguson was dodging questions about a possible clean sweep of trophies but the press were now writing about it being a realistic outcome.

United returned to Derby just 39 days after they had lost there in the Carling Cup, for a fifth round FA Cup tie. Carlos took no part as Sir Alex continued to rotate his squad. The games came thick and fast now. After 20 minutes' play, and with the game goalless, the United fans started calling for Carlos with their now-familiar chant of 'Argentina, Argentina'. This irked the Derby fans, who always had a strong contingent, who followed England home and away. They tried to drown out the Tevez chants with their boos. Tevez was seated behind Sir Alex during the match, but his services were not required. Soon afterwards Nani scored a fine goal that had him celebrating with his famous handstands. United went on to win 4-1 with Ronaldo, Gibson and Welbeck the other scorers.

Three points were obtained from another London team a few nights later when Fulham were mauled 3-0 at Old Trafford. Carlos was back in the line-up with Berbatov. He did not figure among the scorers but his performance earned him 8/10 in the *Manchester Evening News*. His hair was shorter that night, rather than the familiar inky black mop. It was a look that he had sported in recent weeks.

Scholes, who dominated the match, opened the scoring with a classic strike after 12 minutes. Tevez helped set up the second for Berbatov when he took part in a 22-pass move that shredded the Fulham defence. It was a gem of a goal and drew comparisons with the classic goal that the Argentine scored against Serbia in the World Cup in June 2006. That move was two passes longer and Carlos's pal Javier Mascherano was the prime instigator in it. The move ended with him setting up Hernan Crespo to back-heel into the path of scorer Esteban Cambiasso. The ethic and the poetry of the move was the same, though.

Carlos had the ball in the net and it looked a legitimate goal but the referee ruled it out for offside. He was to have his revenge against Fulham in the coming weeks though. Berbatov went off on the hour to be replaced by Rooney, who following his injury was determined to see action after his seven-game absence. He scored almost instantly, just after Carlos narrowly failed to steer in Park's centre. After the match Carlos told the *Daily Telegraph* about his wish to stay with United: 'My idea is to stay in Manchester for a few years more. We have had talks with the board, but nothing has been signed yet. Both sides have decided to wait until June for a definitive solution.'

The win put the Reds five points in front of Liverpool and ten in front of Chelsea; all the teams had played 25 games. At Chelsea, Roman Abramovich replaced Luiz Felipe Scolari with temporary manager Guus Hiddink. Sir Alex, shocked at the treatment of the Brazilian coach, claimed that this action had played into the hands of United.

Blackburn were beaten 2-1 at Old Trafford in United's next game, on 21 February. Tevez was on the bench as Rooney was reinstated, and the England striker duly put United ahead midway through the first half. Blackburn equalised through Roque Santa Cruz, the first goal that United had conceded for a record-breaking 1,334 minutes. Cruz fired in a neat goal after holding off Ferdinand and beating United keeper Tomasz Kuszczak. The goal stunned United: the old freewheeling Reds would have bounced back straightaway, but the 2009 version were more guarded. Blackburn were denied a penalty when Morten Gamst Pedersen appeared to be fouled by the young Brazilian, Rafael Da Silva.

Ronaldo put United back in front with a tremendous free kick. Once again the sheer force deceived the keeper. The speed of the shot was measured at just below 70mph as it swirled and then dipped into the net. Tevez joined the action soon afterwards, replacing Nani. The Argentinean sub was sporting another new haircut; the voluminous hair was shorn. He received a booking for a foul on the Blackburn midfielder Tugay near the end. United held on for the points and withstood a late challenge from Blackburn. At that time, bookmakers had already paid out on them winning the domestic Treble. The best prices were 6-4 on their winning the domestic title by 10 points or more. It looked too easy now.

Carlos remained frustrated by the situation regarding his contact and the fact that he was still sitting out big matches. As always, though, he never moaned and told the *Daily Mail*: 'At this point I am not sure if I will stay, not least because it is not just my decision, it is up to Manchester to decide if they want to keep me – and I have to decide what is right for my career, for my future. Right now I am only focused on the four trophies we are trying to win.'

Carlos had acquired the nickname of 'Sir Charles' from a section of the crowd. Online message boards were jammed with fans discussing his future. He had made it known that after some years playing in Europe, he hankered to return to his first love, Boca, to play out the remainder of his career. The striker's first love never died, but this had hit his value. The worsening economic downturn now meant that his valuation of £30m was a massive figure. The only club in the world that would not baulk at such a figure were United's neighbours, Manchester City, though Real Madrid were still being linked with Tevez. Some reports even told of Corinthians being interested in bringing him back to Brazil. Mario Gobbi, a senior director at Corinthians, told Radio Jovem Pan: 'Carlos does not want to play in England anymore. For a while we have known that he would like to return to Corinthians.'

An even more far-fetched rumour was that Chelsea were lining up a summer move for Carlos. The *Sun* ran an article stating that Abramovich's fortune had shrunk down to £7bn, so a £30m swoop for Tevez seemed unlikely.

A massive week followed in the United calendar. On the following Tuesday, United travelled to Milan for the first leg of their Champions League last-16 tie. Carlos did not participate in the game. Once again he sat out a vital match on the bench and watched as his side earned a 0-0 draw on a frosty, foggy February evening. It was a game that they should have won in a canter. Rooney also languished on the bench as Sir Alex Ferguson just started with Berbatov up front. When the treble was won a decade earlier, Sir Alex had the firepower of Solskjaer, Sheringham, Cole and Yorke, but now he used his striking trio sparingly. Rooney came on in the closing minutes, but there was surprisingly no appearance for Carlos. His presence might have made a difference against a disappointing Inter side.

The truth was, Mourinho had constructed something of a poor imitation of the Chelsea war machine that had won him back-to-back Premier League titles. Their modesty of ambition was in stark contrast to United's attacking policy in the San Siro. Chris Waddle commentated on the game for Radio 5 Live that night and said that Tevez 'pushed teams back.' The ex-Newcastle and England star stated that Tevez's constant chasing and harrying of defenders would have unsettled the Inter rearguard.

The stalemate left things in the balance; it was going to be a tricky return match at Old Trafford. The media made constant references to the fact that Sir Alex had only beaten Mourinho once in 12 games, the famous victory by Porto in 2004 being the pivotal moment in José's meteoric rise. Mourinho once said that he won the Champions League with a Porto side that 'people would not have bet a Euro on to win.' The self-proclaimed 'Special One' would have liked nothing more than to knock out United and wreck the 'quintuple', which was being written up in the press as a distinct possibility.

Carlos ensured the next leg of that quintuple was won, though, when he played a very important part in the Carling Cup final victory over Tottenham Hotspur. As promised, he started the match – after all, he was the joint top goalscorer in the competition. The other top scorer, Roman Pavlyuchenko, who had scored in every round, was in the Spurs line-up. Spurs had four League Cup wins to their name – twice as many as United. Both clubs had made six appearances in the League Cup final. It was billed as a clash between two of the grand old teams of English football. As the economy crumbled and the newspapers were full of stories about teenage knife crime and violence, Manchester United, and particularly Carlos Tevez, were a brazier for people to warm their hands on in that seemingly endless winter of discontent.

Sir Alex omitted Berbatov, Rooney and Carrick from the squad altogether, with Giggs and Vidic on the bench. Danny Welbeck partnered Carlos up front, with Ben Foster in goal and Irishman Darron Gibson midfield. United were nowhere near their best; they had flattered to deceive in the San Siro and once again failed to kill off the game. After 90 minutes the score was 0-0. Carlos had been given a great write-up in the programme but despite putting in another tremendous effort failed to make a defining statement. In the first half he hit the side netting after 14 minutes and just before half-time, he spun in the box and put in a shot the Spurs keeper Heurelho Gomes pushed out. Mark Lawrenson was covering the game for Radio 5 Live and commented on what a 'neat turn' it was. Alan Green, his co-commenter, posed the question, 'I wonder how long he will stay at Old Trafford for?'

Early in the second half, Carlos just failed to divert Jonny Evans's half-volley into the net. A fair number of the crowd in the expensive seats behind the dug-outs missed the incident as they were still enjoying the corporate hospitality well into the second half. Spurs came more into the game but there seemed some inevitability about the extra time and the penalty shoot-out that ensued after two hours.

Carlos put in an incredible shift, tackling back, linking play and trying to set up chances. The clever Tottenham schemer Luka Modric had a fine game and was his side's best player, but Tevez even found time to drop back to mark him. The United fans gave him a tremendous hand when he dispossessed the Croatian near Foster's penalty box, such was the area that he covered. It was Carlos's first domestic

Cup Final and he was desperate to impress Sir Alex and the 88,217 present at Wembley.

It was 10 months on from that rainy night in Moscow, and maybe the stakes were not quite so high, but once again Carlos found the eyes of the world looking at him as he sauntered up to take his penalty in the deciding shoot-out. It was the second United penalty in the sequence, and the only time in the match that the little striker was not running full pelt. Ryan Giggs, on as a sub for Gibson in extra time and looking as if he had just stepped out of the shower, had clipped in the first penalty. Spurs were now eyeball to eyeball with United. Faced with the confidence and self-belief of the Reds, Spurs' nerve cracked, just as the England captain John Terry had in a similar position in Moscow. Tottenham missed their first chance, Ben Foster diving to his left to keep out O'Hara's penalty. Now it was all down to Carlos.

Once again he came up trumps – his kick was perfect, low and hard into the bottom left-hand corner. It was as perfect as the kick he had delivered in the Champions League final – if anything, he hit it even harder and truer. Two-nil, and United had the platform for victory. The Croatia defender Corluka cleverly beat Foster in his attempt to pull one back for Spurs – it was only delaying the inevitable, though. Ronaldo had missed his spot kick in Moscow, and the player voted the best in the world had had a difficult season. The ankle injury and constant speculation about his future were contributory factors to his indifferent form. Had a defender thrown a handful of rice at him the previous season Ronaldo would have dodged it. This term had been harder, but his spot-kick was immaculate. The winger committed Gomes to dive then rolled the ball down the middle. 3-1.

David Bentley took the next kick for Tottenham; for them

to have any chance of salvaging anything he simply had to score. Bentley was another player who was having a difficult season: the ex Arsenal man had struggled to hold his place since his big-money move from Blackburn. Things got worse when he blasted wide. His manager Harry Redknapp later remarked on what a poor kick it had been for a player of his ability. Bentley had at one time been seen as the new Beckham, such was his reputation as a striker of a ball. Recently he had won a £15,000 watch from his agent by drop-kicking a ball into a skip from the roof of a building. That was the point; the reaction to pressure. Tevez had scored twice from the spot in two of the most pressured situations in football. The stakes were so high.

Carlos had recently had his car confiscated – while driving his white £140,000 Bentley GT Continental on the M60 near Stretford to the team's Carrington training ground, he was stopped by the motorway police. They had tugged him because the cops considered that windows on his vehicle were too dark (tinted windows were still fashionable with the players, but the police hated them because the drivers could continue to use their mobiles). When asked to produce his driving licence, Carlos could only produce his Argentinean version and told the officers he had been living in the UK for four years. The law stipulates that foreign nationals can only use a non-UK driving licence for a year. As a result, Carlos's Bentley was impounded, and Patrice Evra had to pick him up on the hard shoulder to make sure he made training. The upshot was that Carlos lost his Bentley – and Spurs lost because of Bentley.

Anderson smashed in his penalty to make it 4-1 and to bring the Carling Cup to Manchester. In 18 months at Old

Trafford the only domestic honour that Carlos did not yet possess was the FA Cup, and he was still working on that. Pictures of the team celebrating with the Cup showed Carlos cloaked in the Argentina flag, which was, of course, obligatory for such occasions. His hair was soaked in champagne. Carlos's overall contribution to the match, however, was greeted with mixed reaction by the press.

The *Manchester Evening News* gave him a high rating of 8/10, citing his 'magnificent work rate', a score equalled only by Ronaldo and Rio Ferdinand. The *Telegraph* only gave him 6/10, though, describing his finishing as 'toothless'. And the *Sun* gave him one point less than that, criticising his end product. Whatever the critics might say, Carlos had another medal to display in a collection that only Ryan Giggs could top.

Another tricky fixture followed, away to Newcastle, who had struggled all season but were desperate for points. Fabricio Coloccini, the Newcastle star, was very anxious to renew his acquaintance with Tevez. The defender's father, Osvado, had coached him at Boca Juniors and had raved about his potential. Fabricio told the *Sun*: 'I played with Carlos in the National team at the Olympics, but I have known him 13 years though because my father Osvaldo was the manager of Boca Juniors youth side, so he knew him when he was very young. It was a very good team that he managed. My father always tells me he is different, he is special. Carlos is a top player and he may not even play. That says everything about their squad.'

Fabricio was to be disappointed as Carlos did not play at St James. Berbatov scored the winner in a hard-fought 2-1 victory. United even went behind to a Peter Lovenkrands, goal after a mistake by Van der Sar. Poor Edwin missed the

European record by 88 minutes for the longest period since conceding a goal. This had been set by the Club Brugge goalkeeper Danny Verlinden back in 1990. Wayne Rooney eluded Coloccini of all people to equalise. The win restored their seven-point lead, with one game in hand over Liverpool and Chelsea. Earlier in the day Carlos had done the touristy thing when he visited the Angel of the North.

Carlos kept up his quest for an FA Cup medal when he scored two first-half goals in the 4-0 thrashing of Fulham at Craven Cottage. Of the dozen goals he had scored, nine had come in cup competitions. The little Argentinean, in for Berbatov, started like an express train and moved up a gear. In the first minute he cut inside the penalty area and fired in a fierce shot that forced Mark Schwarzer to make a superb one-handed save. The Fulham keeper was beaten on 20 minutes, though. Rooney flicked on a corner and Carlos, the smallest man on the field, rose to thread his header home between defender and post. It was the first time that the pair had started together up front since the Boxing Day fixture against Stoke.

The second goal was possibly his best United goal so far in his career at Old Trafford. Deep in his own half, John O'Shea found Darren Fletcher who played a 1-2 with Ferdinand before putting Tevez through on goal. Twenty-five yards out, he let fly and the ball just rocketed into the net. It was a simply unstoppable shot and for the millions watching it at home, it was fabulous entertainment.

There was no stopping Carlos – he hit the side netting once before unselfishly passing to Park, who spurned the chance. Rooney and Park added second-half goals to complete the rout, but the star performer of the match was undoubtedly Tevez. He deservedly won the Man of the

Match award. Praise was heaped on him from all sides. Former West Ham teammate Teddy Sheringham was one of the TV pundits and described Carlos's performance as 'absolutely fantastic.' Ex-Liverpool defender Jim Begin was even more enthusiastic, saying that Tevez, '...had been terrific'. Irish-born Jim stated that he had long been an admirer of Tevez and asked, 'How many goals does he have to score to be in the team?'.

Fabio Capello had given up his early Saturday evening to take in the game and was seated next to Fulham chairman Mohammed al Fayed. Perhaps they were discussing the value of Tevez, or even the price of Bottega Veneta suits in Mr Fayed's local shop.

Despite his exploits at Fulham, Carlos failed to make the team for the next Champions League home game. United won 2-0, but were unconvincing against Jose Mourinho's mundane Milan. Jose looked the part, beautifully dressed in a black Armani raincoat and dark shirt. He had no luck that night, though – there was no Tim Howard to spill Benni McCarthy's last-second shot and no referee's assistant to rule out a vital goal. Headers from Vidic and Rooney were enough to put United into the quarter finals. Carlos sat out the entire game out on the bench but once again it looked as if they could have done with his attacking play as United turned in an uneven performance.

Tevez also missed out on wearing the new badge presented to United before the match by FIFA President Sepp Blatter. This marked their success in winning the Club World Cup in Japan. The problem was that Premier League chiefs would not allow the badge to be worn in domestic combat. Their reasoning was that United only qualified for the Club World Cup through the Champions League. They rather missed the point that United only qualified for that competition by virtue of the fact that they had won their home title.

Liverpool then visited Old Trafford for a Saturday lunchtime Premier League game. Rafa Benitez's team had to win the match to retain any lingering hope of winning the Premier League. The scoreline was an amazing 4-1 victory to the visitors – United's heaviest home defeat in the Premier League and a result that sent shock waves reverberating around Old Trafford and the game of football as a whole. It was a poor performance from the entire United team, though not totally unexpected. United had been getting away with it for some time with narrow, scrappy wins and mediocre performances. Owen Hargreaves was particularly missed as the Reds had no defensive midfielder of his calibre to protect the back four.

Liverpool simply overpowered the United midfield and rained down on the hitherto seemingly impregnable rearguard. Gerrard and Torres, who both scored, grabbed the headlines but the star of the match was Javier Mascherano. Carlos's ex-teammate gave a wonderful display and made the time and space for the grey-shirted duo of Gerrard and Torres to play to their strengths and carve up the United back four. Javier was becoming an increasingly important figure in Benitez's team. It was an indictment of Pardew's coaching abilities that he had been virtually ignored in his spell at Upton Park.

Carlos had started the game but despite his effort there was no end product other than when he chested down a cross and scuffed the shot past the post. Jamie Carragher brought him down as he raced for goal, but only received a yellow card for it. Later in the game, Vidic, who had a nightmare match showing great vulnerability, was sent off for a similar offensive.

The knives were out for United; it was their first defeat in 20 games, but the manner of it was even more worrying. There was a fecklessness that had crept into the team's overall play. Carlos was awarded only 4/10 in *The Times* for his performance though the *Manchester Evening News* gave him a score of 7 and made him the Pick of the Team. One of the criticisms levelled against Carlos was that he was now more effective as an impact sub now than starting a game. Not a good week for him, and it was about to get worse.

Both the Argentineans had risen above the tangled transfer dealings but the fall out from the saga continued to haunt them. On the Monday after the Liverpool game, it was announced that West Ham had agreed to pay compensation to Sheffield United to finally end the squabble over Carlos's eligibility to ply his trade in claret and blue. Depending on what paper you read, the compensation was listed as being anywhere between £15m and £25m. Earlier figures of around £45m had been bandied about. The agreement was to pave the way for the possible sale of West Ham, and it was revealed that the club could also face charges following a further investigation being jointly held by the Premier League and the FA. This related to alleged assurances made that ensured Carlos played in the last three matches.

The Hammers had agreed to pay Sheffield United £10m with an additional £15m in the form of a bond payable over five years. This arrangement was reached after taking legal advice on the case. Former Sheffield United manager Neil Warnock then announced that he was ready to sue West Ham for loss of earnings and the effect that the relegation had had on his career. Warnock had left Bramall Lane by mutual consent three days after Carlos's winner at Old Trafford condemned Sheffield to relegation. West Ham chief executive Scott Duxbury told the *Daily Mail*: 'For everyone concerned, the time was right to draw a line under this whole episode.'

Far from drawing a line, though, the agreement sparked an avalanche of speculation about how many personal claims would be launched. Fulham reportedly claimed £700,000 from West Ham over the affair. They believed that they had missed out on a significant amount of Premier League prize money after finishing just two points behind Tevez's Hammers. Gianfranco Zola admitted that he was fed up with the whole saga and claimed it was not only about Tevez.

A few days later Fulham beat United 2-0 at Craven Cottage to gain revenge for their cup mauling. Fulham knew all about Tevez, following his wonderful performance in that cup match, but two weeks in football is a long time and he and Rooney did not make the starting line-up. Instead Sir Alex used the somewhat bizarre pairing of Berbatov and Ronaldo. United lost Paul Scholes, and a goal, when the midfielder handled the ball in the box. Danny Murphy converted the penalty. When United had been good that season they were very good, but when they were bad, they were sloppy and scrappy. Tevez replaced John O'Shea with 20 minutes left, but the game deteriorated further and in the closing minutes, after Fulham sub Gera had made it 2-0, Rooney was sent off. This was for petulantly throwing the ball back. It was United's first back-to-back loss in 147 Premier League games.

United's title challenge was faltering, but the break for international games gave them much-needed breathing space from the domestic pressure cooker. Not that Carlos could rest, as he faced another endurance test with a marathon trip to South America. In his first match he scored in the 4-0 thumping of Venezuela in Buenos Aires. This was Maradona's first home match in charge. An encouraging performance, but a few days later they were chain-sawed 6-1 in Bolivia, in a World Cup qualifier. This result left Maradona's team fourth in the group and in danger of not automatically qualifying; the rout was Argentina's worst-ever World Cup qualifying defeat.

The match was played in La Paz at the Estadio Hernando, one of the highest grounds in the world. FIFA had previously ruled that as the stadium in La Paz was above 8,200ft, it gave an unfair advantage as players did not have enough time to acclimatise. This was subsequently overruled and Carlos had the added problem of trying to acclimatise to the painfully thin air in addition to the travel fatigue. In any event he did not arrive back in Manchester until late on the Friday before the vital home game against Villa. At the press conference, Sir Alex quipped that Tevez had flown business class so at least he could lie down.

With Rooney serving a one-match ban following his antics at Craven Cottage and Berbatov injured, the onus was on Carlos to kick-start the game. As always he tried his hardest, but even he was understandably feeling jaded. With just 10 minutes left, United trailed 1-2 to Villa and appeared to be about to lose their crown. Both Liverpool and Chelsea had won the day before. Ronaldo had put United ahead with a venomous free kick but the big Norwegian John Carew gave the makeshift United back four a torrid afternoon. The Scandinavian equalised with a powerful header and then set up Gabriel Agbonlahor for the second. That seemed to be it; United struggled to stay in the game. The jet-lagged Carlos looked absolutely shattered but kept going, and with time ticking on, he roused the crowd when he ran 60 yards to win the ball. Ten minutes from time Ronaldo levelled with a fine shot from Carrick's pass. With 3 minutes left, Carlos, who had run himself into the ground, was replaced by Danny Welbeck but it was another substitute, Federico Macheda, who grabbed the headlines. The 17-year-old former Lazio youth player won the game, and possibly the Premier League, with a superb turn and shot. It was a finish straight out of the Ole Gunnar Solskjaer songbook and no surprise as the youngster was a protégé of the master striker. Known to his United teammates as 'Kiko', the Rome-born teenager had spent most of the season playing for Solskjaer's reserves side in the lone striker role. A few days before he had scored a hat trick at Newcastle in a reserve match.

United's power of recovery was typified by that performance. Golf legend Tiger Woods was battling back from a career-threatening injury and had recently won the Arnold Palmer tournament with an incredible long-range putt when all seemed lost. For the greatest sportsmen it was never over, though. Woods's dispassionate maxim, 'Don't feel sorry for your opponent till you are shaking hands with him', could have been Tevez's mantra that day.

Macheda scored the winning goal again in the next Premier League match at Sunderland after coming on as a substitute. Tevez started the match alongside Berbatov and Rooney. Paul Scholes put United ahead but Kenwyne Jones equalised for the Black Cats early in the second half. United hit back and Carlos had two good attempts on goal, one free kick inches over the top and then a blocked shot after Berbatov had put him in. The Bulgarian was then replaced by the young prospect Macheda. Within seconds of his appearance he had deflected Carrick's shot into the Sunderland net to give the blue-shirted away team another precious three points.

Between those two vital Premier League wins, United were held at home by Porto in the quarter-finals of the Champions league. The game was played just two days after the Aston Villa match. Carlos scored what appeared to be the winner near the end against Jesualdo Ferreira's team. Porto's line-up could hardly be compared to Jose Mourinho's side, but nevertheless they put on a brave display of attacking football. Cristiano Rodriguez gave them an early lead after another Cristiano lost midfield possession, but a poker-faced Rooney equalised after 15 minutes and then cleverly set up Carlos's goal 5 minutes from time.

Carlos had replaced Paul Scholes with 18 minutes left. The game definitely needed star quality at that stage and the Argentine ace was greeted rousingly by the home crowd. A petition had been started demanding their cherished number 32 stay at Old Trafford and when the ball flew high into the net, even more signatures must have been added. It looked like the goal had won it, but in the dying seconds another substitute, the unmarked Lisandro, swept the ball home to give Porto a deserved equaliser.

A wonder goal by Ronaldo, hit from 40 yards and timed at 64mph (and voted the best he had ever scored), won the return in the Estadio do Dragao the following week. No English team had ever won there before in front of the rabid Porto fans. Carlos was an unused substitute, sitting on the bench throughout. Sir Alex only made two substitutions. In the closing stages, with legs growing increasingly tired, Carlos would have relished joining the fray.

Meanwhile, there was a growing lobby in the press claiming that Sir Alex did not start Tevez in the real crunch games. The little maestro was becoming increasingly disgruntled with the situation and the fact that the unpredictable, lightweight Nani went on ahead of him in Portugal must have cut deep. Whichever argument was used – rotation, tactics, etc., Carlos had done enough at the club to merit a higher standing.

Carlos was included in the opening line-up of United's FA Cup semi-final against Everton, played at Wembley. The team showed eight changes from the one that started in the Estadio do Dragao and lost on penalties after 120 scoreless minutes. United's dream of a quintuple perished, but by now it was apparent that Sir Alex's priority was just to retain the Premiership and Champions League.

The fielding of a weakened team, whose average age was 22, against a gritty Everton packed with blue-collar technicians produced a riveting spectacle. Carlos had a busy match and missed a chance in the first half. It was highly significant that he did not figure in the penalty shoot-out. Rio Ferdinand and Dimitar Berbatov both missed their spot kicks while Phil Jagielka, of all people, struck the winning penalty to give Everton an unassailable 4-2 lead. Ironic that the ex-Sheffield United defender was becoming something of a bête noir, haunting the man whose superb displays had helped relegate the Yorkshiremen two years before. Jagielka appeared to trip Danny Welbeck midway through the second half, but United were denied what seemed to be a legitimate case for a penalty.

The fact that Carlos did not take a penalty kick in the shoot-out was incredible, considering the beautifully-placed kick he had produced to assist in beating Tottenham on the same ground the previous month. In Moscow the previous May, he had converted the first penalty to help United lift the biggest prize of all. A picture of Rio Ferdinand trudging back after fluffing his kick showed a demoralised Carlos in the background, standing on the halfway line with the rest of the Reds. The striker stood at the end of the row, arms folded, his gaunt features looking sunken with fatigue. Berbatov's horribly casual kick was a pitiful attempt at a penalty and was described by ex-Everton boss Joe Royle as, 'The worst ever taken by a professional.' Everton went on to play Chelsea in the final where, despite Louis Saha smashing the record for the fastest FA Cup final goal, they lost 2-1. Tim Howard, who played superbly against United in the semi-final, was at fault for Lampard's winning strike. Phil Jagielka, who probably would have denied Lampard the space to score, missed the game through injury.

David Moyes's side did United a favour a few nights after their semi-final win, though, when they held Chelsea to a 0-0 draw at Stamford Bridge to put the brakes on the Blues' late Premier League challenge. On the same evening United won 2-0 against Portsmouth at Old Trafford, with goals from Rooney and Carrick. Once again, Carlos did not feature in proceedings, and the *Sun* ran a story the next morning in which he stated that he was quitting United: 'With respect to the fans and the history of Manchester United I don't want to leave, but from a personal aspect my exit will be a best solution. I don't understand my absence from decisive games like those against Chelsea.'

Carlos played probably the best 45 minutes of that astounding season when he came on as a substitute against Tottenham the following Saturday evening. United were two goals down and the Premiership title race looked to be blown wide open again. Goals from Darren Bent and Luka Modric had given Spurs a shock lead against a jaded, nervous United side. Sir Alex introduced a dazzlingly fresh Carlos to the action as he replaced Nani at half-time.

Immediately the mood inside the stadium changed. The

chants of 'Argentina, Argentina' rang around the ground. As the fab four were reunited and proceeded to blow Tottenham out of the water. A tremendous shot from Tevez was superbly saved by Heurelho Gomes, but shortly after Ronaldo scored from a disputed penalty. That opened the floodgates as the champions tore Tottenham apart with their special brand of rat-a-tat-tat football. A 3-goal burst in three minutes, two from Rooney and another from Ronaldo, all but clinched the title for the Reds. Berbatov wrapped it up with a fifth, but the match hero was Carlos, hot-wiring United with his raw energy, versatility and ceaseless running. He gave the Spurs defence no peace at all and put them on the back foot from the start of the second half. Tevez was playing for his future and he had to make every second count. Sir Alex praised the impact of his substitute in an interview with the *Manchester Evening News*: 'We were too slow, too casual in the first half. We needed to speed up in the second half and Tevez was responsible for that. He got the rest of the team playing.'

Then it was another North London side, Arsenal, who stood in United's path to the Champions League final in Rome. The first leg of the first all-English semi-final was at Old Trafford. After his heroics against Tottenham, Carlos started ahead of Berbatov against an Arsenal team unbeaten in their last 20 League games. United started brightly, and a superb double save by the Arsenal keeper Manuel Alumina denied Carlos a certain goal in the 17th minute. Carlos took Ronaldo's pass and interchanged with John O'Shea, and from the return he side-footed towards goal from 8 yards. The bleach-blond keeper made a great stop and then blocked Tevez's follow-up shot.

From Anderson's resultant corner, O'Shea, a 33-1 outsider to score the opening goal, blasted home Carrick's return.

Tevez was later booked when he went for a 50:50 ball with Almunia and ended up colliding with him. Not only did he pick up a card, he was also badly bruised in the clash. When he returned to the game after receiving treatment, he received a terrific reception. Once again his efforts were faultless and he showed his ability to bring his team-mates into the game.

After 65 minutes, almost burnt out by his running he was replaced by Berbatov, but there were no more goals. Arsenal boss Arsène Wenger fancied his team's chances in the return leg at the Emirates. Sir Alex made one change for the return, Ji-sung Park replacing Carlos. This seemed a surprising move considering the excellent press that Tevez had garnered in recent weeks. After his performance in the first leg, Richard Williams of the *Guardian* said: 'Fans love a player who simply wants to play. It is harder for a semi-detached presence such as Berbatov to win their affection – as opposed to their admiration – than it is for a wholehearted type like Tevez, as long as the effort is well directed.'

Brian Reade of the *Mirror* described Tevez as being as fit as 'a butcher's dog' and suggested that Tevez ask Fergie to 'let him stand with Berbatov in front of the Stretford End and ask the fans which striker they would rather keep.'

Park opened the scoring against Arsenal in the eighth minute, and 3 minutes later, Ronaldo effectively ended the tie as a contest when he scored from yet another wonderful free kick. Ronaldo scored again on the hour from a breakaway before Robin Van Persie pulled one back from the spot. The result meant United had the chance of writing their names in the record books by becoming the first team to win the European Cup back to back since its rebranding as the Champions League.

First, there was the matter of clinching the Premier.

Middlesbrough had been disposed of in the period between the semi-final matches. United inched closer to the title with a 2-0 win over Gareth Southgate's doomed team. Ryan Giggs and Park were the scorers in a vital win against a ramshackle defence; Carlos came on 10 minutes in the second half for the photogenic Macheda.

Then it was the big one – the Manchester derby on 10 May. On the morning of the match the *News of the World* ran what they called an exclusive interview. In it an insightful Carlos stated: 'I am very sad about this but I guess what I am saying is goodbye. I do not think I will be a Manchester United player next season. I have done everything I possibly can, but they have never made me an offer so I have to leave. I think I will be at another club next season.'

At that point Carlos had been named in the squad 57 times. He had appeared 47 times, started 32 of those games, and come on as a sub 15 times. A salient fact was that he had been subbed 12 times and played the full 90 minutes in just 20 games.

Carlos started against Mark Hughes's City alongside Berbatov and Ronaldo. Some fans speculated that Sir Alex was putting Carlos in the shop window, following the *News of the World* article. Ronaldo put United in front after 17 minutes with another thunderous free kick that took a deflection on its way in. On a overcast afternoon it was the Carlos Tevez show, though. In the fourth minute Shay Given, the ex-Newcastle keeper, made a great save from a 30-yarder by Carlos, just blocking the ball at the foot of the post. On the half-hour he sent in another tremendous shot that thudded against the crossbar with Given beaten by the sheer pace and power. Thirteen minutes later, he finally scored the goal his efforts deserved; this time Berbatov laid off a beautiful ball for him to lash home.

The goal produced a gesture from him as extraordinary as the dummy incident in the Birmingham match the previous season. This time he waved away his jubilant team-mates and ran to the halfway line with a cosmic twinkle in his eye. When he got there he faced the directors' box and cupped his ears. The message could not have been clearer. Ricky Hatton, the true blue City fan, was in the crowd. A few days earlier he had taken a fearsome beating from Manny Pacquiao. The City defence took a similar pummelling from the Argentine bantamweight in the 151st Manchester derby.

Throughout the match the refrains of 'Fergie, Fergie, sign him up' and 'Argentina, Argentina' rose from all four corners of the ground. Ronaldo flounced off when he was subbed. Tevez hit a post near the end as United moved to within four points of their third successive Premier League title – their 11th since the Premier League's inception in 1992 and their 18th League title in total.

Figures of between £22m and £26m were being bandied about as the fee required to keep Tevez at Old Trafford, at a time when the global financial system was still teetering on the brink of total collapse. That money seemed a reasonable figure, though, when Carlos scored a priceless goal at Wigan, three days later. Once again United were trailing and their title dreams hung in the balance. Hugo Rodallega had put Steve Bruce's team ahead and for long periods on a wet night, United's challenge looked under threat as Wigan wasted a slew of chances.

Carlos once again faced the indignity of sitting on the bench. Perhaps it was for his misdemeanour against City, but after 58 minutes he was sent on for Anderson. Within 3 minutes he had equalised with his 15th – and last – goal of the campaign. This was as neat as any he had ever scored, coolly back-heeling home Carrick's meticulously crafted pass. The Argy warrior stood in the pouring rain – the title was coming home.

Michael Carrick, who had been insisting in the press that Carlos should stay at United, shot the winner against Wigan a few minutes from the end. Carlos's equaliser had broken Wigan's hearts, as it did the millions of Liverpool fans hoping for the slip-up that never came. Liverpool had, amazingly, lost only two games all season in the Premier League. The recalibrated Chelsea, superbly guided by the Dutch master Hiddink, lost only once under his tutelage. That was the measure of United's achievement, withstanding the challenge from two powerful teams while also competing on other fronts.

Eventually they clinched the title with a 0-0 home draw against Arsenal – the third time they had met in less than three weeks. Tevez started this time and played for 67 minutes before being replaced by Park. As he left the field he raised his hands above his head to wave goodbye, a gesture mirrored by the crowd.

It's a pity our fairy-tale story of Carlos's time at Old Trafford doesn't end on a happier note, but Barcelona spoilt the party when they beat United 2-0 in the Champions League final in Rome on 27 May. Barcelona had narrowly beaten Chelsea in the semi-finals. In an interesting game, Chelsea had given them 70% possession and made only 244 passes against the Catalans' 595. In the end, the game finished 1-1 and Barcelona triumphed on the away-goals rule, thanks in the eyes of the Chelsea players and fans to some controversial refereeing decisions by Norwegian Tom Henning Ovrebo. Iniesta and Xavi were the hub of the Barca team, mobile playmakers spinning an ever-changing web of accurate short passes. The warning was there for United.

Buoyed by their easy win over the fragile Arsenal team, Sir Alex went for the same formation in the final, with Park starting ahead of Tevez. Berbatov also found himself on the bench, while Ronaldo was at centre-forward. The pressure on him to score was immense; if he failed, the feeling was United would also fail. In the first 8 minutes, Ronaldo had four attempts on goal. In the ninth minute Barcelona scored, with their first attack. At Chelsea they had one shot on target and one goal. United seemed devastated when Eto'o turned Vidic like a dinosaur in a swamp to score. After that they froze, and legions of fans screamed for Fergie to bring on Tevez and switch Rooney into the middle.

Eventually Tevez came on at half-time, and United flickered briefly into life. With the United midfield obliterated, though, Barcelona were in complete control. The loss of Owen Hargreaves was now apparent – he was the only midfielder on United's books who could possibly have denied Iniesta and Xavi control. Carlos's fellow countryman Messi headed the second from Xavi's pinpoint cross. All season in the Premier League Vidic and Ferdinand had been defending moves like that with ease, but the unmarked forward climbed high to beat Van der Sar.

Carlos Tevez and United wore white that night, a colour that had assumed almost mythical status when worn by the great Real Madrid side almost 50 years before. United had worn white when they beat the Catalans 2-1 in the European Cup-Winners' Cup in 1991. There was no glory for Carlos in Rome, though, and when he had celebrated winning the Premier League against Arsenal, he sported his Argentina shirt. The big question was – whose shirt would he be wearing next season?

CHAPTER THIRTEEN
FLY ME TO THE (BLUE) MOON

Be in control of your self, take control of everything around you,
look big, think big, and be big.
MALCOLM ALLISON, FORMER COACH OF THE GREAT
MANCHESTER CITY TEAM OF THE LATE 1960s

City have got this man with a heart as big as...
as big as a plate.
AN APPRAISAL OF CARLOS TEVEZ BY SKY PUNDIT CHRIS KAMARA (THE QUOTE
WON THE COVETED 'RANDOM COMPARISON' AWARD FOR 2009)

In the end Carlos traded his red shirt for the sky blue of neighbours Manchester City in the biggest and most sensational move of the season. City fans saw the move as getting one over on United, whose fans appreciated the little guy more than the twinkle-toed Ronaldo who had recently relocated to Real Madrid.

Dr Sulaiman al-Fahim, the mouth piece for Sheikh Mansour's Abu Dhabi United Group had recently predicted that City were going to be the biggest club in the world. Bigger than both Cristiano's former and new employers.

Tevez signed a five year deal on a weekly wage of £150,000, after flying in from his holiday in South America for a medical in a Manchester hospital. He became the latest addition to Mark Hughes's star-spangled squad, joining other new summer signings Gareth Barry and Roque Santa Cruz. Hughes told the media what good value Tevez was and how delighted he was to have him at Eastlands, while Manchester United released a statement on their website:

'Disappointingly Tevez's advisors informed the club that, despite the success he has enjoyed during one of the clubs most periods, he does not wish to continue playing for Manchester United.'

Before Tevez, the last player to join City direct from Old Trafford was Terry Cooke. City boss Joe Royle purchased the winger for £600,000 and in his first season at Maine Road helped the club win promotion to the Premiership.

Chelsea had been keen to sign Carlos and their new manager Carlo Ancelotti had bombarded him with calls. At one time it looked like he would be heading down south to join the club that had tracked him since he had first burst onto the scene in South America. They could not match the package of wages and fees offered by City though. Chief executive Peter Kenyon, shortly to leave Chelsea, met Kia Joorabchian at uber-agent Pini Zahavi's daughters wedding in Israel but the deal never too place.

Liverpool had been consistently linked with Tevez. The chance of joining up with his old buddy Mascherano and playing alongside the golden boy Torres may have interested him but the financial restraints placed upon the Scouse side made it impossible. A big deciding factor had been that Tevez's four year old daughter Florencia had enrolled in a private school in Cheshire. The striker was determined that his daughter had the best start in life possible.

In an interview with *Football Punk* Carlos talked about his family life. 'I spend a lot of time at home with my wife Vanessa and my daughter Florencia,' he said. 'I call her

Floppy and she keeps me grounded. Before she goes to sleep at night I tell her I love her, that she is the best thing that has happened in my life.

'I go out walking with her when I have a free day and I often take her to see London.' As a child Carlos himself had sometimes returned home to find very little food on the table. That fear of hunger still drove him on, and in a message on City's website Mark Hughes had talked about Tevez possessing 'All the attributes that will drive this club forward'.

The Times later reported that the total fee for Carlos to cross the Manchester divide was a mind-boggling £47 million. The brother of the ruler of Abu Dhabi had agreed to pay almost twice the £25.5 m fee widely reported in the media. *The Times* revealed that an initial payment of £15 m was to be followed by two further payments of £16 m. A further £3.5 m was factored in should City secure the Champions League trophy while Carlos was still in their employment. At the time that seemed a long shot, but Tevez had already won the domestic title in every country that he played in – Argentina, Brazil and England. He had also assisted in winning the Champions League for United.

The Sheikh was already showing the lengths to which he was prepared to go to take City to the very top. The new owner had simply no concept of defeat. In the coming months the owner's obsession with success made Captain Ahab look like a man on a holiday cruise. Sheikh Mansour's first purchase for City, Robinho smashed the British transfer record but the Tevez deal would eventually obliterate it. Carlos would become the fifth most expensive player ever ranking alongside Ronaldo, Ibrahimovic, Kaka and Zidane. It was also the highest fee paid for an Argentine player beating the £35m paid by Lazio to Parma in 2000.

On a beautiful July morning Carlos arrived at Eastlands in a silver Mercedes to be unveiled as their latest acquisition. Hundreds of fans mobbed the superstar, who was clad in Dior Homme jeans, black shirt and sporting a rather fetching piece of cranial knitwear. Speculation was rife that the headgear was either something that his grandmother knitted for him or else it was one of those wine protection nettings.

Looking like a refugee from Manchester's legendary Hacienda club, Carlos posed for the usual pictures with his new boss Mark Hughes, brandishing his new City home shirt. At the press conference, speaking through a translator, Carlos told the *Sun* that Sir Alex had never spoken to him about his future with United: 'I was there for two years and Sir Alex never called or sent any text messages in that time. The only time he talked to me was after a match against Roma to discuss a situation about going to play for Argentina.

'It does not seem that this is the way to treat a player in two years at the club. It does not seem there is a line of communication.'

Carlos also denied that he had spoken to Manchester City representatives the previous January about a potential transfer. The earliest that the possibility of a move had been mooted was in the now-defunct *London Lite* newspaper. They had reported that Tevez had flown to Abu Dhabi from Rome after United's defeat in the Champions League final. Talks had apparently taken place there between Tevez's mentor Kia Joorabchian and the Arab power brokers to smooth the way for the actual transfer.

Carlos's pre-season preparations at City were not exactly smooth, in a situation similar to his slow start at Old Trafford. A domestic accident meant he missed out on playing on the South African tour. This happened when he slipped over in the shower and damaged his heel. The heel had taken a knock in his last appearance for his country and the fall had aggravated it. He was already carrying a knee problem a legacy from the warfare of the previous season.

As a result Carlos just played for 25 minutes in the pre-season. This was when he was limited to a cameo appearance against Celtic when he was given a rapturous reception by City fans. The famous number 32 was on the back of his shirt; different club, same squad number. Despite the acrimony of his departure from Old Trafford Tevez's confidence was undiminished; he had joined a club with nine strikers but he wanted to be top gun.

Tevez did not play at all on City's three-match tour of South Africa. He also missed out on the team's audience with former South Africa president Nelson Mandela in Johannesburg. It would have been a real thrill for the kid from Fort Apache to have met the 91-year-old, one of the most iconic figures of the 20th Century.

Blackburn away was City's first fixture of the momentous 2009–10 season. After 67 minutes Carlos made his debut for Mark Hughes's team when he replaced Robinho in the pouring rain. For the remaining 23 minutes Carlos buzzed around and only a fine save from England keeper Robinson denied him a debut day goal.

Hughes had beefed up the squad even further by purchasing former Arsenal duo Kolo Toure and Emmanuel Adebayor for a combined fee of £40m. This made a total outlay of almost £215m since his arrival in June 2008. All this had happened as much of the world was teetering on the brink of the biggest economic recession since the late 1920s.

Adebayor opened his City account with an early strike and then Stephen Ireland scored in the dying seconds to settle the game. 7,000 City fans had made the trip to Ewood Park and filled the lower tier of the Darwen End. Some clutched inflatable bananas, nearly all of them wore the new sky blue shirts. When their new hero appeared on the field they started to sing 'Tevez is a blue'.

Hughes fielded a 4-2-3-1 formation against Blackburn with Adebayor pulling the strings behind Craig Bellamy. When Carlos replaced Robinho, Bellamy switched to the left and early glimpses of a promising partnership between the two men were seen. The Welsh manager felt that Tevez was fully capable of playing off one of City's target men, Adebayor or Roque Santa Cruz. Alternatively he could slot into the right side of a fluid attacking midfield including Robinho, Wright-Phillips, Ireland and Bellamy.

The Argentinean gave City an added dimension by helping the forwards become the first line of defence. In essence Tevez was three players in one, focal striker, wide midfielder and defensive midfielder. Fitness was the key to this working and at that time Carlos was struggling to attain the required levels.

Around that time, the infamous 'Welcome to Manchester' poster appeared in Manchester city centre. The huge sky blue poster featured Tevez in a pose that appeared to have been lifted from his celebration when he scored for the Reds against Wigan. It came on their run in for the 2008–9 title and effectively set them up for their third consecutive Premiership title – but now, of course, Tevez was a City player.

Sir Alex was irritated by the provocative poster, calling City 'small minded' and 'a wee bit arrogant'. Some irate United fans daubed it with red paint. The poster attracted headlines worldwide, as newspapers as far afield as

Malaysia and South Korea covered the story. Even the *New York Times* ran a feature on it.

In the autumn Carlos paid £2000 for a huge 20ft digital print of the poster for his Cheshire home, and a further print was purchased for his home in Buenos Aires. The poster reminded Carlos of the banter between the top teams in Argentina.

In his English abode it was hung in the games room of his gadget packed award-winning mansion. Carlos paid £12k a month to rent the luxurious mansion in Prestbury, Cheshire. The new property had been valued at nearly £4m and featured a swimming pool with an underwater sound system. The house was a huge 8,000 sq ft with five reception rooms and five bedroom suites. Other features were a cinema, gym, a custom built wine cellar and textured wall panels.

What was of particular interest was its eco friendly design which included a 60-tube solar heating system which provided 75% of the hot water. Without doubt he was the greenest footballer in the Premier. In an interview with *Football Punk* magazine Carlos talked about the ecology.

'Our generation has not done much for the environment, but today's kids are much more aware of it. I often see them telling their parents off when they throw a bit of rubbish on the ground and that is brilliant. Us human beings should take better care of our Earth.'

In the closing paragraphs of perhaps the greatest novel of the 20th Century 'The Great Gatsby' F Scott Fitzgerald wrote of the journey his hero had made from extreme poverty to a mansion and fabulous wealth: 'He had come a long way to this blue lawn , and his dream seemed so close that he could hardly fail to grasp it'. Tevez had come a long way to his blue lawn in Eastlands, where the streets were now paved with gold.

Wolverhampton Wanderers were the visitors to Eastlands in the next fixture and Carlos made his full debut in the Premiership for City. The only goal of the game was scored by Adebayor after 17 minutes when he finished off an exquisite lay off by Carlos. The match stats indicated that he lasted for 73 minutes made two successful tackles and completed 21 passes out of 26.

The game was watched by the Gallagher brothers, Noel and Liam, of Britpop pioneers Oasis. The siblings were the most high-profile fans of the club and world famous pop stars. Unfortunately, the brothers watched the match from different ends of the ground. A few weeks later Noel was to quit the band as the brothers tempestuous relationship imploded under the weight of their untrammelled egos.

Noel then had his picture taken with Carlos before heading off to play in the V fest at Stafford's Weston Park. It was to be the last time that the brothers played together on stage. This was a great disappointment to Carlos, who had bonded well with them and offered to give the Gallagher boys Latin dancing lessons. The Argentinean told the Sun that he also wanted to play music with them.

'I would definitely jam with them if they were up to it. When they are back in Manchester they can come and watch a City game, then we can go for a jam.'

One of Carlos's all time favourite songs was their mega-hit 'Wonderwall' and he wanted the writer to teach him how to play it. Carlos played an instrument called the Octapad. This was an electronic percussion device which employed eight pads which triggered different sounds via MIDI: 'I am open to lessons and in return I will teach them some Latin style and maybe even some Latin dancing to go with it', he quipped.

The popular TV show *Strictly Come Dancing* was showing at the time and Carlos had hinted that he would not be averse to appearing on it. Such was his sky-high confidence at the time, he even fancied strutting his stuff on national television.

The relationship between Noel Gallagher and Carlos was interesting. Noel had been at City fan all his life not a glory hunter or celeb fan. He had watched games from the Kippax and had based the choruses of his smash hits on the chants from that area. He spoke his mind on all subjects recently describing City target and England Captain John Terry as a 'Cockney cry-baby'. Terry was later stripped of the England captaincy after a series of allegations about his private life.

Tevez was the people's player and Noel being a dyed in the wool fan could identify with him. Even Sir Alex talking about Carlos's departure had stressed how popular his hunch-shouldered, scurrying style had been with the fans.

The first goal Carlos scored for City was in the 2-0 victory over Crystal Palace in the Carling Cup. It came after 70 minutes when unmarked he headed home a corner from Wright-Phillips, who had opened the scoring. Throughout the potentially tricky hurdle Carlos had been abused by the Palace fans and he replied to them with his now famous cupped ear gesture.

Desperate to land some silverware Hughes had fielded his full strength side in English football's second oldest knock out competition. There was to be no slip ups that night unlike the previous season when the Sky Blues had been put out of the competition by lowly League One Brighton. The latest oil money signing the £24m centre-half Joleon Lescott from Everton made his debut at Selhurst Park.

The Carling Cup was always a lucky competition for

Carlos, with happy memories of the part he had played in securing the trophy for United the previous spring. Mark Hughes was delighted with Carlos's performance that night and told the *Sun*: 'I was hoping Carlos would get opportunities here and thankfully he is off the mark now. His general link-up play, his energy and enthusiasm all shone through. He has the ability to retain possession, draw people to him and then release the ball.

'The more he plays the better he will be. We have got Adebayor off the mark, now Carlos. I am delighted.'

Palace were now managed by none other than Neil Warnock, who had been at the helm when Sheffield United crashed out of the Premier League the year Tevez had kept the Hammers up. After the match, Warnock gave a press conference and bemoaned the fact that Tevez had been given a free header. Warnock was tipping cash-rich City to crash the top three though. Neil spotted Tevez in the corridor waiting to board the City coach back to Manchester and confronted him, barking: 'You cost me millions you did.'

Nothing ever fazed Carlos, as a kid growing up in a Buenos Aires ghetto he walked past dead bodies on his way to school. The politics of football, the hype, and the pressure he just eat it up for breakfast. Carlos just stared blankly at the angry little Yorkshire man as if he did not exist.

Warnock was approached by the author of this book for his take on the 'Tevez affair' but he declined to even reply. At the time of writing Crystal Palace were languishing in the lower reaches of the Championship. They press had recently reported that the players' wages had not been paid for several weeks, and the club would later go into administration.

Then it was back to South America to play in Argentina's

World Cup qualifying games. The campaign had turned into shambles as the La Albiceleste (white and blues) stumbled from disaster to disaster. The heel injury meant that Carlos sat out the friendly with Russia a few weeks earlier but he was back for the vital game against Brazil.

They were currently top of the South American qualifying section whilst Argentina were back in fourth spot a mere two points ahead of fifth placed Ecuador. The match had been switched to Rosario rather than Buenos Aires to create a more intimidating atmosphere. Carlos told Sky Sports: 'About the match against Brazil. I think that they are going to come to Argentina being a little bit sacred and we are going to want to beat them.

'But besides my opinion we have to respect them because they are Brazil.'

Respect them was correct, because Brazil ran out easy 3-1 winners and once again Carlos failed to take his club form onto the international stage. In the ratings for the game he only earned a 4.5 rating out of 10 as he failed to play up to his potential. The Argentine FA also confirmed that Tevez had twisted his right knee which would rule him out of the vital qualifier in Paraguay and Manchester City's upcoming games. The situation deteriorated further for Argentina when in a clueless performance they lost 1-0 to Paraguay and slipped out of the four automatic qualifying places. The defeat was there fourth in six qualifiers since Maradona had taken control. There was now a grave danger that his glamorous team would not be playing in the 2010 World Cup in South Africa. There was a huge backlash in the press against Diego. The leading Sports daily *Ole* commentated that the former Argentina Captain '...had made all the mistakes that a coach can commit and which demotivated the players.'

The form of Tevez was proof of this whilst Messi in an Argentina shirt was a shadow of the player who played so imperiously when Barcelona overwhelmed United in Rome. 'The Flea' was shortly to edge in front of Ronaldo as the best player in the world. Meanwhile Maradona, on a $100.000 a month, raged against his accusers in the media: 'Since I was 15 years of age I have feared nobody. I am 48 now and I will continue to fight against them.

'The bearded one [God] saved me many times before, I hope he does this so this time.'

Tevez limped back to England; the pressure was taking its toll on him too. Maradona had checked into a spa to combat stress. The twisted knee ruled Tevez out of the exciting victory over Arsenal. It looked like he would miss out on his return to Old Trafford which was scheduled for 19 September 09. A few days before the game he returned to light training and told the *Sun*: 'I expect to get a good reception from the fans. I always gave my best for United and the fans know I did everything to try to score and help the team win. I do not see why I should get a bad reception.'

Sir Alex had told the *Independent*: 'We made contact with Carlos. We sent him texts and spoke to him when he was in Argentina. Our chief executive David Gill made an offer to his agent Kia Joorabchian. In my opinion I do not think he was worth £25m.'

Michael Owen was the surprise replacement for Tevez, although he was handed Ronaldo's old number 7 shirt. The 2001 European Footballer of the Year appeared to be heading for oblivion when Newcastle were relegated at the end of the 2009–10 season. The latter period of Owen's once golden career had been blighted by injury and the 29-year-old was only offered a one-year deal at United after passing a stringent medical. The key point was that Owen came on a free transfer. The ex-Liverpool striker accepted a significant drop in his former £110,000 per week wages paid by Newcastle. Some reports stated that his United contract was appearance-related, with a basic salary of £20,000 per week plus lucrative bonuses.

Former England boss Glenn Hoddle was of the view that Owen could still be a lethal striker for United. Hoddle, who had given Owen his England debut almost a dozen years before, told the *Sunday Mirror*: 'It is a superb bit of business by Sir Alex Ferguson. I am convinced it could be the shrewdest signing of the summer.

'If Michael can stay relatively fit and be involved in 30 or so games he can be better in front of goal than Tevez.

Perhaps Sir Alex knew in January 2009 that the club would not sanction a £25m fee for Tevez. After all, he had earlier that season spent a king's ransom on Dimitar Berbatov. That would perhaps explain Tevez's dwindling appearances for the club, as Ferguson looked towards a future without him. The young French ace Kharim Benzima had long been Ferguson's replacement of choice but he eventually signed for Real Madrid for £38m. There were to be no marquee signings at that stage; no Ribery or Villa. The signing of Owen appeared to some to smack of desperation, but football has a funny way of making a mockery of even the finest of theories.

On a beautiful early autumn afternoon Carlos Tevez played at Old Trafford; clearly he was not 100% fit but then he hadn't been 100% fit since he had signed for City. In the opening seconds he almost scored a dream goal when he found space behind Vidic to charge down a clearance from United keeper Ben Foster. That set the tempo for a madcap game.

Rooney struck early for United but Carlos quickly set up the equaliser. It was a moment of vintage Tevez when he chased after Gareth Barry's pass that looked over hit. Foster arrived there first but Carlos tenaciously robbed him of the ball. Most players would have tried to score from that position. Particularly if they had a point as big as Tevez's to make but unselfishly he rolled the ball back to Barry who threaded home. That was the high spot of the match for him, just on the break he had a great chance to score the goal that would have been like a dagger through Sir Alex's heart.

Rooney's casual back-heel was snapped up by Kolo Toure, who put Carlos in on goal. It was a dream situation but Tevez's shot flicked the outside of the post and the chance had gone. The whistle blew for half-time and Carlos walked off the field past the Stretford End. Once it had loved him but now it was a sea of hate, angry twisted faces and obscene gestures. Their anger surprised and hurt him; something was thrown out of the crowd, maybe a coin. It missed Carlos but hit his team-mate Javier Garrido. Perhaps that was the moment Carlos realised that his love affair with the red side of Manchester had been shattered. To them he had committed the unforgivable sin of accepting City's millions.

Sir Alex had seemingly attempted to airbrush Tevez out of United's history, only talking about him when asked and making no reference to Carlos in his programme notes. The second half of the match was a blur, and the home crowd continued to boo Tevez every time he touched the ball. Four minutes into the second half Darren Fletcher rose above Barry to nod in Giggs's high cross.

City stormed back and Tevez's short pass was picked up by Bellamy, who cut inside John O'Shea before exploding home a shot from the edge of the box. Both the scorers of the last two goals were to repeat it. Fletcher headed home ten minutes from time to put United 3-2 up. Once again Giggs, playing in his 30th Manchester derby, carved out the chance. That looked to be it, but the drama had some more twists to play out.

In the 90th minute Ferdinand, who had earlier been clattered by Tevez, chipped a careless pass. Barry intercepted and released Bellamy. The Welsh striker ran 60 yards before equalising, and that looked to be it – 3-3.

Bellamy's equaliser appeared to have kept City's unbeaten record intact; he had a fine match, almost a carbon copy of Tevez at his best with his energy and determination. Both players were tenacious and liked to dribble across defences. In the sixth minute of injury time, however, with ex-United legend 'Sparky' Hughes screaming for the whistle, substitute Owen raced onto another Giggs pass, controlled the ball with the outside of his right foot and steered the ball past Shay Given. 4-3. Bedlam broke out. Hughes was furious that the goal had been scored in the 96th minute, after fourth official Alan Wiley had signalled for a mere four minutes of added time.

Carlos sank to the ground, exhausted. The irony of Owen's goal did not escape him. He had played well, made two goals and had been a constant threat to his old colleagues but Owen, who had not come on until the 78th minute, had stolen his thunder and the headlines. There were to be other days, though.

Carlos's next high profile game came against another of his former clubs – West Ham – in a Monday night fixture at Eastlands. Carlos put West Ham ahead after just five minutes when Shay Given's rocket launcher of a clearance was flicked on by Gareth Barry to the explosive Martin

Petrov. The winger tore into the box and squared the ball to the unmarked Tevez who had the simplest of tasks of firing into the roof of the net. It was his first Premier League goal for the 'Citizens'.

Instead of wildly celebrating he jogged behind the goal where the West Ham fans were gathered en masse and held out his hands in apology. A Manchester City player had not been so contrite so since Denis Law had back heeled the goal that had relegated United a lifetime before. Despite their constant struggle for survival in the Premiership the East London team always had a large contingent following them away and tonight was no exception. As one the West Ham fans broke into applause for their former idol. It was a very emotional moment for Tevez, save for kissing the badge on Robert Green's jersey he could not have been more remorseful. If only he could have maintained the same relationship with the faithful at Old Trafford, but things were different. They had not chucked pigs heads at him yet but his status as a United cult hero had definitely been revoked. If his first half shot against United had gone in rather than flick against the post would his celebrations have been so muted?

Comparisons were made between Tevez's behaviour and that of his team-mate Emmanuel Adebayor when he had scored against his old club Arsenal in the previous home match. The striker had run the length of the pitch to taunt the Arsenal fans. Carlton Cole equalised for Hammers with a scrambled effort but Petrov put City ahead again with a curling free kick. On the hour Tevez clinched the game for City when he headed home a free kick from another West Ham striker Craig Bellamy.

After the match West Ham manager Gianfranco Zola

praised Tevez: 'Good players and great players like him are also gentleman and he showed that. And my appreciation to him is great, not only for what he did with the celebration but for the way he played the whole game.'

The win lifted them to fifth place in the league, their best start to the season since 1961, just three points behind Manchester United. They should have progressed from that, but they followed it with a sequence of seven consecutive draws in the Premier League, with Carlos hitting a barren spell during that period. City were not losing, but they failed to click. Disappointing draws followed against lowly Birmingham, Wigan and Burnley. Tevez was occupying the space that Stephen Ireland had occupied the previous season, as he ran through to score numerous goals. Stephen had been voted City's Player of the Year but was struggling to find a starting place in the team.

When Kaka, a previous target for City, joined Real Madrid from AC Milan, he talked of his new team having 'no automatic'. City were the same as Madrid; lots of new players with no fluency, no 'automatic'. Arsenal had that fluency; City were yet to play as a unit and show any cohesion.

Sandwiched between the Premier League fixtures were appearances for Argentina, the first of which came in a friendly game in Spain. Xabi's double strike salvaged a narrow win for the home country. Messi, again very disappointing, scored for Argentina from the penalty spot. Carlos looked desperate to impress when he entered the fray but apart from some rash tackles he found it hard to get started. At that time he was searching for both form and fitness.

Carlos also came on for the lat three minutes in the World Cup qualifying win against Uruguay. His former West Ham colleague Mascherano was the first name on the team sheet these days. Manchester City assistant manager Mark Bowen was puzzled by the decision to leave his star man on the bench after he had made the 14,000-mile round trip to Buenos Aires, and explained to the *Manchester Evening News*: 'We are a bit mystified by the situation. To make all that fuss about him going over there and then to leave him on the bench does not seem to add up.

'Carlos is not operating at 100% per cent yet. He is carrying bumps and bruises to his ankle and back, but he is playing well enough despite that.

'In terms of his sharpness and match fitness he will get better, so the best is yet to come from Carlos in the weeks ahead.'

Bowen's forecast was to be chillingly accurate. One of the problems Carlos faced was his struggle with the English language. Considering his background and the fact that his education consisted mainly of street football, what did the media expect? At the press conference at Eastlands when he signed for City, much was made of the fact that he still used a translator and spoke in Spanish after being in the country for nearly four years. There must have been precious little time in that period, though, for Carlos to learn a new language.

But help was at hand in the form of the country's longest running soap opera, *Coronation Street*. Carlos became a devoted fan and, like Dimitar Berbatov, started picking up the English language from the show. Of course the accents were a problem but who knows, maybe one evening we will tune in and see Carlos ordering a pint in the Rovers.

The Argentina situation was worrying him, though, and exhausted by the constant travelling he poured his heart out to the *Guardian*: 'I am a bit tired of so much football, so much football. I want to enjoy my family a bit. I am very keen to stop and get a bit of calm. I have already won a lot. Living for football has saturated me.

'We were criticised a lot sometimes rightly so, but to have people say we did not play well because of the money or we do not love the [Argentina] shirt, do not sing the national anthem, there is a lot of ill will.'

There was speculation that Carlos may follow in the footsteps of one of his peers Juan Roman Riquelme and quit Argentina for good. Juan had starred in the classy Villarreal side but his whole career had been dogged by controversy and discord. Eventually the disenchanted play maker quit the national side after a quarrel with Maradona.

Argentina eventually scraped into the 2010 World Cup with their lowest ever total of qualifying points. To many, though, they were still global heavyweights. Carlos pledged that he was determined to turn the situation around and was even threatening to hang up his boots for good if Argentina won the World Cup for a third time: 'At the World Cup they are going to see the best Carlos Tevez', he said.

Despite their faltering form in the Premier League, City made progress in the Carling Cup. A stubborn Fulham side were beaten in extra time, and City then beat Scunthorpe 5-1 at the end of October to put them into the quarter-finals. The fourth goal was Carlos's as he thrashed a pass from substitute Vladimir Weiss into the net. It came at an important time as the battling Championship side were refusing to yield. But the turning point in the early days of his City career came for Carlos against Liverpool away. Mark Hughes omitted him from the original line-up, citing tactical reasons for the failure of his number 32 to start the match. With Liverpool leading by a Martin Skrtel goal, Carlos's introduction turned the whole game. Gareth Barry was withdrawn on the hour and Carlos galloped on. Almost immediately Liverpool's Lucas was booked for a crude foul on the substitute. Liverpool, aware of the threat of the new arrival, retreated into their defensive shell whilst City pushed up. Adebayor equalised soon after when he headed home a swirling corner from Bellamy.

Carlos helped put City in front when he set up Ireland to flick the ball past Reina. The Argentinean had stolen possession from Skrtel and deftly fed Ireland to score a neat goal. Liverpool where there for the taking, They had only won one of their last 10 games and had crashed out of Europe. Within a minute though the City back four got into a terrible tangle and Benayoun stabbed in the equaliser.

Hughes explained to *The Times* about his decision not to start with Tevez. The Welshman made it clear that the knee injury and fatigue that had limited his initial impact was not the major factor: 'Carlos is an experienced player and he understands that on occasions you need different personnel…He has had a little bit of a problem with his knee, he has been playing with a little discomfort but today it was a tactical thing. You are not going gung-ho with all guns blazing because the likelihood is you will concede goals.

'When we conceded, that was the time to introduce Carlos. It was always my intention to bring him on because of the impact Carlos can have from the bench. I thought he was excellent.'

The Hughes era was drawing to its close around then, although few realised it at the time. In 27 matches the previous season, Carlos had started or finished on the Manchester United bench; in a further 10 he was an unused sub. The main reason he had moved across town was that

Mark Hughes had sold him a vision of Manchester City's future in which he would play an integral part. Had he jumped from the Old Trafford frying pan into the fire at Eastlands? Was he destined now to be a nomad, travelling from club to club, just a glorified impact player?

Perhaps the greatest asset of Carlos Tevez was his mental strength. It had taken him so far, and now he had to call on it again. In the next few weeks he was to hit the form of his life as he went on a goal spree that was to lay waste to everything in his path.

City were now 7th in the Premier League; they had drawn their last seven games and their next opponents were Arsenal in the Carling Cup. Carlos opened the scoring in the 50th minute with a superb goal. Arsenal's Alexandre Song played the ball out from his box to Tomas Rosicky but Carlos robbed him of the ball. There followed a quick interchange of passes with Bellamy and Carlos then charged down the wing. There was only one intention in his mind as he swerved past Emmanuel and Song and cut into the penalty area before firing in a terrific right foot shot that went across goalkeeper Fabianski and in off the bar.

It was a marvellous goal of pace and power, and the *Manchester Evening News* awarded Tevez with a rating of 8/10 for his performance. Shaun Wright-Phillips fired in the second goal and promising young sub Weiss wrapped it up with a third in the dying moments. City Chairman Khaldoon Al Mubarak punched the air with delight as the final whistle blew. It was almost a year to the day that Tevez had scored four times in the same competition for United against Blackburn.

By a quirk of fate, Manchester United were City's next opponents in the two-legged Carling Cup semi-final which was to be played in January 2010. Speaking through an interpreter Tevez spoke of the match as being a 'Classico' and, in a bid to defuse the bad feeling between fans of the two clubs, he stated that in the event of him scoring he would not celebrate.

The games were coming thick and fast. League leaders Chelsea came to Eastlands on a wet Saturday evening and Carlos scored the winner with a beauty of a free kick. Tevez started like an express train and kept going. In the opening minutes he left Terry standing but his cut back cross went wide of the goal. Chelsea went in front with an untidy goal that went in off Adebayor's back. Emmanuel equalised for City after 37 minutes when he swept home the rebound from Wright-Phillips's fierce shot.

The match was billed the 'Battle of the Billionaires' and, roared on by a record crowd of 47,348, City took the game to the London side. Eleven minutes into the second half, Carvalho was booked for a high challenge on the nimble Tevez. A free kick was awarded, which Tevez elected to take. Twenty-five yards out, Chelsea built a wall while Petr Cech patrolled the goal line. Up strode Carlos – it was a crucial moment in his career. The ball was just a blur as it curled past the wall and beat Cech, who had opted to go in a different direction. It was a marvellous free kick, scored with that lovely technique Carlos has of opening his foot to make an angle. It was as good as anything Ronaldo or Messi could have conjured up. The goal proved to be the match winner, as Shay Given administered justice and made a great save from Lampard's late penalty that united both sides of Manchester in ecstasy.

Roman Abramovich left the stadium frowning; there were new kids on the block now and their spending power was superior to even his. City's worth had been estimated at a staggering £500bn.

City shared six goals against Bolton in their next match at the Reebok. Carlos scored two equalisers in the game, both fired home from the edge of the penalty area with great power and accuracy. The first came when Bellamy, later sent off, crossed and Tevez glided past Muamba to smash home. His second goal was even better than the first, surrounded by a posse of Bolton defenders he took a pass from Ireland and beat keeper Jussi Jaaskelainen from an acute angle. It was the sixth time Carlos had scored a brace in the Premier League.

After these great wins over Arsenal and Chelsea, many City fans thought that they had turned the corner, but the defects were easy to spot, the defence's inability to keep a clean sheet being the most glaring. It still looked a big ask for City to dislodge one of the quartet who habitually filled the top four. But Mark Hughes was delighted with Carlos's form. He told the *Metro*: 'I thought Carlos was outstanding, he led from the front. He is getting to a level of fitness that allows him to have a big impact on games.' The City boss also thought that Tevez's decision to quit Old Trafford had been vindicated: 'Carlos made a big decision but is not fazed.'

The pressure was growing on Hughes though; it was City's thirteenth game since they had last lost but eight of them were drawn. The following Wednesday, City travelled to White Hart Lane for a Premier League clash with Tottenham Hotspur. In a woeful performance City were crushed 3-0. Carlos was the pick of the team battling on with precious little support. It was the end for Hughes, the press speculated that his days were numbered.

The day before the home game with Sunderland, Carlos made a statement in the *Daily Telegraph* urging the club to keep faith with their manager: 'I support him 100% because I believe that we made a great deal of progress towards reaching our goal.

'We need to have stability and calm to allow the club to move forward. People should not panic.'

In just a few games, as he had done at West Ham, Carlos had achieved the status of a cult hero to rank alongside the likes of Georgi Kinkladze, Shaun Goater, Paul Lake and Rodney Marsh. In Hughes's swansong match City beat Sunderland 4-3 and Carlos scored the second goal from the penalty spot. He hadn't missed from the spot since his arrival in English football. It was to no avail though as after the match it was announced that after 563 turbulent days in charge Mark Hughes contract was terminated. Roberto Mancini was immediately confirmed as his successor.

Jose Mourinho had been identified as the type of manager City wanted to run their billion-dollar operation. Roberto was cut from the same mould, beautifully dressed, tough, and highly organised he had led Inter Milan to success before 'The Special One' had replaced him.

Carlos Tevez scored three times in his first two games for his new boss. Stoke were the first victims, he made the opening goal for Petrov then clinched the points with another spectacular goal, leaping high in the air to acrobatically steer a cross into the back of the net.

Two days after Christmas, City travelled to an icy Molineux to take on newly-promoted Wolves. It was another tricky fixture but City looked very strong and motivated. Already Mancini was giving the side organisation. The team in old gold were brushed aside 3-0, with Tevez scoring the first and third. The last was a real gem. Substitute Robinho carving out a chance for Carlos to blast home, a real touch of South American class on a bitter winter evening in the Midlands.

The freezing weather continued, Carlos hated it, he was named among the subs for the third round FA Cup visit to Middlesbrough. A FA Cup winner's medal was the only domestic medal not in his treasure trove. City won 1-0, amongst the highlights of the game shown on TV was an amusing clip of Carlos shivering on the bench. His face all but covered with a scarf and a balaclava ensemble.

The next day United lost at home by the same score to one of their oldest and bitterest rivals – Leeds United. In a toothless display the Reds had deployed Rooney, Berbatov and Owen up front in the closing stages in a frantic attempt to save the game. It was a massive humiliation for the champions; the first time in Ferguson's 23-year tenure that his team had been knocked out in the third round. And the player who would have best suited the cut and thrust and the extreme physical conditions of the game was on the other side of town.

Tevez's scoring spree continued unabated in a Monday night Premiership match against Blackburn. Mancini, the 17th City messiah in 20 years, had given Carlos the lead role in football's latest and glossiest soap opera. He had now scored 10 goals in his last seven Premiership games. Carlos scored after just 6 minutes when keeper Paul Robinson missed Petrov's corner. Benjani returned the ball to Tevez, who tapped it into an empty net. Benjani was playing in place of Emmanuel Adebayor, who was on compassionate leave after being caught up in the terrible attack on the Togo team's bus prior to the African Cup of Nations.

Micah Richards put City two up in the first half and after 48 minutes Carlos scored their third. Cleverly playing the ball into the right hand channel he found Benjani who cut it back to the edge of the area where Carlos arrived to curl a wonderful shot past Robinson from 18 yards. Blackburn's classy winger Pedersen pulled a goal back, but Carlos had the last word.

As Blackburn folded like an origami swan Carlos's third goal was perhaps the best he had scored in English football. Substitute Robinho played the ball to him in the D and with no back lift curled in his hat-trick. City leapfrogged Tottenham to gatecrash the top four and their place in the upper echelons of English football seemed assured.

CHAPTER FOURTEEN
BEST SERVED COLD

A cynic knows the price of everything and the value of nothing.
OSCAR WILDE

Our story has one more twist in it before this volume of Carlos Alberto Tevez's amazing odyssey draws to an end. The first leg of the Carling Cup semi-final, re-arranged thanks to the Arctic weather that swept Britain in January 2010, was played at Eastlands. Ryan Giggs scored his first Manchester derby goal since 1996 when he tapped in from close range after Wayne Rooney's shot had been parried by Shay Given. United appeared to be in control, but two minutes before the break came the incident that changed the pattern of the whole game and then threw up one of the most controversial incidents in the history of the Manchester civil wars.

Tevez flicked a short pass to Craig Bellamy, who raced into the box. Rafael da Silva, the United defender, impetuously tugged the Welshman's arm and a penalty kick was awarded. Up strode Carlos to take the kick. The ground was hushed; given the recent history between Carlos and his old team it was a critical moment in an incendiary atmosphere. Carlos's former strike partner Wayne Rooney started to chatter to him. Carlos looked completely unfazed by the whole matter.

It was all about state of mind, and Carlos was in the mood to score. You could have bet your mortgage on Carlos that night. He fired home a textbook penalty, a magnificent rising drive that ripped into the net. Carlos then made a beeline for the United dug-out, cupping his ears in celebration. Ironic that it was an exact reprise of his behaviour when he had scored against City at Old Trafford the previous spring.

Gary Neville, warming up on the touchline, was the target of Carlos's anger as he gestured that he talked too much. In the build-up to the match Neville had stated that he agreed with Ferguson's assessment that Tevez was overpriced at £25m. The United sub gave Tevez the finger in response, a gesture that got him in trouble with the FA.

As the game restarted Carlos made the alligator hand to Rooney to inform him that he was another United player who talked too much. And the Argentinean made a mockery of the statement about his worth when he grabbed the winner in the second half with a neat header. Van der Sar's punch only took the ball as far as Pablo Zabaleta, who nodded down for Kompany to chip into the box. El Apache nipped in front of the United keeper to nod home.

After the match, shown on the BBC, Carlos was interviewed live on air. It was the first time he had appeared in such a situation in England and he seemed more nervous than he had been when he stepped up to take the penalty. He only managed a few words in faltering English – 'It's OK' – when he was asked how he felt.

The fall-out from the incident with Neville dominated the

sports headlines for the next few days. On ESPN radio in Argentina, Carlos hit back at the United veteran calling him a boot-licker, and a *tarado* (moron). Few outside Old Trafford would have doubted him. 'It was a lack of respect for a *companero*', Carlos said. 'I feel he was a boot-licker when he stood by Ferguson's comments that I was not worth the money. Just as I was running off to celebrate the penalty, I came across Gary and I said to myself "Shut your trap, keep quiet".'

Sir Alex told the media that he 'did not see the incident'. The debate was opened up again on internet messageboards, blogs and radio phone-ins across the land. Should United have kept Carlos? The *Guardian* posted a poll asking that question to its readers. It received an overwhelming 'Yes'.

And Carlos went on to score another superb goal upon his return to Old Trafford in the second leg of the pulsating Carling Cup semi-final. It came after 75 minutes when Bellamy sent over a curling cross and Tevez somehow flicked in a shot from a difficult angle. It beat Van der Sar and made the score 3-3 on aggregate.

After a bright first half, in which City comfortably held the champions, Carlos almost scored with a diving header. In the second half, though, United rolled back the years and played their best football since Carlos and Ronaldo had left. Goals from Scholes and Carrick had put the reds back in front until Carlos had equalised. The whole of the country was looking forward to the mouth watering prospect of extra time until Rooney headed a winner in the 92nd minute.

Carlos was devastated – he had scored three goals in the tie and had been the outstanding player. But he put the niggles of the first leg aside as he found time to wish his former team-mates good luck in the final. So City were denied their first final in nearly 30 years, but it has to be said that the future remains bright for the kid from Fort Apache. If he continues to perform at the level he has shown in 2009–10, it surely won't be long before he and City are challenging at the very top of English football.